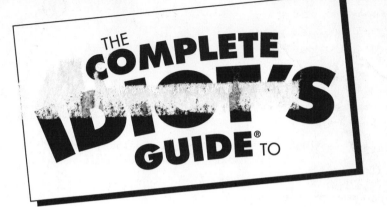

THE COMPLETE IDIOT'S GUIDE® TO

The Paranormal

by Nathan Robert Brown

ALPHA

A member of Penguin Group (USA) Inc.

6/2/10

This book is dedicated to all those who seek to find the hidden truth behind the many mysteries of our world, and to those brave enough to do battle with the forces of evil.

ALPHA BOOKS

Published by the Penguin Group

Penguin Group (USA) Inc., 375 Hudson Street, New York, New York 10014, USA

Penguin Group (Canada), 90 Eglinton Avenue East, Suite 700, Toronto, Ontario M4P 2Y3, Canada (a division of Pearson Penguin Canada Inc.)

Penguin Books Ltd., 80 Strand, London WC2R 0RL, England

Penguin Ireland, 25 St. Stephen's Green, Dublin 2, Ireland (a division of Penguin Books Ltd.)

Penguin Group (Australia), 250 Camberwell Road, Camberwell, Victoria 3124, Australia (a division of Pearson Australia Group Pty. Ltd.)

Penguin Books India Pvt. Ltd., 11 Community Centre, Panchsheel Park, New Delhi—110 017, India

Penguin Group (NZ), 67 Apollo Drive, Rosedale, North Shore, Auckland 1311, New Zealand (a division of Pearson New Zealand Ltd.)

Penguin Books (South Africa) (Pty.) Ltd., 24 Sturdee Avenue, Rosebank, Johannesburg 2196, South Africa

Penguin Books Ltd., Registered Offices: 80 Strand, London WC2R 0RL, England

International Standard Book Number: 978-1-59257-988-4
Library of Congress Catalog Card Number: 2009934677

12   11   10   8   7   6   5   4   3   2   1

Interpretation of the printing code: The rightmost number of the first series of numbers is the year of the book's printing; the rightmost number of the second series of numbers is the number of the book's printing. For example, a printing code of 10-1 shows that the first printing occurred in 2010.

Printed in the United States of America

Note: This publication contains the opinions and ideas of its author. It is intended to provide helpful and informative material on the subject matter covered. It is sold with the understanding that the author and publisher are not engaged in rendering professional services in the book. If the reader requires personal assistance or advice, a competent professional should be consulted.

The author and publisher specifically disclaim any responsibility for any liability, loss, or risk, personal or otherwise, which is incurred as a consequence, directly or indirectly, of the use and application of any of the contents of this book.

Most Alpha books are available at special quantity discounts for bulk purchases for sales promotions, premiums, fund-raising, or educational use. Special books, or book excerpts, can also be created to fit specific needs.

For details, write: Special Markets, Alpha Books, 375 Hudson Street, New York, NY 10014.

Publisher: *Marie Butler-Knight*
Editorial Director: *Mike Sanders*
Senior Managing Editor: *Billy Fields*
Executive Editor: *Randy Ladenheim-Gil*
Development Editor: *Megan Douglass*
Production Editor: *Kayla Dugger*
Copy Editor: *Nancy Wagner*

Cartoonist: *Steve Barr*
Cover Designer: *Kurt Owens*
Book Designer: *Trina Wurst*
Indexer: *Johnna VanHoose Dinse*
Layout: *Becky Batchelor*
Proofreader: *John Etchison*

Contents at a Glance

Contents

Introduction

The paranormal is an extremely broad subject, and writing any single book that covered every aspect of it would be nearly impossible. This book is meant to serve as an introduction to understanding the vast and fascinating world of paranormal phenomena.

Also, as you read this book, it is important to understand that much of what we know about the paranormal world is still based on theory, speculation, and first-person accounts. Rarely is one solid theory or concept thought to definitively explain any paranormal phenomenon. So there could be times when the ideas, theories, and concepts you read in this book might contradict your own personal beliefs. Please note that this book is meant to offer available data on the paranormal and is in no way intended to denounce anyone's belief system, nor is it meant to tell you what to believe.

If you are seeking truth, remember that the best place to look is often within yourself. Never just take someone's word for it—not even this book's. Only by thinking for yourself and seeking your own truth will you be able to learn anything of value.

How to Use This Book

In order to make a more effective and user-friendly reference on the subject of the paranormal, this book has been separated into four main parts and further broken down into chapters by focus subject and type as follows:

Any discussion of the paranormal usually begins with the subject of spirit phenomena, and for good reason. The majority of cases being handled by today's paranormal investigators involve alleged ghost phenomena or spirit activity. In **Part 1, "Ghosts, Spirits, and Paranormal Investigation,"** I discuss in detail the various forms and phenomena related to the spiritual realm. You are also introduced to the tools, methods, and tactics of modern paranormal investigation.

Angels have long been a part of human myths. For every light, however, there is always dark. In the paranormal world, evil forces are often identified as fallen angels or demons. **Part 2, "Angels, Demons, and Spellcasters,"** offers you a closer look at the darker side of the paranormal world.

Not all paranormal entities are spirits, of course. Every year, there are reports of human encounters with the strange and monstrous. However, where do we draw the line between monster and animal? In **Part 3, "Monsters, Shapeshifters, and the Undead,"** we take a look at the physical entities of the paranormal world. From hairy humanoids to sea creatures to walking dead guys, this part familiarizes you with the monsters of our world.

Many paranormal phenomena are as difficult to define as they are to explain. In **Part 4, "Unexplained Phenomena,"** many of these strange occurrences are presented in detail. Can some humans really move objects with their minds? Why have so many people vanished without a trace, never to be seen or heard from again? These are just a sample of the many mysteries we explore in our final part.

Sidebars

As already explained, the paranormal is a very broad subject, so it is sometimes easy to find yourself confused. To better guide you along the way, I provide a number of sidebars, which clarify key terms, ideas, concepts, and facts.

The Bermuda Triangle

These sidebars offer clarification for easily confused concepts, events, and words related to the paranormal, such as common misperceptions or similarities in spellings, plots, purposes, and actions.

Conjuring Words

These sidebars offer definitions and explanations for the various terms, objects, and names you'll encounter while reading the text.

Stranger Than Fiction

These sidebars offer facts related to the content of the text. Some of these will simply offer interesting but extraneous side notes, while others will directly relate to the subject matter.

The Scary Truth

Sometimes, especially when dealing with the paranormal, the line between reality and fiction can become a little difficult to see. These sidebars will act as reality checks from time to time, offering rational explanations for the many spectacular and historical situations you'll encounter throughout your reading.

Acknowledgments

As always, I would like to thank everyone at Alpha Books who made this project possible. A special thanks to Randy Ladenheim-Gil and Megan Douglass for their confidence and effort in helping make this work the best it could be. I would also like to thank the staff of the Southwest Blvd. I.H.O.P. in Wichita Falls, Texas, for being so accommodating to me while I used their restaurant as a temporary office space.

Trademarks

All terms mentioned in this book that are known to be or are suspected of being trademarks or service marks have been appropriately capitalized. Alpha Books and Penguin Group (USA) Inc. cannot attest to the accuracy of this information. Use of a term in this book should not be regarded as affecting the validity of any trademark or service mark.

Part 1

Ghosts, Spirits, and Paranormal Investigation

Before you can truly have an understanding of the paranormal, you must know how to tell the difference between a ghost and a spirit, a haunting and a poltergeist, or a following specter and a demonic presence. Once you can properly identify these phenomena, you'll need to have the proper equipment and be knowledgeable in the methodologies of paranormal investigation. Before you go chasing down ghosts and spirits, these chapters will tell you the basics of what you need to know.

Chapter 1

The Haunts of Lost Souls

In This Chapter

- The differences between a spirit, a ghost, and an apparition
- The forms assumed by ghosts and spirits
- The various frequencies and schedules by which ghost and spirit activity occurs (or reoccurs)
- The traditional definition of a "lost soul" ghost
- The many new theories about the ghost phenomenon
- Encounters with evil forces and demonic spirits pretending to be ghosts

Any discussion of the *paranormal* world must begin with a discussion of spiritual entities. Before you can understand and identify any kind of paranormal activity, you must first know how to tell the difference between them to figure out what you are dealing with. Only then can you develop a plan on what to do.

What Is That Thing?

People who experience paranormal phenomena throw the word "ghost" around a lot. However, in many cases these individual *percipients* haven't encountered ghosts at all. That's not to say they did not have an experience with some paranormal *agent*; it just wasn't a ghost.

Conjuring Words _____

Paranormal literally means "above/beyond normal." The term refers to events, abilities, and phenomena which cannot be explained, identified, or understood through normal/scientific means or methods.

In the paranormal world, a **percipient** is someone who witnesses a spirit apparition. In recent years, some paranormal investigators have replaced this word with simpler terms such as "subject" or "client."

In terms of paranormal phenomena, an **agent** refers to the spirit phenomenon a percipient witnesses. This word has largely come to be replaced by "entity," as agent implies a certain amount of intent, which recent theories suggest may not apply to all spirits or apparitions.

In general, there are three primary types of spiritual entities that one may encounter when dealing with the paranormal:

+ Spirits

+ Ghosts

+ Demons or other evil forces

Any of these entity types will usually manifest, or at least make their presence known, in one or both of the following manners:

+ **Perceivable activity:** The spirit might make sounds or move certain objects (though this is somewhat rare, especially if you're dealing with a ghost) but not make itself visible.

+ **Apparition:** A spirit can assume a visible form that you can see with the naked eye or record in photos/videos. Apparitions can range from looking human to shadowlike to assuming various shapes of light.

Spirits

While a particular spirit might turn out to be a ghost, this won't always be the case. In basic terms, a ghost is a specific type of spirit. Therefore, all ghosts are spirits, but not all spirits are ghosts. Then what are spirits? Well, as is often the case when dealing with questions about paranormal phenomena, it's rather difficult to pin down a definitive answer for this.

A spirit, which we can more specifically refer to as a *disembodied* spirit, is best described as any nonphysical entity that seems to have a mind, will, or force of its own. This doesn't mean that all spirits are intelligent or interactive, however. Some experts believe that some spirits, especially in certain theories regarding ghosts, have a very limited will (if they have any will at all).

 Conjuring Words

Generically speaking, **disembodied** means "released/separated from the body." In paranormal terms, it refers to spirits, such as ghosts, that are at any point thought to have occupied a physical body. (In some situations, this also applies to any human-possessing demonic entities known to have been exorcized from a human body.)

Ghosts

As already stated, ghosts are a specific type of spirit. But how so? Unlike other spirit entities, ghosts always mimic, behave like, have the personality of, or appear in the form of a person who was at some point among the living. Ghosts, basically, are largely considered spirits of the human dead (or at least spirits that are trying to act as such).

Ghosts, like most spirits, don't always manifest in visible apparition forms. The word ghost also has a number of synonymous terms, many of which we use interchangeably, including but not limited to:

♦ Phantom

♦ Specter (or spectre)

♦ Spook

♦ Lost soul (specifically the ghost of a once-living person who does not realize that he or she is dead)

- Spirit vision/ghost guide (the ghost of a person who has returned in order to deliver a warning, advise the living, etc.)

- Wraith/vengeful ghost (the restless ghost of someone betrayed or in some way irredeemably wronged, usually resulting in the person's death)

Since ghosts are supposedly the spirits of those who were once alive, their frequency of activity changes from one case to another. The most common schedules for the activity of ghosts are as follows:

- **Isolated occurrence:** The ghost is only seen, experienced, or otherwise encountered on one occasion.

- **Predictable reoccurrence:** The ghost appears or is active at the same time or day of the week or month. For example, a ghost who always appears at 3 A.M. on the second Saturday of each month.

- **Anniversary reoccurrence:** The ghost shows up on the same date each year, commonly on the date of his or her death.

- **Localized reoccurrence:** The ghost seems attached to a room, house, structure, or place and may follow a less regular activity schedule.

- **Personal ghost:** The ghost follows a specific living person. For example, the ghost of a dead husband follows his grieving widow because he desires to take care of or protect her (neither of which he can do, of course, as a ghost). This ghost type is very rare, and there are some in the paranormal field who do not agree that they exist.

Theories About Ghosts

Are ghosts, in fact, the wandering, returned, or lost spirits/souls of human beings who were at one time alive? Some would say they most definitely are. In fact, until the rise of paranormal research and investigation over the last few decades, this "lost soul" concept was very commonly accepted as the cause of the ghost phenomenon. After all, ghosts often seem to act like or resemble people who have died. However, many new theories in the paranormal community offer alternative explanations for ghosts.

Many of these new theories regarding ghost phenomena come from the realm of *parapsychology*. This new area of study has led to breakthroughs in paranormal research, including new technology and improved methodology in dealing with certain phenomena. According to some parapsychologists, what we have long called ghosts are not the lost souls of the dead at all. Some in this field would argue that ghosts are, in fact, not even a supernatural occurrence.

Conjuring Words

Parapsychology is the study of unknown or unexplained mental phenomena, often called psychic phenomena (see Chapter 16). The work of parapsychologists often overlaps with that of paranormal research. Therefore, they're sometimes referred to as "paranormal psychologists," though this term doesn't really make sense if you think about it.

Many of these new ideas are actually based on an ancient Eastern belief that all things, physical and nonphysical, are ruled by the flow of a secondary life force or energy, which the Chinese refer to as *Chi*, and the Japanese, *Ki*. They believe it flows out from a center point in the abdomen and makes its way throughout the body by traveling along a complex series of intersecting *Chi/Ki* points, which are often called "meridians" in English. Hindus believe this energy flows through a series of circular or spherical "inner gates" called *chakra*.

Stranger Than Fiction

For years, many in the medical and scientific community scoffed at the idea of *Chi/Ki*. Because of this skeptical perception, doctors and scientists long dismissed the Chinese art of acupuncture as "experimental" at best. Acupuncture involves inserting thin needles at certain body points to "unblock" *Chi* meridians in order to improve healing, control pain, and even alter habitual behaviors. However, when data strongly supported that acupuncture produced very real and consistent results, this view changed. Today, acupuncture is considered a legitimate medical procedure, and therefore is now covered by most insurance companies.

The first new theory is that ghosts are not lost souls but residual energy left behind by the living after death. It is believed that people who die violently, traumatically, or in a moment of extreme stress release an extremely strong amount of energy in the process. When their bodies die, this energy remains behind and produces a phenomenon that is mistakenly thought to be a ghost. Ghosts almost never interact with the living, at least not directly or intelligently, but instead endlessly repeat the events/behaviors they performed at the moment of their deaths. Perhaps what a percipient sees when witnessing a "ghost" phenomenon is actually a strong amount of human energy that has left behind a kind of residual imprint that will mark the space where it occurred until it finally burns out.

A second, but rather similar, theory suggests that humans leave behind energy during life. This is especially true with habitual behaviors or repetitious actions. For example, if a person does a particular action every day, in the same place, over and over, for decades upon decades, the idea is that he or she is involuntarily leaving behind a minute amount of energy each time. As the years pass, the energy builds. As long as the living person continues these repetitive, regularly performed actions, the energy continues to build a charge … often entirely unnoticed. When the individual passes on, however, the theory is that the energy starts to release or dissipate, often following the same schedule by which it was charged.

This concept is not that hard to accept, especially when you consider the fact that many ghosts (especially visible ones) are often seen performing repetitious or habitual actions. For example, an old man who once lived in a home spent every evening sitting in his favorite chair, smoking a pipe and reading the paper. For 50 years, he did this every day at roughly the same time. After he died, the new occupants of the house saw apparitions of the deceased old man sitting in his chair, smoking his pipe, and reading the paper. When they tried to get his attention, he ignored them or just disappeared.

The next theory is also similar to the idea of residual energy but runs more along the lines of physics. As you'll read in Chapter 16, recent advancements in science have revealed the existence of "memory molecules." That's right. Our memories are not just intangible data; they have an actual, physical molecular form. This theory begs a question—if memory can exist in molecules, then where do those molecules go, both during life and after death? Well, it's now believed that some of these molecules pass down in our DNA. However, this doesn't explain where *all* of them go. This theory suggests that ghosts are actually molecules of memory that the dead (and in some cases, even the living) leave behind, which somehow travel their way into the minds of other people. These people mentally receive a "secondhand" signal as a result of interaction with these memory molecules. The rather unusual experience that this causes may often be mistaken as either a ghost or spirit encounter.

Lastly, there is a psychic phenomenon known as retrocognition, which causes people to see things that have happened in the past right before their very eyes. For example, a person staying in an old house looks outside to see an army of seventeenth-century soldiers walking across the yard. The person is seeing an event that happened in that very spot several centuries before. However, no one really knows how or why this happens. In truth, any of the preceding theories could just be different ways of explaining what might later turn out to be the same phenomenon.

Spirit/Ghost Activity vs. Demon Activity

When interacting with spirit entities, one must always remember one crucial piece of information: *a ghost cannot and will not harm you.* True ghosts, 99.9 percent of the time, are not known to be dangerous. However, this doesn't mean that all spirits are harmless. As you will see in Chapters 6 and 7, certain evil forces and demonic spirits exist that certainly can and will bring harm to the living if they can.

But just because a ghost or spirit is loud, rude, or even frightening, don't automatically assume you have a demon on your hands. Sometimes it is thought that ghosts get a bit cranky when unfamiliar people occupy their space, likely because this reminds them that they are not alive. However, they're just trying to frighten you and will often leave if you tell them to. Many believe that ghosts could not physically hurt people even if they wanted to—that they are actually incapable of making any physical contact. But remember this: the moment a spirit intentionally harms a living human being or animal, you can rest assured that it's definitely *not a ghost.* In all likelihood, it is a demon ... which means you should consult an exorcist or demonologist as soon as possible.

Many cases of spirit phenomena have been initially misidentified as either being a ghost or "friendly spirit," only to be discovered later that this was not the case. It is not unheard of for evil forces or demonic spirits to pretend to be ghosts or harmless spirits. In many cases of home hauntings, such malevolent entities have identified themselves at first as being people known to have died in the house. By doing so, they're able to strengthen their hold on the house before they turn ugly. And you better believe things can and will get very nasty in such cases. As you will learn in Chapter 4, carrying out a proper and methodical paranormal investigation is crucial in order to avoid mistakes such as these, which are likely to come back to bite you in the rear later on.

Just because demonic spirits sometimes pretend to be ghosts, this does not mean that *all* spirits are actually demons in disguise. Many of the more rigidly conservative Christian groups are often fond of making all-inclusive claims such as these when it comes to spirit phenomenon. They insist there are no such things as ghosts or even spirits (which is odd, especially since they openly express their belief in the nonphysical human soul), but only demons in disguise. Of course, these claims almost never address the fact that, if all spirits are demons, then what about angels? If a demon were to manifest itself, claiming to be an angel, how would one know the difference? Because of the situation, right? Well, it's no different when one is dealing with spirits.

The truth is that every single case of paranormal activity is different and must be handled based on its evidence and behavior. Not all cases of paranormal activity can be resolved with exorcisms, nor can they all be handled by spirit mediums. Whether you are dealing with ghosts, spirits (good or bad), or demons, trying to place concrete labels on something as abstract as spirit entities is never a very good idea.

The Least You Need to Know

- While all ghosts are spirits, not all spirits are ghosts.

- Ghosts always resemble, in action or appearance, humans who were at one time alive.

- New theories among paranormal researchers suggest that ghosts are not the lost souls of people but illusions caused by residual energy/life force.

◆ Another theory suggests that memory molecules may somehow make contact with others, causing an experience that could easily be mistaken as "ghostly."

◆ *Ghosts do not hurt people,* but evil forces and demonic spirits certainly do.

◆ If a spirit entity turns physically violent, it's time to consult a demonologist or exorcist.

2

Poltergeists and Hauntings

In This Chapter

- ◆ The difference between a haunting, a poltergeist, and demonic activity
- ◆ Different ways of dealing with poltergeists, hauntings, and demonic activity
- ◆ The theories behind what causes the poltergeist phenomenon
- ◆ The renowned case of the Enfield Poltergeist
- ◆ The haunted Toys R Us store in Sunnyvale, California
- ◆ Encounters with the infamous spirit who haunts Japan's Sendagaya Tunnel

Are chairs tumbling over, as if by themselves? Do drawers spontaneously open and slam shut? Are rocks falling from the ceiling, as if materializing from thin air? Well then, it's quite possible that you have a poltergeist on your hands!

The poltergeist phenomenon is probably one of the most widely misunderstood paranormal concepts. As a result, people often mistake ghost phenomenon for poltergeist activity, and vice versa. So how do you tell the difference between these sometimes similar yet distinctly different paranormal phenomena?

Haunting, Possession, or Poltergeist?

A haunting specifically refers to the presence of ghost phenomenon. In all honesty, sometimes ghosts are just something residents/occupants have to learn to deal with or move out. Ghost phenomena have never been known to bring intentional harm to a person. In a handful of cases, people have been so startled by ghosts that they've either died from the shock (quite literally "scared to death") or as a result of some freak accident that occurred during their flights of panic. However, in these cases, it's believed that the ghosts involved did not directly hurt anyone. Also, true ghosts have been known to move stuff only in rare cases.

The Bermuda Triangle

When dealing with spirit phenomena, it is important to keep this in mind: scary does not always equal dangerous. Ghostly agents can often do some very disconcerting things, but this doesn't necessarily mean they're trying to harm you or anyone else (nor even that they're capable of doing so). Ghost phenomena can *act* violent at times, but that's about all it really is—acting.

If the phenomenon being experienced has begun to do more extreme things, such as moving objects or hurting people, then this is probably not a traditional ghost haunting. In this case, the phenomenon is going to be either a poltergeist or a demonic/evil spirit (sometimes called area possession, which you can read more about in Chapter 7). These two very unique phenomena require far different methods to deal with them.

The Truth About Poltergeists

Many of the common misperceptions regarding the poltergeist phenomenon began in 1982, when Steven Spielberg and Tobe Hooper
released their frightening special effects masterpiece called *Poltergeist*.
The movie was a hit at the box office and has since come to be seen as
a classic of the horror cinema genre. There's just one problem with this
film ... it has absolutely nothing to do with poltergeists.

The Scary Truth

Movies about the paranormal can be very entertaining, but keep in
mind that these are works of *fantasy*. Movies and TV shows (even
those based on true events) are often sensational in nature because this
makes them more interesting to watch. However, they also play with the
facts and details of the events they're based on. Therefore, you probably
shouldn't go to movies if you are hoping to increase your understanding of
paranormal phenomena.

The word *poltergeist* comes from the German language and roughly
translates as "noisy ghost/spirit." Although it is no longer believed that
spirits or ghosts have anything to do with poltergeists, the use of the
original term has continued for the sake of familiarity.

You may be wondering why this phenomenon first came to be called a
"noisy spirit." Well, the answer to that one is simple. One of the most
common attributes of poltergeists is that they are *loud* like you would
not believe. They slam doors, toss objects (they seem especially fond of
rocks and silverware), turn over furniture, bang on walls, and violently
yank open and slam shut kitchen cabinets and drawers. Sometimes a
poltergeist will even make faucets turn off and on or spontaneously (and,
as one might guess, rather disconcertingly) cause electrical devices to
turn on and off. In some of the most extreme cases, it has seemed as if
the entire home had gone crazy. You can probably imagine what it would
look like if *all* this poltergeist activity happened in one house simultaneously. To say the least, it'd probably scare the wits out of most people.

Apparitions, however, are not a part of the poltergeist phenomenon.
Witnesses see the activity it causes, of course, but no one has ever actually seen a poltergeist with their own eyes. You hear and see what it does,

but if you see an apparition, then it isn't a poltergeist. In which case, you probably have an area possession on your hands, meaning you're dealing with evil forces or demonic spirits. For details on how to proceed in the case of area possession, refer to Chapter 7.

Five Stages of a Poltergeist

There are generally five primary stages by which the level of a poltergeist is identified. These stages range from mildly annoying to downright dangerous. Basically, the more extreme the poltergeist activity becomes, the higher the number by which it is classified.

> **The Scary Truth** _____
>
> Sudden drops in temperature have long been associated with various forms of paranormal/spirit phenomena. However, this doesn't mean that just because a room gets cold that you have something paranormal on your hands. Look for a normal cause before you start freaking out. For example, you may just be sitting under or near an air conditioning vent. Also, unexplained cold does not exclusively occur with poltergeists. Just about all spirit phenomena are believed capable of causing these sudden temperature drops.

The five main stages of a poltergeist, in order of frequency and extremity (weakest to strongest), are as follows:

- Stage 1: Latent/dormant/passive stage
- Stage 2: Obvious/detectable presence
- Stage 3: Increased kinetic activity
- Stage 4: Intelligent/individual targeting
- Stage 5: Dangerous/life-threatening kinetic activity

Let's discuss each of these stages in detail.

Stage 1: Latent/Dormant/Passive Stage

Nothing all that remarkable occurs at this stage. In fact, most people aren't even aware that anything is awry, and they certainly aren't thinking their house is under the influence of a poltergeist. The activity is minimal and often dismissed as coincidence or a series of "freak occurrences."

However, there are certain things one can look for in order to identify such phenomena. Animals are usually more in tune to paranormal activity than humans. As a result, your pet may begin to act strangely—for example, a dog may stare, growl, or bark at a spot when nothing is there. Another telltale sign is noticing cold spots, meaning the temperature will suddenly seem to drop in certain places for no reason.

Stage 2: Obvious/Detectable Presence

This stage occurs when those experiencing the phenomenon become aware that something is not quite right. Of course, this is not true of everyone. There are always those individuals who will continue to dismiss the unusual activity with the usual excuses, such as it's all "just their imaginations," "just the wind," or caused by "the house settling."

The cold spots will usually increase at this point. For example, entire rooms may suddenly be engulfed by frigid air, often more intensely in certain rooms than in others. Also, unexplained scratches, gashes, or cuts may begin showing up on walls and/or furniture at this point. Sometimes, one person in the house might start experiencing light but unexplained scratches on his or her skin. Needless to say, these are not good signs.

Stage 3: Increased Kinetic Activity

Probably the best way to describe a stage three poltergeist is that this is the "holy crap phase." There's no more ignoring the phenomenon by now, because its presence is far more obvious. You see, at this stage the really weird stuff starts happening. Most of the time, owners/inhabitants are finally convinced to seek out the help of a paranormal investigation team (or a religious figure) by this point. Can you blame them?

Lights and appliances sporadically turn off and on. Closed and sometimes even locked doors and windows may suddenly come open, and unexplainable rapping and banging sounds may also begin to occur.

People in the house may begin to feel as if unseen hands are touching or scratching them.

Stage 4: Intelligent/Individual Targeting

This is where things start to get really, *really* scary, because the activity turns from disrupting to violent. At this stage, poltergeists often behave as if they're targeting one or more specific individuals in the home. For unknown reasons, most of the violent activity seems to specifically target adults (especially parents) and teenagers in the home more often than young children.

Objects may fly at people from places unseen. Doors may suddenly slam in people's faces (or *into* them) as they enter certain rooms. Sharp objects, such as kitchen knives, may even shoot out of open drawers. However, these often don't seem aimed at anyone or at least don't have enough force to be lethal.

Stage 5: Dangerous/Life-Threatening Kinetic Activity

If a poltergeist reaches this stage, you should get out of the house … *right now.* This thing isn't playing around anymore and has the potential power to seriously injure, or even kill, someone in the house. The safety of everyone inside the house, no matter if they live there or not, is now in serious jeopardy. If you haven't sought professional help by now, what in the heck are you waiting for—an invitation?

The scratches are now drawing blood from the skin, or ripping deep gashes through walls and furniture. Knives are flying hard enough to imbed deeply in countertops. And what's worse, small fires spontaneously spark up in different places and spread out all over the house (fire extinguisher, anyone?). Needless to say, this stage is about as bad as a poltergeist can get … and they can get very *bad.*

The thrown objects now move with far more force, making them capable of serious damage. Also, the size and weight of the objects can increase. For example, the poltergeist may have started by tapping you lightly in the back with the occasional tossed, but still relatively small, rock. By stage five, it's more likely to send a 40-pound dumbbell flying straight at your head.

Theoretical Causes of Poltergeists

No one can say with absolute certainty what causes the poltergeist phenomenon. However, comparative studies of known cases have turned up some very interesting clues. The one thing just about everyone in the paranormal research community now agrees about is that poltergeists are definitely *not* disembodied spirits or ghosts.

In fact, most experts now agree that all poltergeist phenomena are actually caused by human beings, namely a specific secondary individual (usually someone living in or near the house where the activity is occurring). The theory explains that this individual who causes poltergeist phenomenon is usually (but not always) unaware that he or she possesses psychokinetic or telekinetic abilities. These latent abilities, many agree, are released in periods of extreme mental stress, emotional distress, and trauma.

At one point, it was popularly thought that females entering or in the middle of puberty specifically caused poltergeists. This theory stemmed from the fact that many of the initially investigated cases of poltergeist phenomenon were found to be caused by teenage girls releasing some kind of involuntary psychic energy. While it's true that poltergeists have frequently occurred in homes with teenage females, there have been many recorded poltergeists where this was not the case.

The most widely accepted nature of this involuntary psychic energy, which has been developed and endorsed by some of the world's most prominent parapsychologists, is something called *Recurrent Spontaneous Psychokinesis*, also referred to as *Repressed Psychokinetic Energy*. The idea is that if an individual who unknowingly possesses psychic, telekinetic, or psychokinetic abilities suddenly experiences some kind of traumatic event (which, most people would agree, certainly includes puberty) then he or she could accidentally unleash a large amount of psychic energy. Unfortunately, the person isn't aware he or she is doing this, and certainly can't control it. In fact, the individual might even harm themselves or be afraid of the poltergeist, despite the fact that it's coming from their own psychic energy.

Conjuring Words _____

Recurrent Spontaneous Psychokinesis is a regularly reoccurring release of psychic energy, capable of moving physical objects, usually released by someone who is unaware that he or she is doing so. Some believe this to be a cause of poltergeist phenomena.

Repressed Psychokinetic Energy is believed to be psychic energy unknowingly released by an individual who possesses psychic abilities but does not know it. This form of energy builds as a result of stress or trauma until it eventually reaches a peak and is released, resulting in a poltergeist phenomenon.

The idea that poltergeists are caused by humans was first proposed by renowned parapsychologist Dr. William G. Roll, Ph.D. He developed this idea during a 1984 case, often called the "Columbus Poltergeist" (it took place in Columbus, Ohio), in which he believed a teenage girl named Tina Resch was accidentally causing a poltergeist phenomenon to occur in her home. He first dubbed this unusual psychic phenomenon as "Spontaneous Telekinesis."

A veteran photojournalist named Fred Shannon came to the scene to document the phenomenon with his camera and produced a number of impressive pieces of photographic evidence. The validity of the pictures is, as one would imagine, still being challenged by skeptics and continues to be debated among many of today's paranormal researchers and parapsychologists.

Of course, a number of people still insist that poltergeists are caused by malevolent spirits. Some claim that evil spirits may be drawn to a place by the large amount of psychokinetic energy being released there. Others go the whole nine yards and claim the entire phenomenon is caused by demonic spirits. However, there is one rather large hole in this theory. In multiple cases of poltergeist phenomena, demonic exorcisms were performed (sometimes being repeated several times) and absolutely nothing changed. If demonic spirits were responsible for the phenomenon, then the exorcism should have at least had an effect. However, research suggests that exorcisms are pretty ineffective against poltergeists (for more on exorcisms, see Chapter 7).

The Enfield Poltergeist

In 1977, a poltergeist case began at a home in Enfield, England. The first event took place one night when a woman named Peggy Harper was told by her 11-year-old daughter, Janet, and 10-year-old son, Peter, that their beds had jolted and turned suddenly. The mother was convinced her children were simply playing a prank and refused to believe their story. This would soon change.

Not long after the first event, again in the evening hours, Janet and her sister were playing in their bedroom before bedtime. They were stunned when a large chest of drawers began to drag its way across the floor. At first, the girls thought it was coming at them, but it then moved toward the door as if to block them in the room. Luckily, Mrs. Harper entered the room just in time and pushed the chest back against the wall. However, it started pushing back. Mrs. Harper realized that some nonphysical force was involved. In a panic, she quickly gathered up her children and got them out of the house.

When she went to her neighbor and explained what had happened, some of her male neighbors went over to search the house and found it completely empty. They then started to hear loud rapping, as if someone were banging on every wall in the house at regular intervals. They called the police, who arrived on the scene at 11 at night. The policemen also heard the rapping, and one officer watched in astonishment as a chair suddenly moved across the floor right in front of him. All the men, including the officers, later signed sworn statements that what they'd reported was absolutely true.

This is what makes the Enfield Poltergeist case so unique. There were a lot of witnesses, many respected members of the community, to the phenomenon. For roughly two years the paranormal activity continued. Before it ceased, as many as 30 independent people had witnessed the poltergeist activity in the Harper home.

Despite the large number of witnesses and an impressive body of video and photo evidence that was collected by the British Society for Psychical Research, many skeptics continue to insist that the Enfield Poltergeist was a hoax, orchestrated by Janet Harper. They claim that this 11-year-old girl had somehow duped everyone. There are even some vehement skeptics who find this claim a little hard to swallow.

Since poltergeist phenomenon is believed to be caused by people, it certainly is possible that Janet (who was just entering the age of puberty) was causing the kinetic activity—not by a hoax, but by accidentally releasing repressed psychokinetic energy. This theory is further supported by the fact that when the poltergeist later revealed itself, it did so by speaking through Janet.

Some claim that the fact that spirits revealed themselves by speaking through Janet proves the theory that evil spirits, not people with psychokinetic abilities, cause poltergeist activity. However, a big enough amount of psychic energy is believed capable of manifesting in the form of an entity. Such poltergeist agents are thought to be intelligent manifestations of the psychokinetic person's psyche or unconscious mind.

In truth, no one can say for certain who or what caused the Enfield Poltergeist. However, in 1978, the activity suddenly stopped. In 1980, there was a brief resurgence of the activity, but since that time, there've been no further reports of paranormal activity at the Harpers' Enfield home.

The Amityville Horror

The famous paranormal case that is commonly referred to as the "Amityville Horror" is probably one of the most widely known and discussed paranormal events in recent decades. Despite the large body of evidence that was compiled during the case, many people have come forward, for various reasons, claiming to have proof that the Amityville haunting was really just a hoax. Discussing the various personal and legal conflicts surrounding the case would offer little to no insight, however, into what actually transpired. Therefore, what follows is simply a summary of the strange phenomena that was encountered by Ed and Lorraine Warren, paranormal investigators, demonologists, and co-founders of the New England Society for Psychic Research (NESPR). (See Chapter 4 for more details on the Warrens and NESPR.)

Stranger Than Fiction

Many of the hoax accusations surrounding the Warrens and the Amityville case stem from a man named Steven Kaplan. Kaplan heard of the activity at the house, and arrived unannounced with a Channel 7 camera crew and seven self-proclaimed "witches." Mr. Lutz immediately threw them off the property. It is generally believed that this began a personal vendetta for Kaplan against both the Warrens and the Lutzes. He later recanted his accusations and publicly apologized.

At 6:50 P.M., on November 13, 1974, 23-year-old Ronald "Butch" DeFeo Jr. came crashing through the door of Henry's Bar in Amityville, New York. He yelled "You got to help me! I think my mother and father have been shot!" He then fell to his knees, sobbing and hysterical. Butch's best friend, a local masonry worker named Bobby, along with a group of other bar patrons, followed him back to the house. They found his entire family dead and called the police.

At the DeFeo home, 112 Ocean Avenue, in Amityville, New York, police discovered the bodies of almost the entire DeFeo family—the father, mother, and four of their children. In fact, only one member of the family was not among the dead—Ronald, their oldest son. It was soon discovered that Ronald had murdered his entire family. Apparently, Ronald's father had recently learned of his son's drug habit. The confrontations between them were often heated, and Ronald began to hate his father. Under the influence of drugs, and also claiming to have been guided by a "shadow spirit," Ronald hatched a plot to murder his father with a .35 caliber rifle.

The Scary Truth

It has been confirmed that Ronald DeFeo Sr. was known to have been physically abusive, especially toward his oldest son, Ronald. In all honesty, this is likely what led Ronald to drug abuse. It also explains why he hated his father enough to murder him. This does not mean that some evil force was not involved, but it does mean that there were non-paranormal motivations in the DeFeo killings.

But why, then, if he'd only planned to kill his father, did he also murder his mother and siblings, who had done nothing to provoke him? Under police interrogation, Ronald claimed that after he'd killed his father, the "shadow spirit" convinced him to kill his four siblings (two brothers and two sisters) and his mother. He later told detectives that these killings had occurred around 3:15 A.M. (nearly 14 hours before he came to Henry's Bar). Ronald was later convicted of murdering his family and sentenced to life in prison without the possibility of parole. He is currently serving out his sentence at the Green Haven Correctional Facility. Even from prison, Ronald has carried out numerous (and usually frivolous) lawsuits against nearly every person involved in the Amityville case in order to extort money for himself.

There was one weird detail that baffled everyone, however. All the victims had been shot, but no one in the neighborhood (even in the nearest houses, only 40 feet away) had heard any gunfire. Also, no one heard so much as a scream during the hours in which the killings occurred. Also, all of the victims were found lying face down on their stomachs. However, they had not been moved after they were shot … and there was no evidence that they had been forced to lie down before they were shot.

Based on the evidence regarding the state in which the bodies were discovered, the Warrens and NESPR members later came to the conclusion that the shadow spirit may have put them all into a state they call "phantomania," which leads to a state of involuntary movement (caused by the acting spirit's influence) and/or total paralysis. This means that the DeFeo family may not have even known what was happening to them, and that they were likely incapable of pleading with their deranged son or even crying out for help. The influence of phantomania, according to the Warrens' theory, would certainly explain why no one in the surrounding area reported hearing any shouts or screams coming from the house during the murders.

According to the data collected by the Warrens and members of the NESPR during their initial research regarding the history of the house, the property on which it was built had previously been used as a sanitarium of sorts, exclusively for Native Americans who were sick, insane, or terminally ill. The conditions of the place, however, were horrible and inhumane. Many paranormal experts believe demons and other malevolent inhuman spirits are attracted to such places, where humans are suffering (especially if it occurs on unholy, cursed, or unconsecrated ground).

In December of 1975, George Lutz and his family moved into the home at 112 Ocean Avenue. Shortly after, they began experiencing frequent, violent, and frightening paranormal activity. They consulted a priest, Father Ralph Pecararo, who was so convinced that he in turn contacted Ed and Lorraine Warren. During a violent fit of paranormal activity on January 14, 1976, the Lutzes had totally abandoned their new home in terror. They were now staying with Mrs. Lutz's mother in Deer Park, New York. They had left in such a rush that they'd abandoned all their possessions in the house, leaving with only the clothes on their backs. They had not returned to the house since. During the Warrens' initial interview with the Lutzes, they were so frightened that they didn't even seem to want to speak about what had happened.

The Warrens decided to go to the house and conduct an initial investigation. But the Warrens did not venture there alone. They were accompanied by a Duke University professor, a camera crew from the local Channel Five News, and Mary Pascarella, the president of the American Society for Psychic Research. When they reached the house, Lorraine was immediately bombarded with vivid and disturbing psychic messages and visions. Her husband Ed was eager to confirm the phenomenon, and so ventured down into the home's cellar. There, he was physically attacked by a group of shadowy spirits that appeared covered with what he described as "pinpoints of light." Ed had to use religious chants to resist the spirits' attempts to force him down to the ground. By Ed's own admission, he had never before (and has never since) been as severely affected by a case as he was by the one in Amityville.

Lorraine ventured upstairs and immediately felt psychically drawn to the room where the Lutzes' children had slept. She revealed that the beds and furniture in the room (which the Lutzes had found there when they first moved in) had belonged to the two murdered daughters of the DeFeo family. The Lutzes' children, they realized with horror, had been sleeping in the very same beds where the two girls had been killed. When she went to the master bedroom, it was the same story. The bed in the room (which had also been there when they moved in), she revealed, was the same bed in which the DeFeo parents had been killed. As Lorraine continued to go through the other rooms, the situation only got worse.

The Scary Truth

Sometimes, there are three sides to a story—one side's version, an opposing side's version, and the truth. When it comes to the Amityville case, it is hard to tell where the lies end and the truth begins. This is largely because so many people have come forward with false claims and fabricated evidence, both confirming and debunking the case, in attempts to "cash in" on its fame. In all honesty, there is sufficient evidence to support both sides of the debate on what really took place at 112 Ocean Avenue. In the end, you should just make up your own mind about what you want to believe.

Later, Lorraine used her abilities as a medium to communicate with any spirits in the houses. Odd noises seemed to come from nowhere and shadows moved swiftly along the walls of the room. The professor from Duke University became so overcome with fear that he fainted. Mary Pascarella fell violently ill, and had to be carried out of the house (and she never went back into the house … but can you really *blame* her?).

Ed and Lorraine Warren, based on what they'd witnessed, felt strongly that there was little that could be done to effectively exorcise and "cleanse" the Lutzes' home, because they claimed it was totally saturated with evil forces, malevolent energies, and demonic spirits. They left the house and vowed never to go back inside its evil walls. However, they later reconsidered this vow and courageously returned to assist in the long and difficult exorcism and cleansing of the possessed property. To this day, the debate rages on about what occurred from this point. Some say the spirits were forced out. Some claim that the whole thing was a hoax from the start. Who's to say? When all was said and done, however, the negative paranormal activity at the Lutzes' home ceased. The home remains a place of interest for paranormal enthusiasts and movie fans, but has never since been the site of any malevolent spiritual phenomena.

The Haunted Toy Store

There is some debate as to what is causing the strange paranormal activity that has long plagued the Toys R Us store in Sunnyvale, California. Some say it is a poltergeist, while a majority of others insist it is a traditional ghost haunting. Either way, there's no denying that a lot of weird things have happened in this toy store since the 1970s.

If you ask anyone who's worked at the store, they'll probably tell you the place is haunted by the ghost of a man named Johnson. Apparently, this man sometimes takes a visible apparition form, wearing a pair of riding knickers (suggesting that he died no later than the early twentieth century, and definitely before the store was constructed on that spot). Many claim he haunts the store because of some romantic tragedy he experienced during his life. This, however, is based on claims from employees and not from any documented evidence. Even so, Johnson's ghost is freaking out some of the women who work there. For example, many refuse to enter the women employees' restroom, claiming that when they do, the faucets suddenly turn on and off for no reason.

Some claim this is a poltergeist, based mainly on the fact that on several occasions managers have opened the doors in the morning to find the place in total disarray. But they're forgetting one important fact: the Johnson ghost has never once harmed anyone. Sure, he's weirded them out with some harmless pranks, but not once has he ever done anything mean or violent to anyone in the store. In fact, he hasn't even threatened anyone.

Just so you know, don't go to the Sunnyvale Toys R Us begging them to let you spend the night inside. And don't go sitting outside the front door with your Ouija board at 4 in the morning, trying to conjure up Johnson's ghost, either. The managers of the store really hate that kind of stuff and will promptly kick you off the property. As any paranormal investigator will tell you, always be respectful of other people, their property, and (perhaps most importantly) the law.

Sendagaya Tunnel (Japan)

The Sendagaya Tunnel runs directly beneath Japan's Ao-Yama Cemetery of the Senjuin Temple. So perhaps it's no surprise that the tunnel is said to be home to some rather strange ghost activity. Many motorists have had run-ins with a number of these paranormal traffic hazards.

Many taxi drivers in the area tell stories about being hailed by a young woman walking through the tunnel. Believing her to be a stranded motorist, the taxi driver pulls over, but when the young woman opens the back door, she suddenly disappears into thin air as she enters. As a result, many drivers won't even stop if they see someone walking in the tunnel (which is not good news for any *living* stranded motorists).

On top of this, a number of accidents have occurred due to other ghostly encounters. Many drivers have reported that, while making their way through the tunnel, they've looked in their rearview mirrors to see young children sitting in the backseat, staring back at them. The sudden panic caused by some of these child ghost experiences has caused drivers to lose control of their vehicles. Obviously, suddenly seeing a ghost kid in one's rearview mirror would be enough to make most people spaz out a little.

The Least You Need to Know

◆ While hauntings, area possessions, and poltergeists produce similar activity, they are very different phenomena.

◆ If you believe you have a stage five poltergeist, get everyone out of the house immediately.

◆ Many now believe that poltergeists are caused by humans who unknowingly release repressed psychokinetic energy.

◆ Exorcisms have proven ineffective in dealing with poltergeists.

◆ The Enfield Poltergeist case is unique because it produced more evidence and had more witnesses than any other in history.

Chapter 3

Japan: From Beyond the Grave

In This Chapter

- The "Ghost Season" of the Japanese *yurei* spirits
- The vengeful Japanese spirits known as the *Go-Ryo*
- The lost ghost mothers called the *Ubume*
- The *Funayurei* ghosts of lost mariners
- The spirits of the tragic fallen warriors of the Genpei War and the fearsome spirit of Taira no Masakado

Japanese culture is quite possibly the most "ghost-savvy" in the entire world. The myths and folklore of Japan, spanning the entire breadth of the country's history, are rich with stories about human encounters with members of the spirit realm. Many paranormal researchers consider Japan the most densely haunted country on the planet. After all, Japan has been home to a plethora of traumatic events, not the least of which were the catastrophic atomic bombings of both Hiroshima and Nagasaki during the final days of World War II.

In addition, statistics show that, on average, 30,000 Japanese citizens commit suicide each year (that's roughly one suicide every 15 minutes), giving it one of the highest suicide rates in the world. These suicides are often the results of either bullying or overwhelming personal/financial stress. So we shouldn't be surprised to find that a multitude of modern Japanese ghost tales exist that deal with disgruntled students or employees who violently haunt their former schools or places of business. In the Japanese point of view, the dead do not always rest in peace.

Japan's "Ghost Season"

From August through September, two of the warmest months of the year, Japanese commonly believe that *yurei* spirits are especially active. While there is no specific Japanese term for it, some refer to these months as Japan's "Ghost Season." Many of the more superstitious Japanese people take special care during this period to give honor to the dead, ward off the wrath of evil or vengeful spirits, and protect their homes and families against supernatural harm in general.

Conjuring Words

Yurei literally translates as "hazy/faint spirit," but is often interpreted in English as "ghost." In ancient times, they were considered good, but as time passed, they came to be regarded with a certain amount of fear.

The Japanese belief that August is a month when spirits are most active may have arisen shortly after the introduction of Buddhism into the country. In the Japanese Buddhist tradition, a special ceremony (sometimes referred to as "Bon") is held during mid-August to honor the spirits of family ancestors and lost or angry spirits in general. On the first night of this ghostly ceremony, many Japanese families (Buddhist and Shinto alike) light bonfires called *mukae-bi*. This first bonfire is supposed to draw up ancestral spirits from the realm of the dead and out of their permanent resting places.

The Bermuda Triangle

Shinto and Buddhism are the two primary religions of the Japanese people. The nature-focused tradition of Shinto was the original indigenous religion of the country, but eventually, Japan came to accept both religions. Today, a great number of Japanese people integrate the beliefs and practices of both the Shinto and Buddhist religions, so it is not at all uncommon for a Japanese person to openly practice both.

Over the next few days, the *mukae-bi* bonfires are kept burning because, during this time, the families believe the spirits vacate their graves/tombs and stay in or near the flames. While the spirits are absent, family members go to their burial sites to clean them. After each grave has been cleaned, the family members offer respect by chanting special *sutras*, making prayers, and preparing special meals for the honored dead. By the evening of the final night, the sites should already be properly cleaned, repaired if damaged, and maintained as necessary.

Conjuring Words

Sutras, in both Hinduism and Buddhism, are short summarizations of key teachings from their religious texts. In Buddhism, sutras are often recited from passages believed to have been the words of the Buddha.

On the final night of Bon, the family creates a new bonfire, which they call *okuri-bi*. As they allow the initial *mukae-bi* bonfire to die out, they believe the spirits transfer to the rising flames of the new *okuri-bi* fire. This second bonfire offers a way for the spirits to return to their newly cleaned and restored resting places. Not doing so risks a frightening alternative.

Practices such as this are meant to satisfy and respect the resting spirits of the dead. By performing these rituals, the family can avoid having their ancestral spirits turn into dangerous supernatural creatures (who can often bring grief and terror to their living family members). The idea that the spirits of the human dead can, under certain circumstances, transform into powerful evil spirits is a common element in Japanese belief. When a *yurei* makes itself visible to the living, the outcome is usually not a good one. Although it is believed that *yurei* were considered entirely benevolent in ancient Japan, this view changed sometime during or shortly after the eighth century C.E. Today, when *yurei* show themselves, their appearances are rather terrifying—white clothes, pale faces, eerie expressions, contorted postures, dark eyes, and cavernous mouths are all common elements in descriptions of the *yurei*.

The Night of 100 Spirits

The ritualistic game of *Hyaku Monogatari Kaidankai*, or "The 100 Supernatural Stories Gathering," has been a part of Japanese culture for centuries. Nobles are thought to have first played the game during the Edo Period (also known as the Tokugawa "Peace Period," lasting from 1603 to around 1868), which marked the end of the long and violent "Warring States" period. For the first time in many years, the samurai nobility (many of whom were given administrative positions after the war) found themselves with time on their hands. And what better way to pass the sweltering hot evenings of the summer months than to spook the living daylights out of each other?

Originally, the game, which was meant to be played indoors and during the nighttime hours, involved the telling of 100 spooky stories. Before the game began, 100 candles were lit. As each person completed the telling of a story about a personal experience with the supernatural, he or she blew out one candle. This meant that, as more stories were told and the "spookiness factor" increased, the room got progressively darker. When the final story was told, the last candle would be blown out, suddenly plunging the room into total darkness. At this point, it was believed that as many as 100 spirits had been attracted to the room, and that something frightening or supernatural should occur. Telling the stories, you see, was thought to have called forth the responsible spirit.

Stranger Than Fiction

The *Hyaku Monogatari* game as well as other similar ghostly exploits are commonly used rites of courage among today's Japanese youth. Another such test of courage involves a group of boys going to a graveyard and daring one another to turn their backs to it. Turning your back to the resting place of a spirit is considered a risky act of disrespectful spirit provocation in Japanese culture.

Eventually, it became okay to just have one story told by each person present. The game, however, is still called by its original name. Today, Japanese teenagers looking for a thrill continue to play this storytelling game. In the modern version, each person in the group brings a candle and assembles at a predetermined location—spooky-looking, abandoned, or haunted places are considered the best. The candles are then lit after nightfall.

The result of the last candle being blown out is often total chaos. Girls start screaming, some of the braver boys start laughing, and (of course) the least courageous members of the group make a hasty, stumbling run for the nearest exit. So if you ever walk past a dark house in Japan and suddenly hear screaming and laughing, followed by terrified young people darting from the exits, try not to be too alarmed—especially if it's August or September (though the game is sometimes played during the summer months in general).

Revenge Spirits of Japan

When people die violently or meet their ends due to acts of betrayal, the Japanese commonly believe they will become an *Onryo* or *Go-Ryo* in death. Both *Onryo* and *Go-Ryo* are basically revenge spirits who will often vent their anger by tormenting the individual(s) who killed or betrayed them in life. The spirit exists for one purpose and is fueled by one overwhelming motivation—to make life a living hell for those responsible for their demise. It will not find rest until its one desire has been fully satisfied ... the desire for revenge.

Conjuring Words

Onryo means "angry ghost/spirit." These are most commonly female, and frequently are the vengeful spirits of wives/women who were murdered, abused, betrayed, or otherwise severely mistreated by their husbands/lovers when alive. They usually torment their living husbands/lovers in retribution.

Go-Ryo roughly means "honorable ghost." While these spirits are still vengeful, they are often male members of the noble warrior classes (especially those who were betrayed or martyred in some way). According to lore, a *Go-Ryo* can only be commanded by a *Yamabushi* (a mountain-dwelling warrior monk of Zen Buddhism or Shinto).

Finding yourself the target of an *Onryo* or *Go-Ryo* is, to say the least, one seriously bad situation. These spirits never rest and never stop until they have exacted their revenge. Sometimes, if you are relatively lucky, the spirit will bring just enough terror and ruin to your life to satisfy its anger. Most of the time, an angry *Onryo* or *Go-Ryo* at least wants to see you permanently maimed. Worst-case scenario: it won't stop coming after you until you are dead. In this case, it's best to get your affairs in order since no one is known to have ever escaped from one.

Oiwa-San: Hell Hath No Fury

The *yurei* known as Oiwa-san is certainly among the most feared and revered *Onryo* in all of Japan. Ask almost any Japanese person about her, and they will likely be able to recite her entire tragic story for you. The figure of Oiwa-san represents a common theme of stories about *Onryo;* that of wives who turn into revenge spirits because they were abused, betrayed, murdered, or otherwise mistreated in some unforgivable way by their living husbands.

The Bermuda Triangle

Technically, Oiwa-san's given name is just Oiwa. The addition of "san" is an honorary Japanese term, which is similar to (but not really an equivalent for) the English titles of Mister/Miss/Misses. The name should always be said with the "san" in order to show respect, especially in the case of Oiwa-san. Even modern legends state she can be rather nasty to those who do not show her the proper respect.

When she was alive, it is said that Oiwa-san was one of the most beautiful women one could ever hope to lay eyes on. She lived in the Yotsuya district near the capital city of Edo (modern-day Tokyo). When a handsome young samurai fell head-over-heels in love with her, he wanted nothing more than to marry her. She accepted his proposal, but there was one issue. Her family was poorer than most, so her dowry would be very meager. Believing he would soon be able to rise to higher rank and increase his revenue, the young samurai chose love over money, and the two were soon married. For the first few years, they lived happily together in marital bliss.

As the years went on, however, the samurai's career didn't turn out as he'd planned. His *daimyo* (meaning "feudal lord") was an exceptionally stingy fellow and refused to acknowledge the samurai's many years of devotion, service, and loyalty. As a result, his promotions were few, and his financial means remained limited. Eventually, his need for financial gain outweighed his love for the beautiful Oiwa-san. One day, the lovely daughter of a local, very wealthy merchant caught his eye. He soon won the girl's affection and convinced her to agree to marry him. However, he had to deal with one problem in order to secure the new marriage—Oiwa-san. So the samurai consulted an apothecary, acquired an especially dreadful poison, and sprinkled it over Oiwa-san's meal that evening. As she fell into a seizure, grasping at her throat, her husband only stood by, doing nothing as she writhed before him in excruciating pain. One side of her face became gruesomely contorted by the effects of the poison, and remained that way even after she had drawn her final breath.

Oiwa-san's murderous husband quickly carried her lifeless corpse outside and dropped her into an old well he no longer used. Some versions of the story claim he then filled it in with dirt to ensure that no one would ever discover his crime. As weeks passed, he claimed his wife had run off, possibly with another man. His *daimyo* gave him permission to remarry as he pleased. Overjoyed, and believing he had gotten away with murder, the samurai soon married the merchant's daughter and received a hefty dowry from his new bride's wealthy father. This greatly improved his financial situation and allowed him to increase his status. In his mind, he thought his future looked pretty bright. He could not have been more wrong.

One night, some weeks after his marriage, a bloodcurdling shriek shocked the samurai from his slumber. The terrifying sound continued to grow louder and louder with every passing moment. Eventually, the samurai got up the courage to draw a blind and peek outside. What he saw made his blood run cold. Oiwa-san was standing in front of the house, ghostly pale, shrieking and howling at him. He feared others would soon hear her and come to investigate. Not wanting to be discovered, he took up his sword and rushed outside to the wailing apparition. He made one strong cut with his blade and was shocked when it cut through Oiwa-san as if she were alive. With a final howl, she fell to the ground front first. She did not, however, disappear as the samurai had expected.

With trembling hands, the samurai rolled the body over and was horrified to discover that the face was no longer Oiwa-san's, but his current wife's! He had cut down his new (and very much alive) wife, mistakenly believing her to be Oiwa-san resurrected. He screamed into the night with a cry of horror and terror. According to some versions of the story, he was soon discovered holding the slashed corpse of his new wife, with his blood-drenched sword beside him, and was ruined. Branded a murderer, he was ordered to commit suicide (or was executed in some versions). The good news, one might say, was that he never saw Oiwa-san again.

This was definitely not, however, the end of Oiwa-san's story. Many people still claim to see her spirit wandering the streets of modern Tokyo. A number of movies have been made about her, all bearing the title *Yotsuya Monogatari* (meaning "The Yotsuya Story").

A number of strange phenomena have always been associated with the production of these "Yotsuya Story" films, especially when it comes to strange accidents (which seem to have plagued the set of every film). In one case, the acting director is said to have scoffed at how some members of the crew feared the ghost of Oiwa-san might be provoked by the work. His humorous skepticism ended, however, when a freak on-set accident resulted in both his legs being badly broken (nearly paralyzing him for life). As soon as the director was able, he immediately assembled the entire cast and crew, and everyone went to her shrine to pay her their respects. No further accidents occurred during the rest of the film's production. Was his accident a coincidence? Perhaps it was. Then again, maybe it wasn't.

Ubume

Stories about these spirits are a common part of Japanese folklore. Certain sources interpret *Ubume* (pronounced *Oo-boo-may*) as meaning something like "mother ghost" or "spirit mother," but the word literally translates more along the lines of "childbirth lady" or "child-having woman." *Ubume* are the spirits of mothers who died, often suddenly or unexpectedly, without making proper arrangements for their surviving children.

Often, an *Ubume* will not turn violent unless someone threatens or harms her child. Doing so is not a good idea because you know what they say: "The most dangerous being in existence is a mother protecting her child." In the case of *Ubume*, this saying applies even beyond the grave. Before an *Ubume* can find rest, she must find a way to ensure that her child/children will be cared for in her absence. Sometimes, she'll take the child/children to a safe place (in some stories, a cave or hut). She then searches for a suitable guardian, and once found will lead that person to the location of her hidden children. In other stories, an *Ubume* will continue to watch over her children herself. For example, some stories tell of a certain *Ubume* who enters a store and buys food for her children with coins. Shortly after the *Ubume* leaves, however, the coins turn into dried-up leaves. When the unlucky store owner rushes out to catch up to her, however, the *Ubume* has already vanished.

Funayurei: Lost at Sea

Funayurei (roughly pronounced *Foo-nah-yoo-ray*) translates as "mariner's spirit/ghost." These ghosts are those who perished at sea, their bodies often lost to the watery deep. Since they didn't receive the proper last respects and funerary rites, these lost seafarers are believed to eternally wander the ocean. But we all know how misery loves company, and a seagoing vessel that encounters a *Funayurei* can quickly find itself in a good bit of trouble.

Funayurei often present themselves as sailors who were somehow thrown from their vessels. When well-intentioned sea captains come by, they often unknowingly welcome the disguised *Funayurei* onto their ships. At first, nothing seems amiss (aside from, of course, finding some guy floating alone out in the open sea). At some point, though, all *Funayurei* make the same request: they ask for a deep, ladlelike tool called a *hisyaku*. Never, under any circumstances, should you give this object to a suspected *Funayurei!* Why? Because once it gets its hands on one, it will turn the bowl-side over, and water will begin to pour from it rapidly. In some stories, however (usually those about *Funayurei* who encounter smaller fishing boats), it just scoops water from the ocean into the boat. Soon the vessel will take on too much water and begin to sink. If the crew can't find some way to get the troublesome ghost overboard (and do so rather quickly), it won't be long before the entire ship is forever lost to the dark depths of the sea.

Samurai Ghosts

Samurai are unquestionably one of the most significant parts of the culture and history of the Japanese people. For thousands of years the samurai were the exclusive members of the warrior class, who defended, fought for, and even ruled over the islands of Japan. The samurai lived for nothing more than to die gloriously in battle for the sake of their *daimyo*.

A good many samurai met with violent, tragic, or unjust ends at the hands of their enemies ... and sometimes even at those of the very lords they so loyally served. Violent or tragic deaths, no matter where they occur, often leave behind residual energies that manifest as ghostly specters. Perhaps this explains why there are so many legends about human encounters with the restless spirits of fallen samurai warriors.

Ghosts of the Genpei War

Many so-called "ghost samurai" are said to be the fallen warriors who died during the terrible conflict known as the Genpei War. The Japanese refer to this war as *Jisho-Juei no Ran*, which can be roughly translated as "The War of the Jisho and Juei Eras." This conflict raged for only five years, from 1180 C.E. to 1185 C.E., but cut a bloody path across the two brief historical eras of Jisho (which lasted from 1177 until 1181) and Juei (which began in 1182 and ended in 1184). Before this war, an ongoing power struggle between the two greatest samurai clans—Taira and Minamoto—had divided Japan. This struggle escalated until it finally resulted in all-out war between them when, in 1180, the two nominated different candidates for the next imperial ruler of Japan.

When the Taira's nomination was endorsed, they succeeded in gaining favor with the new ruler of Japan and assumed a very powerful new status. They used this new power to order the executions of their rivals, almost all of whom were members of the Minamoto clan. As a result, it is said that headless samurai are often seen at the sites of these executions. They are headless because, at the time, the acceptable method of execution for a samurai was to have a special executioner, called a *Kaishakunin*, cut off the condemned warrior's head with a *katana*.

One of the most interesting stories about these samurai ghosts of the Genpei War tells about those who were lost in a vicious sea-battle called *Dan-no-Ura*, which ended in a decisive victory for the Minamoto clan. The opposing ships of the warring clans quickly closed distance and tossed hooks until they could engage in close combat. Any samurai knocked into the sea quickly drowned since their heavy armor made it nearly impossible to swim (that is, of course, if they even knew how to).

Ever since this terrible battle, it is said that at certain times (often during full moons or on the anniversary of the battle, April 25, 1185 C.E.), if you stand before the shoreline of the Shimonoseki Strait near Honshu, you may see the spirits of these drowned samurai emerge from the waters and come lumbering onto the shore. They are said to wander right past those who see them, not even acknowledging the presence of the living, and then disappear into thin air once they reach a certain distance inland. Needless to say, seeing this happen would be the kind of thing that keeps one up at night years after.

The Wrath of Taira no Masakado

The legendary samurai Taira no Masakado, or "Masakado of the Taira clan," is known throughout Japan as one of the most fearsome warriors the country has ever known. He was so fearsome, in fact, that following his death many people believed he became one of the godlike *Kami*. However, many Japanese have another belief about what Masakado became after his execution.

In 939 C.E., long before the violent years of the Genpei War, Masakado executed a daring and bloody coup d'état on his own clan (the Taira). This incredible act of rebellion is known to Japanese history as *Johei Tengyo no Ran* (or "War of the 12th month/*Johei* of the *Tengyo* Year"). Masakado kicked off his uprising by taking a government outpost in the Hitachi province. From there, he marched forth with his army and quickly conquered two entire provinces—Shimotsuke and Kozuke. He then declared himself *Shinno* ("The New Emperor") of the conquered region. Had he stopped there, some wonder if he would not have eventually succeeded in taking the entire island. However, his fate was sealed when he killed his own uncle (and a fellow member of the Taira clan), Taira no Kunika.

The Imperial government in Kyoto took notice of Masakado's uprising and immediately placed a reward on his head. Taira no Sadamori, the son of the murdered Kunika, assembled a vast army and defeated Masakado's forces at the Battle of Kojima in the early months of 940 C.E. He beheaded the defeated Masakado and delivered his head to the emperor. The head was later buried (without his body, the whereabouts of which remain unknown) in Edo. This, however, does not appear to have been the end for Masakado.

The place where Masakado's head is buried is now near Exit C5 of Tokyo's Otemachi Station. To this day, the region has been host to a number of strange occurrences believed to be the work of Masakado's vengeful spirit. In the hopes of pacifying his spirit for not burying his body with his head, a shrine has even been erected in the Otemachi district, an area primarily considered a financial district. From time to time, witnesses claim they've seen a ghostly, headless figure in full samurai armor wandering the area. Every witness is certain that the figure is indeed the spirit of Masakado.

Back in 1923, during the reconstruction efforts that followed the devastating Kanto earthquake that killed well over 125,000 people, Japan's Ministry of Finance began to execute plans to build their new office structure right on top of where Masakado's shrine had been. They soon abandoned these plans entirely after no less than 14 ministry officials were killed, in frighteningly close succession, during the early stages of construction. Included among the dead officials was the Chief Minister of Finance himself. Once again, this could have been a coincidence … but 14 deaths in a row is enough to make one wonder.

Shortly after World War II, engineers from the American Occupational Forces began making plans to construct a parking structure over the same location. When they saw the terror in the eyes of locals and cooperating Japanese officials, many of whom turned ghostly pale every time the spot was mentioned, the engineers decided to think twice about the venture. Soon enough, they scrapped the plans entirely.

To this day, those who work in surrounding office buildings in Otemachi's financial district remain silently aware of the nearby shrine that still entombs Masakado's severed head. Subtle evidence of this can be seen if one knows where to look. For example, few employees have their desks facing in any direction that might require their backs to be turned toward the shrine. Turning one's back to a person, and especially to a spirit, is considered an act of disrespect. This intentional method of desk arrangement is done in order to avoid provoking the wrath of the Masakado's spiteful spirit. After all, no one wants to be chased around by the headless apparition of an angry, dead samurai.

The Least You Need to Know

◆ In Japan, the summer months (especially August and September) are considered the "Ghost Season."

◆ In mid-August, many Japanese families hold the spirit veneration ceremony of "Bon" in their homes.

◆ Not all *yurei* are mean, but revenge spirits like the *Onryo* and *Go-Ryo* usually are (especially if you are the target of their revenge).

◆ The betrayed and murdered bride, Oiwa-san, is one of the most well-known revenge spirits in Japan.

◆ Never give a *hisyaku* ladle to a *Funayurei*, no matter what he says.

◆ Never turn your back to a Japanese spirit or grave, as this is considered an act of disrespect and could provoke a spirit's wrath (or at least offend living Japanese people).

Chapter 4

Paranormal Investigation

In This Chapter

- The fascinating field of paranormal investigation
- Famous paranormal investigators Ed and Lorraine Warren, Dr. Hans Holzer, and Ryan Buell
- Three of the world's top paranormal societies
- The primary methods for conducting a valid paranormal investigation
- How to put together a basic paranormal investigator's kit
- Some of the basic data and evidence-collecting tools used by paranormal investigators

When confronted with the paranormal, most people tend to run in the opposite direction (oftentimes while frantically screaming in terror). On the other hand, a number of unique individuals, commonly called paranormal investigators, face such things head on. These men and women dedicate their lives to seeking out the hidden truths behind the many mysteries that continue to defy explanation. It takes a special breed of person to become a paranormal investigator. Do you think you have what it takes?

What Is Paranormal Investigation?

Paranormal investigation is the research of events or phenomena that science can't or won't explain. Sometimes, this means investigating a suspected haunting. In other cases, paranormal investigation means looking into what is causing people to report sightings of a strange creature. In certain cases, it could even mean chasing down UFOs. No matter what the case might be, paranormal investigation is rarely a boring field.

The field of paranormal investigation, first and foremost, requires one to possess a rational mind, a calm disposition, and (perhaps most importantly) a set of very calm nerves. Often, things that seem paranormal at first turn out to have rational explanations. Therefore, while it is important to keep an open mind, it's doubly important not to go rushing to conclusions without the proper evidence. Those who are quick to draw conclusions are often not cut out for paranormal investigation.

As you'll see later on in this chapter, much of paranormal investigation has to do with finding the *normal* truths behind those things that initially seem *paranormal*. For example, imagine being brought in to investigate a house suspected to be experiencing poltergeist activity. The main piece of evidence is that the people in the house report hearing constant knocking sounds at night. You could not (or at least should not) begin your investigation with the assumption that this is a true poltergeist.

First, you'd need to search the house from top to bottom during the nighttime hours in order to seek out a normal source for the sound. It may just be a tree limb striking the roof or a rodent moving in and out of a hole. It might even be the mischievous trick of neighbors or kids living in the house. Only after you've completely exhausted such rational explanations can you begin investigating the possibility that the house is experiencing a poltergeist.

Famous Paranormal Investigators

In almost every field, paranormal or not, there are those who have achieved extraordinary feats and are seen as legends by those who work in their fields. In the paranormal world, a select few have achieved such a legendary status. These men and women have walked into the terrifying darkness and trod where few would dare. When other investigators have failed, given up, or simply been scared off, these famous figures have persevered and succeeded.

Ed and Lorraine Warren

The husband and wife team of Ed and Lorraine Warren have been involved in some of the most dangerous and extreme cases of paranormal phenomenon. They were first brought into the public spotlight for their roles in the famous case now referred to as the "Amityville Horror." They also jointly founded their own paranormal organization, the New England Society for Psychic Research (NESPR), in 1952.

Stranger Than Fiction

The Amityville Horror case was the focus of a 1979 film, *The Amityville Horror*. The movie, under the same title, was remade in 2005, starring Ryan Reynolds. It is important to note that both of these films are *very* loosely based on the real case and should be taken for what they are: entertaining movies and nothing more. If you want to know the facts, see Chapter 2 (or go to the Warren website, www.warrens.net).

Ed, a leading paranormal investigator and psychic researcher, died on August 23, 2006, at the age of 79. His wife Lorraine, a world-renowned demonologist and talented medium, continues to do paranormal work. She is now regularly assisted in investigations by her son-in-law, Tony Spera. She is also a regular consultant on demonic or otherwise malevolent cases for the Penn State Paranormal Research Society's documentary series *Paranormal State*.

Dr. Hans Holzer

Hans Holzer was born in Austria on January 26, 1920. Dr. Holzer was very interested in the supernatural/paranormal from a very young age and often laughed about being nearly expelled from his kindergarten class for telling ghost stories to his fellow students. Despite this early academic hurdle, he grew up to develop an impressive academic repertoire.

Dr. Holzer initially graduated with a degree in journalism from the University of Vienna, which he often called a "total waste of time." He then studied ancient history and archeology, also at the University of Vienna, and later spent a number of years studying Japanese at Columbia University. Finally, he attended the London College of Applied Science, where he earned a Master's degree in comparative religion and a Ph.D. in parapsychology (which, at the time, many scholars did not consider a legitimate area of academic study).

For eight years, Dr. Holzer taught parapsychology courses at the New York Institute of Technology. Like Ed and Lorraine Warren, Dr. Holzer is most well known for his role in the paranormal investigation of the infamous Amityville Horror. Throughout his career, Dr. Holzer proved to be one of the most prolific writers on the subjects of the paranormal. He penned a total of 138 books on various paranormal issues and an additional 7 creative works (many of which were screenplays).

On Sunday, April 26, 2009, Dr. Holzer passed away at the age of 89. The entire paranormal research community mourned his loss. He is often referred to as the "grandfather of parapsychology."

> **Stranger Than Fiction**
>
> Dr. Hans Holzer's 1979 book, *Murder in Amityville*, is the inspiration for the 1982 film, *Amityville II: The Possession*. However, one must keep in mind that this film is a work of fiction and, though entertaining, was only *loosely* based on Holzer's non-fiction work.

Ryan Buell

Many in the world of paranormal research see Ryan Buell as a shining example of the new generation of paranormal investigation. Born on

July 8, 1982, in Corry, Pennsylvania, Buell is one of the youngest para-normal investigators in the world at only 27 years of age.

For much of his childhood in Sumter, South Carolina, Buell experienced an unusual amount of paranormal phenomena. As a little boy, these strange experiences terrified him, but eventually he learned to accept his gift and his fear turned to resolve. When he began his higher education at Penn State University, Buell realized he was not alone in his para-normal experiences. At only 19, Buell founded Penn State's Paranormal Research Society (PRS) in 2001. Over the past seven years, Buell and his PRS team (made up primarily of Penn State students) have come to be viewed as some of the most prestigious paranormal experts in the world.

In 2006, Buell graduated from Penn State with a degree in anthropology and is currently pursuing an additional degree, also from Penn State. In 2007, Ryan and the PRS team became the subject of the documentary series *Paranormal State* which still airs on A&E. A bold investigator and tireless researcher, Buell's many cases range from simple to downright dangerous. He has fought many impressive battles against some of the darker forces one encounters in the world of paranormal investigation. (For details on one of his cases, see Chapter 7.)

Paranormal Societies

Most people would agree there is safety in numbers, and in the world of paranormal investigation, this is especially true. It is unwise to tackle paranormal investigations on your own. After all, in certain situations it's difficult to produce physical evidence. If you are the only witness, you might find it difficult to convince others to believe your story. With an entire team, however, the number of potential eyewitnesses increases.

There are far too many paranormal research societies in the world to give a basic summary of them all, so we'll only discuss some of the most prestigious groups in this chapter. For a more detailed list of paranormal societies in the United States and around the world, see Appendix B.

New England Society for Psychic Research

Ed and Lorraine Warren founded the New England Society for Psychic Research in 1952. Since Ed's death, Lorraine and her son-in-law Tony

Spera have led the group. According to the group's official website, www.warrens.net, the NESPR's mission statement is as follows:

> Our mission is to seek answers to previously unanswered questions. We endeavor to find the truth in matters relating to the supernatural, preternatural, and occult worlds.
>
> To assist in any way we can to free those persons who suffer the pain and despair that comes from dabbling in occult practices, or who innocently have fallen victim to the forces that emanate from the dark side.
>
> To share our knowledge with others, because we believe that knowledge is power, and power used correctly can overcome all obstacles.

For more than five decades now, the Warrens and their NESPR team of special investigators have been involved in a number of the world's most famous paranormal cases, including but not limited to the following:

- The Annabelle "Rag Doll" Case (1970s)
- The West Point Academy Haunting (1972)
- The Lindley Street Case (1974)
- The Smurl House Case (1985–1987)
- The Southend Werewolf Possession (1987–1988)
- The Stamford Case (1998–1999)
- The White Rose Case (1999)

The Paranormal Research Society (PRS)

Ryan Buell officially founded the Paranormal Research Society in 2001. Originally, the group was formed as a student organization at Penn State University, where Buell was attending college. The aim was to create a new kind of paranormal research society by integrating field work with experimental, scientific, and technological resources. The Paranormal Research Society's longstanding motto is "To trust, honor, and always seek the truth."

In 2007, A&E created a series around the PRS team, called *Paranormal State*. The show, which sends camera crews to follow Buell and his team on some of their most extreme cases, was a big hit and was picked up for further seasons.

Recently, the Paranormal Research Society chose to split into two separate groups. One group, the original student organization at Penn State, will continue as it has for nearly seven years. The new group, containing the members of PRS's original team who have now graduated, will become an independent organization. The new group has become incorporated, now called the Paranormal Research Society, LLC. Both groups will remain on close and friendly terms. Buell's "graduate team" has created a new base of operation located on College Avenue in College, Pennsylvania.

Stranger Than Fiction

The PRS organized and booked an annual paranormal convention, which they dubbed UNIV-CON. This convention has become one of the largest paranormal-focused gatherings in the world. Originally just a convention for paranormal enthusiasts, Buell recently announced that from now on the event's format will have a far more academic/scientific focus.

The Atlantic Paranormal Society (TAPS)

Originally called the Rhode Island Paranormal Society (RIPS), The Atlantic Paranormal Society (TAPS) was jointly founded by friends and researchers Jason Hawes and Grant Wilson in 1990. This primarily "ghost-activity-based" group's main headquarters is located in Warwick, Rhode Island (hence its original name). However, when the group began to take multiple cases outside of the state, they chose a name that suggested a wider geographical range.

One of the most notable things about the TAPS group is that they have a strict "no money" policy. From the beginning, they have done all their work on a pro bono basis. The only thing they've ever asked from their clients is the permission to use, as they please, any data or evidence they gather during the course of an investigation.

In July of 2006, Hawes and Wilson went public with some of TAPS' most impressive evidentiary findings by creating a radio show called

TAPS Para-Radio. Later, in April 2007, they started a new show called *Beyond Reality Radio*. The medium of radio, however, offered them a rather limited platform since they couldn't present photo or video evidence.

Eventually, the group came to the attention of the producers from cable's Syfy channel. They found a new, far broader platform for their work. Their weekly "reality styled" show, *Ghost Hunters*, debuted in 2004. The show quickly became one of the channel's most popular programs, and remains so today.

Seek the Truth, Not the Illusion

When paranormal investigators enter a scene, they often encounter people who are already frightened, sometimes to the point of hysteria. Despite what the truth may turn out to be, if people have called in a team of paranormal investigators, they're already convinced that what they are experiencing is truly paranormal.

It's all too easy for a paranormal investigator to get caught up in the hysteria of one's clients, and falling into this surprisingly tempting snare can seriously cloud any paranormal investigator's judgment. This can be further complicated when one is presented with impressive evidence but fails to properly validate it. These are just a couple pitfalls into which even the most seasoned of investigators have sometimes fallen. We'd all like to think we're above being bamboozled by pranksters and fame-seekers, but assumptions such as this can be dangerous. Never assume that anything you are told or shown is true until you have experienced, investigated, documented, researched, analyzed, and validated it properly.

The Scary Truth

Sometimes enthusiasm can turn out to be the greatest enemy of any paranormal researcher/investigator. Sometimes it is difficult not to let enthusiasm overtake better judgment. Always keep in mind what you might call the credo of all paranormal investigators—*simply because you want something to be true, that doesn't make it so.*

To avoid these case-destroying mistakes, here are some of the most basic rules that all legitimate paranormal investigation teams strictly follow:

1. Seek the truth above all else, and always seek to shatter any illusions, no matter how impressive.

2. Always attempt to disprove phenomena first, but always treat your clients with sympathy and respect. Remember, these people are often legitimately scared.

3. Always keep a log (written or recorded) of any paranormal phenomena or unusual experiences.

4. Always conduct initial interviews, gather evidence, and compile your research *before* you start drawing conclusions, *not* the opposite.

5. *Never* accept a piece of evidence as real until you have properly analyzed and validated it.

6. *Never falsify evidence* or make untrue statements about a case.

7. Keep both an open mind and a level head.

8. If you encounter a phenomenon with which you are totally unfamiliar, consult an appropriately educated/trained/experienced expert.

9. If any team members (yourself included) find that they cannot control their fear, they should be immediately removed from the case at hand.

10. If a case turns out to be a purposeful hoax, don't waste anymore of your team's time on it—just walk away.

Conducting Interviews

When a paranormal investigation team enters a scene of suspected paranormal phenomenon, they usually start by interviewing everyone involved. Doing this often helps investigators identify reasonable, people-related explanations. For example, if during the initial interviews investigators realize that one or all of the clients are under the influence of LSD or some other psychedelic drug, then it's a good bet that paranormal phenomenon has nothing to do with their experiences. Also, there are times when initial interviews reveal that a person suffers from a serious mental-health issue, such as schizophrenia (which causes a person to hear voices or experience visual hallucinations). So interviews are the first line of defense in identifying whether or not the situation is paranormal in nature.

There are three basic rules for conducting initial interviews during a paranormal investigation:

1. Separate everyone immediately (in different rooms if possible) *before* conducting any interviews.

2. Always record the initial interviews in audio or video format.

3. *Never* be condescending or disrespectful (no matter how crazy what a client says may sound), and always conduct yourself with courtesy, compassion, and understanding.

Once you've separated everyone, begin the interviews. If you have enough team members, these can be done at the same time. In any case, keep those not being interviewed separate while the interviews are going on. The power of suggestion can become a very real problem, and if the clients are discussing what has happened, this might alter the details of their testimonies. I cannot stress this enough: *never interview clients together!*

It's best to ask everyone the same series of questions. Certain questions may seem odd to your clients, and some might get defensive or even feel insulted that you asked. Don't be hostile when this occurs. Remember, these people called because they need help. Always do your best to assure clients that you're not asking these questions because you're making assumptions or judgments, or "think they are crazy." Reassure clients that you're just asking routine questions, while emphasizing to them that honesty is crucial. Always remind the clients that your team is there to help, not judge.

The Bermuda Triangle

While there is nothing wrong with taking notes during client interviews, it's important to always have a complete and concrete record. This means using either a video camera or audio recorder (tape or digital). Always inspect any and all recording devices/equipment to make sure it has a sufficient power supply and is in proper working order before you begin any interviews.

Start with these basic informational questions, which will help identify each client's unique state of mind as well as which specific client was being interviewed when the team later consults the data:

1. Please state your full name, age, address, and occupation.

2. Are you taking or have you recently taken any kind of mind-altering drugs?

3. Are you taking any prescription medications? If so, please specify type and dose.

4. Have you been, or are you being, treated for depression or mental illness?

5. Do you feel that you are of sound mind?

Once you've addressed these questions, begin asking about the phenomenon itself. Every paranormal group has its own unique series of interview questions, so you might add or create some of your own. However, here are some of the more common phenomenon-specific interview questions paranormal investigators ask:

1. Can you give me a rough estimate as to how long this has been going on?

2. Do you know if the previous occupants also experienced any strange activity?

3. Are there any specific times, days, or periods when most of the activity seems to occur?

4. Have you heard any unexplained sounds? If yes, where do they seem to be coming from?

5. Have you or anyone else in the house been attacked, injured, or physically touched by the entity? If yes, please explain.

6. Are you afraid for your safety or that of others in the house, or do you feel at all threatened by what is happening?

7. Have you noticed that you or anyone else in the house has recently been behaving differently or in ways that are out of character?

8. Do you feel, or have you ever felt, that whatever is in the house might try to force you or anyone else to do something violent? Do you believe it has the power to force you to do something against your will?

9. Does the strange activity seem to focus on any one person in the house more than anyone else?

10. Have you personally experienced any unusual phenomena? If the client answers yes, follow up by asking "Do you mind telling me about your experience?" If the client doesn't want to talk about it, then don't press the issue. Just note that the client didn't wish to discuss it.

11. Is there anything else, no matter what it is, that you would like to tell me that you think is important or relevant to this investigation?

Once you've conducted the initial round of interviews, place the records in a secure location, such as a sealed folder or lockbox. Then assemble the team in a closed room or somewhere else well away from the clients (even if this means leaving the property). Do not analyze the interviews in the presence of your clients, because they may become defensive if you point out certain inconsistencies. At this point, the entire team should listen to all the interviews together. As they listen, everyone on the team should take notes of anything they consider relevant in their log books, notepads, etc.

Once the interviews have been analyzed, every member should offer their own take on the situation and bring up any inconsistencies or contradictory details or facts he or she may have noticed. It is human nature to remember things differently, so you should expect a few minor inconsistencies. However, there's a limit. The more consistent the interview details are, the more likely that all the clients are telling the truth. If *big* details aren't matching up, however, then you may be dealing with a hoax or, at least, something that has a rational explanation. The preceding two lists of questions are designed to check consistency. If someone is lying or just imagining things, then he or she is likely to make multiple mistakes during the initial interview.

You should also view the opposite as a red flag. As already stated, it is human nature to remember things differently. Too much consistency, where everyone seems to be describing the same thing (especially if everyone is using the exact same words), could also be a warning sign that you are dealing with a hoax. Unusually high consistency between interviews, however, should not be considered solid evidence of a hoax. As with inconsistencies, just be aware that there is a limit to how well everyone's stories should match up. For example, every person in the house reports a nearly identical experience. They all tell the story in the same order, and use a lot of the exact same words. Descriptive words are a big warning sign, since it is very rare for everyone in a group to describe things the same (again, humans remember things differently).

Sometimes a single client may say one thing early on in the interview and then something entirely different as the interview progresses. In other cases, the clients' stories as a whole may not match up. One client might say the activity has been occurring for weeks, while another says it's been months. One client might claim that most of the activity occurs in the evenings, while another claims that it frequently happens in the late night/early morning hours.

The interviews should first be considered individually, then as a whole because some of the potential inconsistencies may have a legitimate cause. Everyone wants to fit in, especially in extraordinary situations. Sometimes, if some of the individuals involved in the case haven't experienced anything unusual, they might make something up because they don't want to feel left out. Inconsistencies or contradicting details are not, by themselves, enough to immediately dismiss a case (unless there are so many obvious issues that fraud is the only explanation). However, you need to clear them up before you move on.

Once the team makes a collective choice as to whether or not they wish to continue the investigation, consult the clients again, this time as a group. Point out any issues of confusion or concern (being respectful and nonconfrontational, of course), and ask the clients to clear them up. At this point, many of these issues may become clearer. Also, this is a good time to ask any of the clients who claimed to have experiences but did not wish to discuss them in the initial interview to talk about them. Sometimes, they might be more inclined to tell their stories in the presence of friends or family. If the group consultation reveals the case is a hoax, it's time to pull out your team. If not, then you should certainly continue.

Stranger Than Fiction _____

In any team, paranormal investigators or not, there are always going to be differences of opinion. It's hard for everyone to always agree on what to do in every single situation. Even if you disagree with the conclusions of everyone on your team, perhaps you should take this as a sign that you're not seeing the situation clearly for some reason. Never alienate your team members just because they disagree with you. Also, it is unethical to force or guilt-trip any member of your team to remain on a case to which they have objections, no matter what their reasons might be.

Once you've completed this secondary group interview/consultation and resolved as many issues as possible, it's okay to offer the clients one or more potential causes for what they are experiencing. However, it is crucial that you make it very clear to the clients that nothing is certain until the team has finished the rest of its work. At this point, the team should carry out any necessary initial research and investigate the location.

Initial Research

You can never know too much, especially when conducting a paranormal investigation. Initial interviews will often provide revealing clues as to where the team might begin their research. For example, if one or more clients mentioned that previous owners/occupants had reported unusual experiences, then it might be a good idea to track down and interview them.

Here are some of the most important questions any paranormal investigator must consider while conducting initial case research:

◆ What is the property's history? On what was the current structure built? Was the property/house/building ever used for a different purpose?

◆ What's *under* the property? This is a commonly overlooked, but potentially crucial, piece of information. For example, strange noises may be coming from an underground installation, subway tunnel, large sewer pipe, etc.

◆ Have any significant or historical events occurred on or near the property?

◆ Have any murders, suicides, or other such traumatic or violent events occurred on/in the property/house/building?

◆ Is there evidence that any previous occupants ever practiced devil worship, dark magic, necromancy, or any similar forms of "curse dabbling," demon conjuring, or spirit invocation?

◆ Do any of the clients or individuals involved have a criminal record for fraud or similar offenses?

While one member or section of the team researches for answers to these questions, the rest of the group should begin an initial search and inspection of the property (inside and outside).

Possible Explanations

No matter what kind of evidence the team collects or strange activity they experience, they must never stop looking for rational explanations. From beginning to end, every member of the team should be on the lookout for anything out of the ordinary, and this includes potential explanations.

If there is a normal cause for the activity, it will usually become clear during the initial client interviews and research. However, the team needs to check the house thoroughly and leave no stone unturned. They must closely inspect the entire property, inside and outside, from wall to wall, ceiling to floor … every nook and cranny. This will allow the team to eliminate the possibility that hidden speakers, illusion devices, or other nonparanormal causes are involved during the engagement step of the investigation.

If during the search anyone on the team discovers any unusual, questionable, or suspicious items, these should be confiscated, documented (and photographed, if possible) in the case log, and brought to the attention of the clients. Do not return such items until you have concluded the investigation. It may turn out that one of these suspicious items has been causing the strange noises or other suspected paranormal activity. Worst-case scenario, you might find that these items, unbeknownst to the other clients, are being used by someone in the house as some kind of twisted prank. If any of these items points to a normal cause, it would be best to finish the investigation before dismissing the case entirely unless it is painfully obvious that no further investigation is necessary.

Engaging the Phenomenon

Now that you have the necessary initial data and have been unable to prove this is not a paranormal case, it's time to attempt to engage the phenomenon, entity, or the … well, whatever it turns out to be that's causing all the weirdness for the clients. By now, you should have enough information to come up with one or two potential identifications for what you are dealing with.

If the entity is just a wayward ghost or some form of residual apparition or energy, both of which are completely harmless, then you may just need to explain to the clients that they're not in any sort of danger. The good news is that ghosts will usually leave when asked or commanded to do so. Often, the clients just want to know whether or not they are seeing things. They need to know that what they are experiencing is real, and that you believe them. Also, clients will feel more secure in knowing that the paranormal activity is not something that's trying to harm them or otherwise jeopardize their safety (or the safety of their family members and loved ones).

If it is a poltergeist, a violent/interactive haunting, or demonic activity, then you'll need to appropriately engage the responsible entity before you can remove it. In recent years, more and more groups have employed a method called "Dead Time," a tactic created and developed by Ryan Buell of the Paranormal Research Society. It involves turning off any and all electronic devices in the house and turning off all primary lighting. Once this has been done, investigators employ recording devices and motion sensors and ask questions over short intervals. For example, the first question to put out to whatever is in the house is usually, "What do you want?" This is often followed by, "If you are here, give us a sign of your presence." At some point, however, the questions need to turn to commands. For example, "The people in this house do not want you here. You are commanded to leave this house." If more than 30 to 45 minutes pass with no activity, then it's probably time to conclude the Dead Time session. If the paranormal activity begins, increases, or interacts/answers, then continue to engage until it ceases.

The Bermuda Triangle

Paranormal investigation isn't something you just wake up one morning and decide to do. Trying to take on cases without the proper knowledge, training, and experience could soon get you in over your head. If you really want to get involved in paranormal research or investigation, then contact an already established and experienced paranormal organization in your area and volunteer your time (these groups are almost always looking for volunteers to assist with grunt work). Don't just get a bunch of your friends together and run off to "chase ghosts." For a list of paranormal organizations, see Appendix B.

If the activity turns violent or dangerous, however, stop Dead Time immediately and get the clients to a safer location for the time being (remember, you are there to help and protect them, not to needlessly put them in harm's way). Violence likely means you're dealing with something demonic or evil in nature, which means it's time to call in an exorcist or demonologist (for more information on demons and exorcisms, see Chapter 7). After you've concluded Dead Time, have the team collect the data recording devices for review and analysis. First, however, you need to know what tools to use.

Tools of the Trade

A paranormal investigator can do very little without the proper equipment. Evidence is the key, and anyone in the field will tell you that just your word (or even the word of many people) is not going to cut it. Not to mention that, depending on what kind of entity you are dealing with, you should always have some protective and useful items on hand.

Before you can conduct a proper paranormal investigation, you must have the proper equipment. After all, any true plumber would never attempt to fix a leaky pipe with nothing but his or her bare hands. In the same way, any legitimate paranormal investigator would never attempt to take on a case with nothing but his or her hands.

Basic Paranormal Investigation Kit

When equipping yourself for paranormal investigation, it is prudent to strictly follow the motto, "Always better to have something and not need it, than to need something and not have it."

Just as regular crime scene investigators carry large cases containing basic evidence-gathering items, so do paranormal investigators. Any well-equipped paranormal investigators will bring a kit with the following items:

◆ Logbook or notebook and plenty of extra pens and pencils

◆ Watch, stopwatch, and compass (for recording time and direction details in your log, and because paranormal activity has been known to disrupt such instruments)

◆ Pocketknife (for use as a tool, *not* a weapon)

◆ Several pieces of chalk, to identify or mark off certain areas of activity or evidence

◆ Several pairs of latex or plastic examination gloves (be sure to get the nonpowdered kind to avoid contaminating evidence)

◆ Box of clean, unused/uncontaminated zipper bags or containers for collecting physical evidence

◆ A minimum of two flashlights with extra batteries for each, as well as candles and matches (just in case)

◆ A well-stocked first-aid kit

◆ A thermometer and/or thermal camera to record temperature changes (temperatures often drop drastically during paranormal activity)

◆ Either a 35mm high-speed camera with plenty of extra film or a high-pixel, high-speed digital camera with plenty of extra memory cards/sticks

◆ At least one video camera, preferably with a tripod

◆ Audio recording devices, preferably of high quality, both tape/analog and digital types (digital recorders allow sound data to be stored as electronic files, making it easier to e-mail for analysis if necessary)

◆ Protective items of the investigator's choosing, such as crosses; holy water; or anything you personally consider a sacred, blessed, or holy object

Remember, a paranormal investigator's kit is only useful when it is properly maintained. Inspect, replace (if necessary), and restock all items before any new case. New items, when reasonable, are always recommended. Obviously, this doesn't apply to something as expensive as a camera or recording device, unless it is malfunctioning.

Especially when it comes to items used in evidence preservation (such as plastic bags, gloves, and containers), don't recycle your equipment. Doing so could jeopardize the validity of your next case by contaminating evidence. In the paranormal investigation field, solid physical evidence is *very* hard to come by. Therefore, always handle it in an intelligent, careful, and (most importantly) secure manner. Every team should create a strict protocol for how to document and handle evidence.

EVP and RVP

The use of EVP tools is the primary reason that you say all questions and commands at intervals while conducting a Dead Time session. EVP stands for Electronic Voice Phenomenon, and RVP stands for Radio Voice Phenomenon. Both techniques are still relatively new but are gaining acceptance among those in the field of paranormal investigation.

EVP, roughly speaking, is done by running audio recording devices and then asking questions to the paranormal entity at intervals during a Dead Time session. After the session, the easy way to look for EVP is to replay the recording at a higher volume. The idea is that the voices of spirit entities can be heard among the white noise of the recording. In professional circles, special sound equipment is used to amplify the white noise. This makes finding EVP much easier but requires a certain amount of knowledge and electronic expertise.

The Bermuda Triangle

Even among paranormal investigators, there are many who question the validity of EVP and RVP. They point out that, when one employs such techniques with the intention of recording spirit voices, then one is likely to hear what one expects to hear. The subjective nature of such evidence, which often requires the presenter to tell the listener what to listen for beforehand, does not help. Therefore, don't rely on EVP or RVP evidence to prove your paranormal case.

RVP is a newer technique similar to EVP. The basic idea is to tune a radio to an unoccupied station. The theory is that, like with EVP, the voices of any paranormal entities present can be heard among the white noise.

Photographic and Video Evidence

Many of us are familiar with the old saying, "Seeing is believing," or "The camera doesn't lie." Well, these days, sayings like these are no longer true. In this new digital age of Computer Generated Imaging (CGI), Photoshop, and video-streaming websites, you can make just about anything look shockingly real. However, when it comes to video and photo evidence, you need to know exactly what your cameras have captured. Sometimes it's easy to get excited when something unusual pops up on your videos or photos during an investigation. However, making premature conclusions now can cause you to lose credibility later.

Consider, for instance, a case that occurred in Parma, Ohio, in 2007. An attendant at a gas station, while looking at the outdoor security camera's monitor, noticed a strange, whitish-blue object that appeared to be flying around sporadically. He went outside but couldn't see anything; when he went back in, he saw the unidentified object again. Soon after, the attendant went public with claims that he'd witnessed a blue ghost floating outside with his very eyes. As proof, he presented a copy of the security video.

It didn't take long for a number of amateur ghost hunters to come on the scene, many claiming that the video was proof of a ghost's existence. Soon, even more people got in on the act. One man came forward, claiming that he'd had a psychic vision that the station had been built on an Indian burial ground. (And, just for the record, the whole "Indian burial ground" shtick has been so overused that it's nearly a cliché at this point, even to the most naïve of paranormal investigators.)

All these "eyewitnesses," as well as the many would-be investigators who endorsed the video evidence, felt extremely foolish later. When a group of experienced investigators came on the scene, it took them less than a day to figure out what was really going on. As it turns out, the so-called blue ghost was nothing more than a bug. That's right—it was an *insect*. Apparently, when the bug landed directly on the camera's lens, it could not be focused, which caused the bug (a beetle) to look like a whitish-blue blur on the monitor.

So what's the lesson to be learned from the Parma incident? Good paranormal investigators should never assume they have solid evidence of a paranormal entity just because the cameras come up with something unusual. Analyze and confirm your visual evidence first, and present it later. Honestly, it's better to do this than to suffer the grief of the alternative.

The Least You Need to Know

◆ Paranormal investigation is the fascinating field of seeking the truth behind that which science cannot explain.

◆ Ed and Lorraine Warren, Dr. Hans Holzer, and Ryan Buell are among the world's most famous paranormal investigators.

◆ Paranormal research societies (such as the NESPR, PRS, and TAPS) are found all over the world.

◆ Paranormal investigators always seek to discover the truth and to shatter illusions.

◆ A paranormal investigator must keep an open mind, but a level head.

◆ Never start a new case before inspecting and restocking your equipment and kit.

Part 2

Angels, Demons, and Spellcasters

All realms of existence have a balanced nature, and the spirit
realm is no different. These chapters deal with the powerful
and often darker sides of the paranormal world. You'll learn the
names and roles of the angels (many of whom are considered
guardians of paranormal investigators). In turn, you'll learn the
natures, names, and roles of fallen angels and other demonic entities. In addition, you'll learn about the dark arts of necromancy
and the illusive practices of faith magic. These dark powers and
principalities seek to ruin humankind, so proceed with caution.

Chapter 5

Angels

In This Chapter

- The angelic Metatron, the acting agent of the voice and will of YHVH
- The Seraphim and Cherubim classes of angels
- The angelic watchers known as the Grigori
- The highest order of angels, the mighty archangels
- The roles of the high-ranking archangels Michael, Gabriel, Raphael, Orifiel, Zachariel, and Uriel

Beyond the imperfect realm of the physical world lies the realm of the spiritual world. Our world, some say, is but a flawed reflection of this perfect spiritual world. Our struggles reflect theirs. Angels are the guardians and watchers of the human world, the divine agents of the supreme being. These unseen warriors battle against the evil demonic forces that seek to destroy us.

The Metatron

The Metatron, whose name is sometimes spelled Mittron or Metaraon, is known by many names. He bears the titles of the Voice of *YHVH*, Chancellor of Heaven, King of Angels, Prince of the Divine Face, and Tetragrammaton. The simplest way to understand the Metatron is as the angel who acts as the physical voice of YHVH. In the Jewish Talmud, the Metatron acts as an angelic link between the physical and spiritual worlds. He carries out the will of YHVH, often by bringing divine messages to human beings.

Conjuring Words

YHVH is the Hebrew title for God, which is often seen spelled in its more anglicized forms of Yahweh or Jehovah.

The Book of Enoch describes the Metatron as the tallest and greatest of all angels. Interestingly enough, this text also claims that the Metatron was once a mortal being. The story goes that when the Metatron's immortal soul was first received into Heaven, it was given a new form as a divine angel of light and fire. From the Metatron's back spread 36 pairs of giant wings, and he had more eyes than one could count. The home of the Metatron is in the seventh level of Heaven, where the throne of YHVH stands.

The Metatron is difficult to label with a definitive role, however, because his nature is rather multifaceted. In fact, many of his tasks and roles seem to contradict. For example, his angelic domain is said to include light, dark, wisdom, wrath, fate, and death. Adding to the enigma is the fact that the origin and exact meaning of the name Metatron is hard to pin down. There are many theories, but most of these are at best speculative, and none can be concretely verified.

Seraphim or Cherubim?

The Seraphim (which is the plural form of the singular Seraph) is considered the highest of angelic orders, just above the Cherubim. The Seraphim angels surround the holy throne of YHVH in the seventh level of Heaven, constantly and eternally calling out the triple cry of "Holy! Holy! Holy!" Admittance into the order of Seraphim is supposedly reserved for angels who exhibit attributes related to light, fire, or love. In appearance, when angels are carrying out their roles as Seraphim (some Seraphim have other roles, which require them to assume alternate forms), they have four faces and six wings. Interestingly enough, although Seraphim are said to have three pairs of wings, they are rarely depicted this way in works of art.

Just below the ranks of the Seraphim is the order of the Cherubim. Human perceptions of Cherubim have changed drastically from ancient times to the present. Cherubim is thought to be Assyrian in origin, and the singular form, Cherub, is believed to have originally meant something like "one who intercedes" or "one who knows." The ancient Assyrians described the Cherubim as titanic, winged beings with the heads of lions (although sometimes they were depicted with the heads of men) and the bodies of either bulls or eagles. They were eventually absorbed into the *angelology* of the Jews, and the Talmud explains that the Cherubim are an order of "Holy Beasts" that reside in the sixth level of Heaven.

> **Conjuring Words**
>
> The term **angelology** literally means "the study of angels." However, the term has come to mean any religious or theological doctrine that involves the roles, hierarchies, or arrangements of angels.

Later, the perception of Cherubim changed drastically in the angelic lore of Christianity. In modern Christian depictions, Cherubim are commonly portrayed as fair-faced, childlike angels and are often shown playing classical stringed instruments such as harps or lyres.

The Grigori

The members of the Angelic Order of the Grigori (also spelled *egregori* or *egoroi*) are commonly referred to as the "Watchers." They are called such for good reason, since their responsibility is to stand watch over the entirety of humankind. According to the Judaic tradition, the Grigori are well suited to this task because they've been granted the ability to *transubstantiate* and assume the appearances and forms of humans, which allows them to blend in and walk among humans without suspicion. While this human appearance is what most human eyes see, these angels can also choose to reveal their true forms from time

to time (though this happens *very* rarely). A Grigori's true form is said
to be overwhelming, and they are as brilliant in appearance as they are
enormous in size.

Conjuring Words

Transubstantiate literally means "to move across substance," and
the simplest definition of the word is changing from one substance to
another. In spiritual terms, especially in the Catholic and Eastern Orthodox
traditions, the term refers to the miraculous changing of substances. For
example, Jesus transubstantiated water into wine. In regard to angels (and
sometimes to demons), it means the ability to shift from their true spirit
forms to substantial physical forms. Spirit entities can use this ability to
either blend in among or physically interact with figures and elements in
the human realm.

The watcher angels of the Grigori are held by one very strict rule, one
which can only be bent or broken in very certain circumstances: they
may observe, but not interfere, with human affairs. This means the
Grigori are not supposed to speak to humans … *ever.* The reason why is
uncertain. Some say the Grigori *can* speak, but simply do not because of
the rules surrounding their angelic order. Others believe that YHVH
simply did not create the Grigori with the ability to speak.

The leader of the Grigori is Salamiel, whose name means "the one who
rejected God." This, in addition to certain passages from the Book of
Enoch, has led to claims that at least some (if not all) of the Grigori
were a part of a failed uprising of angels that spawned a war in Heaven.
This implies that at least a certain number of the angels in the Grigori
Order are fallen angels (for more on fallen angels and the war in
Heaven, see Chapter 6).

Some lore, in contrast, states that Salamiel (and other Grigori who were
involved in the angelic uprising) is no longer a watcher angel, although
he seems to have retained his title as Prince of the Grigori. According
to at least one myth, Salamiel was not a part of the uprising led by
Lucifer. This story claims his rejection of YHVH was personal, and
one he perpetrated on his own. However, why he did this is unclear.
His expulsion from the Grigori ranks could simply mean that, at some

point, he may have refused to obey an order from YHVH. Then again, Salamiel may have followed a path similar to Lucifer's by rejecting his creator altogether.

Archangels

Many people misunderstand the nature of the order of archangels, believing them to be only a group of warrior angels. While some certainly are warriors, the title of archangel is actually given to any of the highest-ranking angels. In truth, an archangel is any angel who has risen above the generic rank of an angel. Among the archangels, seven "Archangels of the Throne" (although this term is not used in canonical texts) hold the highest ranks in the order—Michael, Gabriel, Raphael, Orifiel, Zarachiel, Uriel, and Simiel. These privileged angels may also stand or kneel before the Throne of YHVH, the divine presence.

The Bermuda Triangle

You may notice that there is not a section that elaborates on the Archangel Simiel. Unfortunately, little information survives about this particular archangel (especially when it comes to Christian texts). This is mainly due to the fact that in 745 C.E., a council of the Roman Catholic Church deemed that Simiel's name should be removed from their authorized list of angels that were fit for veneration. Some on the council claimed that Simiel was actually just an alternate spelling for Samael. It also appears that there were suspicions that Simiel was one of the rebel angels, and therefore among the Fallen. The same fate also befell the Archangel Uriel. Luckily, however, there is still a body of lore about Uriel that exists in the texts of Judaism (which is why a section on him is still included).

Michael: The Angel Prince of Israel

The name of the Archangel Michael means "the one who is as God/ YHVH." In almost all angelic lore, regardless of text or denomination, Michael is the most powerful of all the angels. In human terms, Michael is often considered the "General of the Angels." This stems from the fact that, during the war in Heaven, Michael stepped forth and led the loyal angelic ranks into a fierce battle against the would-be usurper Lucifer and his rebel angels.

The Bermuda Triangle

The Muslim lore regarding the Archangel Michael differs somewhat from the Christian. According to Muslim tradition, Michael's spiritual home is in the seventh level of Heaven (not the fourth, as stated in the Christian tradition) beside the throne of YHVH. It describes him as having emerald-colored wings and a splendid body covered with saffron hairs. On these hairs are millions of mouths that speak in all the languages in existence, all crying out in praise to Allah and appealing for pardon of humankind's sins.

The Archangel Michael is a natural leader, and assumes this role across various planes of existence. His authority is not solely restricted to the angelic ranks, but extends into the realms of both Heaven and Earth. Michael is the Chief of the Order of Virtues and the Prince of the "Presence." He is also the patron angel of righteousness, mercy, justice, repentance, and sanctification. He is the natural enemy of all that is evil and unjust. However, Michael's most prestigious titles were bestowed upon him as a result of his loyalty and devoted service in the war in Heaven, for which YHVH appointed Michael as the holy ruler of the fourth level of Heaven and declared him the Angelic Prince of Israel. In addition, Michael serves as one of the Ten Angels of the Holy *Sefiroth*.

Conjuring Words

Sefiroth, also spelled Sephiroth (singular forms are sefira/sephira), refers to two polar opposite angelic orders. One half is the Ten Holy Sefiroth, made up of Heaven's most powerful archangels. The other half is the Ten Unholy Sefiroth, a group of evil counter-entities (mostly fallen angels). In Jewish mysticism, Holy Sefiroth represent the divine elements—Metatron (Crown), Raziel (wisdom), Tzaphqiel (understanding), Tzadqiel (mercy), Michael (beauty), Raphael (splendor), Gabriel (foundation), Camael (strength), Haniel (victory), and Shekinah (kingdom). In some texts, Metatron simultaneously assumes the role of both Crown and Shekinah/ Kingdom (as these two angelic entities are sometimes thought of as one and the same).

Although Michael is the holder of many angelic titles, his most well-known title is that of "The Conqueror of Satan" because his role is to do battle with the great adversary of YHVH, Lucifer. The word Satan actually means "adversary," a title given to Lucifer (and many other fallen angels) after the war and his fall from Heaven. In art, Michael is most commonly portrayed in his role as The Conqueror of Satan.

For centuries, artists have created visual works depicting the final moment of Michael's victory over Lucifer in battle. While these works sometimes differ in minor details, their themes are generally the same. Lucifer is usually shown on his back (often disarmed, with his weapon lying nearby or falling out of his hand) while the Archangel Michael stands over him victoriously, sometimes even pinning his rebellious brother down with his sandal-clad foot. Michael is often wearing shining armor (which usually closely resembles the armor styles of the specific periods in which the works were created) and pointing the tip of either a sword or spear at Lucifer's throat or chest. Many consider this scene the ultimate symbol of good triumphing over evil.

If ever there were a patron warrior angel, it would certainly be the Archangel Michael. His role as an archangel has long been one of battle, and he is almost always depicted holding a sword or spear. While Michael is benevolent in nature, his role as a warrior often requires him to be wrathful as well. Judaic lore credits him with the destruction of the ancient city of Babylon, although he acted under the divine orders of YHVH.

In the recently transcribed Dead Sea Scrolls, there is a tale of a terrible war between the Sons of Light and the Sons of Darkness. In this tale, Michael is the Prince of Light, and leads the angelic ranks into battle against the Sons of Darkness, led by the demon commander Belial (for more on the fallen angel Belial, see Chapter 6). While certain elements of this story somewhat resemble those from the war in Heaven, this doesn't necessarily mean they are the same. Some claim the "war in Heaven" and the "war between the Sons" are actually two separate heavenly conflicts.

Gabriel: The Divine Trumpeter of Heaven

The name Gabriel means "My strength is from God/YHVH" (although it is sometimes interpreted as "Hero of God/YHVH"). In the angelic lore of both the Muslim and Judeo-Christian traditions, the Archangel

Gabriel is second in rank only to the mighty Archangel Michael. In the biblical Old Testament, he is one of only two angels referred to specifically by name (the other being Michael).

The Bermuda Triangle

Some might say that three angels are referred to by name in the original texts of the Old Testament. This belief is based on a passage from the Book of Tobit, which specifically names the Archangel Raphael. However, the validity of this text is widely disputed among Catholics, Protestants, and even Jews, so this is why the Archangel Raphael is not included here among those mentioned by name in the Old Testament.

Gabriel's angelic role is often thought of as YHVH's announcer, or as Heaven's messenger or trumpeter, which has led some to consider Gabriel as a Judeo-Christian equivalent to the Greco-Roman messenger god Hermes/Mercury. But while acting as a divine messenger/announcer is among his responsibilities, the entirety of his collective roles is far more complex. He is certainly more than just an angel who blows a trumpet, which is a common misperception.

The Archangel Gabriel's nature is as fascinating as it is unique. When compared to his fellow archangels, Gabriel displays an amazingly balanced set of roles. These balanced, and sometimes paradoxical, attributes give him a very unique and somewhat dualistic nature. Gabriel assumes many roles that could be, at first glance, perceived as contradictory (or, at best, very uncomplimentary). For example, Gabriel is the patron angel of both mercy and vengeance. He is also the patron angel of death and resurrection and of annunciation (telling) and revelation (revealing). In all these cases, Gabriel seems to be performing tasks contrary to one another. However, this can also be seen as a metaphor for the divine balance that allows contrary forces to exist harmoniously (light and dark, life and death, etc.).

In Islamic angelic lore, Gabriel is the patron angel of Truth. According to the Qur'an, the dust thrown up by Gabriel's holy steed found its way into the mouth of the golden calf the Jews erected during the absence of Moses. When this occurred, the blasphemous statue suddenly became animated as though it were alive. In the lore of Judaism, Gabriel was the one tasked with raining down fiery destruction upon the cities of Sodom and Gomorrah, which were doomed for their rampant debauchery.

Stranger Than Fiction _____

In the world of mythology, many scholars view the Archangel Gabriel as the Judeo-Christian version of the Greco-Roman figure Hermes/ Mercury. Both are portrayed as the messengers/announcers of a god, as well as patron figures of wisdom, truth, justice, and mercy.

Gabriel also plays an important role in Christian mythology. In the New Testament (Luke 1:26–38), Gabriel is sent to Nazareth to deliver a message to the Virgin Mary that she will give birth to Jesus the messiah. This scene of the New Testament is referred to in Christianity as "The Annunciation":

> And the angel came to her and said, "Hail, you are highly favored and the Lord is with you; blessed are you among women."
>
> When Mary saw him, she was afraid and troubled by what she saw and heard, and wondered what manner of salutation this should be.
>
> And the angel Gabriel said to her, "Fear not, Mary, for you have found favor with God. And behold, you shall conceive in your womb and bring forth a Son, and you will name him Jesus. He shall be great and will be called Son of the Highest; and the Lord God shall give to Him the throne of David, and He shall reign over the house of Jacob forever; and His Kingdom will be without end."
>
> Then Mary said to the angel, "How can this be, seeing as how I have never yet known the touch of a man?"
>
> Gabriel answered and said to her, "The Holy Spirit will come upon you, and the power of the Highest shall overshadow you. Therefore, the Holy One that will be born from you shall be called the Son of God. [...]"
>
> And Mary said, "Behold the handmaiden of the Lord; so let it be according to your words." And the angel departed from her.

This scene serves to solidify the general view of Gabriel as the messenger of YHVH. However, this is a rather narrow perception of the Archangel Gabriel when one considers the various other titles he holds.

Raphael: Protector of the Eden Tree

The name of Raphael, who is commonly considered the third highest in angelic rank, means "God has healed." The oldest known text to mention him by name is the Book of Tobit, which is not considered part of the Judeo-Christian canons and whose validity has long been a matter of religious debate.

According to the Book of Tobit, the Archangel Raphael was charged with the task of being the guide and guardian protector of Tobias, the son of Tobit, when he journeyed to the mighty ancient city of Nineveh. In this role, Raphael assumed the guise of a mortal human so as not to cause Tobias alarm and did not reveal his true form until after they reached Nineveh. Once they arrived, Raphael uncased his wings and explained to Tobias that he was one of the Seven Holy Angels who stood/knelt before the throne of YHVH.

As with his fellow archangels, Michael and Gabriel, Raphael is known by a variety of titles, names, and roles. First and foremost, he is known as the Protector of the Eden Tree for his role as the guardian of the sacred tree after the transgression of Adam and Eve (who ate its fruit after being forbidden to do so by YHVH). In addition, he is also the Guardian of the Western Horizon and the Prince of the Second Level of Heaven. The Archangel Raphael is also the patron angel of light, love, happiness, and prayer. A member of almost every possible angelic order, he is a Cherub as well as a Seraph and stands as one of the Ten Angels of the Holy Sefiroth.

As his name suggests, Raphael is widely considered an angel of healing, medicine, science, learning, and knowledge. There is a flip side to this part of Raphael's nature, however, and one day his time for healing others will reach its end. When this time comes, Raphael's attribute of healing will turn to one of destruction, and he will appear ominously as one of the Seven Angels of the Apocalypse.

Orifiel

The name Orifiel is a rather odd one, and it is often translated as either "My neck is God/YHVH" or "I am the neck of God/YHVH." Above all, the Archangel Orifiel is the patron angel of the forests/wilderness.

His domain is over the uncultivated, wild areas of the earth, which he does his best to protect against the ravages of evil men and urban development. (The ancient Jewish tribes, who were widely nomadic, greatly opposed the rise of cities and the concept of land ownership.)

Since Orifiel frequents those places that have remained untouched since God/YHVH created them, his usual haunts are said to be in deserts and oceans. This is likely because both are places to which men rarely try to make any permanent claim of ownership. Orifiel is considered the angelic enemy of greed, deception, and worldliness.

Zarachiel: Angel of Prayer

The name Zarachiel means "The command of God/YHVH." Zarachiel is also commonly referred to (especially in the Roman Catholic tradition) as Salaphiel, which has the somewhat similar meaning of "The one who prays to God/YHVH." No matter what name you call him, he is the patron angel of prayer.

In artistic depictions, the Archangel Zarachiel is most frequently portrayed in the act of his patron role and, interestingly enough, as male in gender (which is somewhat odd since angels are generally thought to have no specific gender or sex). The Archangel Zarachiel, usually shown assuming various states of prayer with his hands folded and his head bowed reverently, is credited with teaching humankind the proper methods by which to pray to God/YHVH.

Uriel: Angelic Light of God

The name Uriel (sometimes spelled Oriel) means "Fire of God/YHVH" or "Light of God/YHVH." As with his fellow archangel, Raphael, the oldest mention of Uriel's name is found in an *apocryphal* text, the Book of Enoch. In this text, Uriel is specifically referred to as the "leader of them all [the angels]." This suggests that, at least at some point, Uriel outranked Michael in the angelic hierarchy.

In the text, Uriel reveals to Enoch the truth of the workings of the planets and other celestial bodies. Uriel is tasked with the keeping of the mysteries of existence, deep within the depths of the earth and well beyond the known recesses of the cosmos. Of the seven "Throne

Archangels," Uriel is said to assume the closest position to it. Uriel is closely associated with the Sun (as his name would suggest) and in ancient times he was said to be the angelic guardian of the "great light" as it passed into the dark realms thought to exist between sunset and sunrise. During the daylight, Uriel exercises his greatest influence during the second hour of sunlight.

Conjuring Words

The term **apocryphal** literally means "probably not true." In religious terminology, however, the word refers to those writings/texts considered questionable by a religious body. These texts are sometimes set aside, but not completely forbidden, by some religious denominations. In other cases, however, they may be read but not cited. In extreme situations, even the mention of an apocryphal text is strictly forbidden.

The Least You Need to Know

♦ The Metatron acts as the agent of YHVH's voice and will on Earth.

♦ The three highest-ranking angels, in Judeo-Christian and Islamic texts, are Michael, Gabriel, and Raphael.

♦ The Grigori are the "watcher" angels who are supposed to observe but not interfere with human affairs.

♦ The seven "Archangels of the Throne," who stand in YHVH's presence, are Michael, Gabriel, Raphael, Orifiel, Zarachiel (also Salaphiel), Uriel, and Simiel.

6

Fallen Angels

In This Chapter

- ◆ The Judeo-Christian accounts of the war in Heaven
- ◆ The fate of Lucifer, leader of the rebel angels
- ◆ The demon Beelzebub's role in Hell
- ◆ The hostile demon lord of chaos known as Belial
- ◆ The many destructive roles of Azazel
- ◆ The Nephilim, said to be the sons of the fallen

According to Judeo-Christian lore, a violent conflict once raged between the ranks of Heaven like an angelic civil war. While the most detailed of the extant chronological accounts of this war are not universally accepted as part of the Christian canon, all Christians know the basics of the story cited in the New Testament. The bold rebels, known as fallen angels, were cursed to live as demons until the end of times for rising up against their creator.

The Book of Enoch

We can find the most complete chronological account of the war in Heaven in the noncanonical text of the Book of Enoch. Most sources agree the only complete version of this text was likely transcribed sometime around 300 B.C.E. However, this text is believed to be a written account of a much older orally transmitted myth (possibly by thousands of years). The complete text was written exclusively in the dead language of Ge'ez. However, a number of additional fragments also exist that recount parts of the original text, though they are written in either the ancient *Aramaic* language or in Hebrew quadratic script.

> **Conjuring Words**
>
> **Aramaic** is an ancient language widely spoken by the Semitic tribes of the Near East around 400 to 300 B.C.E. Eventually, it was almost completely replaced by the Hebrew language. Today, it is known only by roughly 75,000 people worldwide.

The Enoch text claims to be a written account of a divine vision experienced by the Jewish prophet Enoch, the father of the Hebrew leader Methuselah. He was also the ancestor of Noah, who preserved the Judaic ways of life and civilization during the Great Flood.

When a group of angels took Enoch to the heavens, they revealed the truth behind the great mystery of existence. He learned of the oneness of YHVH, the arrangements of the hierarchies of Heaven and Earth, and the story of the fallen angels and the war in Heaven.

The Light Bringer

When it comes to fallen angels, Lucifer is the undisputed top dog. His name literally translates as "Light Bringer," but it is also often read as "Morning Star." In ancient Judaism, spiritual entities were often associated with specific celestial bodies, and it is believed that Lucifer was identified with the planet Venus. Later, however, some interpreted his name as related to the description of his fall from Heaven, commonly said to have looked like a fiery star falling from the sky.

The Bermuda Triangle

One common misconception is that Lucifer and Satan are two names for the same entity. Actually, Satan means "the enemy/adversary." While this title is often applied to Lucifer, it is not exclusively used to refer to him. A number of other demonic entities are also referred to by the title Satan. In addition, the word has a figurative meaning sometimes used to refer to human temptations and the inner conflict of good versus evil within the human soul. This broad use of the term has led to a number of misinterpretations over the years.

There are multiple, sometimes differing versions of the specific details regarding what led Lucifer to rebel against YHVH. However, almost all agree that he was initially the most beautiful and radiant of all YHVH's angels. He was blessed with the title of being YHVH's most favored angel. But at some point, even his exalted position and high angelic title were no longer enough for him. Some versions of the myth claim that Lucifer was angered because YHVH granted souls and free will to humans (both gifts that were denied the angels).

The Bermuda Triangle

Fallen angels do make up a good chunk of the vast array of Judeo-Christian demons. However, it is important to note that while all fallen angels are considered demons, not all Judeo-Christian demons are fallen angels.

With promises of glory and power, Lucifer convinced one third of Heaven's angels to join him in an uprising against YHVH, the very God who had created them. As you might guess, the battle did not turn out well for Lucifer and his force of rebel angels. When the war was over, Lucifer was judged harshly for his crimes. He was stripped of his angelic title and cast down from the heavens to the realm of Earth, where he will remain until final judgment.

The Demon of the Flies

The name of the Judeo-Christian demon Beelzebub (sometimes alternately spelled Belzebud or Belaboul) translates as "God of the flies." This title comes from the time when the ancient Syrians worshiped

Beelzebub as a deity likely associated with disease and death. When Judaism waged a bloody campaign against all non-YHVH religious cults, however, Beelzebub was annexed into their mythology and transformed into a demon. In the demonological lore of the Judaic mystical practice of *Kaballah*, this fallen angel is identified as the high demon lord of the Nine Hierarchies of Evil.

> ### Conjuring Words
> **Kaballah** is a tradition of mystical spiritual practice in Judaism. However, the specific texts associated with Kaballah mysticism are not considered a part of the Jewish canon.

Of all the 200 fallen angels found in the traditional Judeo-Christian demonology, Beelzebub is the one most frequently mistaken as being an alternate name for Lucifer. In truth, however, Lucifer and Beelzebub are two completely different demonic entities. The confusion of these two usually occurs because they are both commonly referred to by the title Satan.

The Wicked Lord of Darkness

As the appointed Angel of Hostility, it is not surprising that Belial sided with Lucifer. Before the war in Heaven and the fall of the rebel angels, Belial was an angel of war, chaos, and conflict. By nature, he stood contrary to order and peace. His name is usually translated to mean something like "God's Wicked One" (although because of his current demonic status, many religious texts translate the name as simply "Wicked One").

> ### The Bermuda Triangle
> It is a common misperception that the fallen angels were banished to a specific place called "Hell." However, neither the apocryphal or canonical texts support this interpretation. The fallen angels were quite clearly banished to the physical realm, a terrible fate for beings who had always lived in the blissfully perfect realm of Heaven. However, some fallen angels who were too powerful or troublesome were sealed *within* the earth until Judgment Day.

Some apocryphal texts claim that Belial was created as a side-by-side, polar opposite to Lucifer. He was as horrifying in his appearance as Lucifer was beautiful. Whereas Lucifer was given an angelic title of Light, even as an angel Belial ruled over all of that which was Dark. In fact, in the *Dead Sea Scrolls* it is written of Belial that "All his dominion is Darkness." When the pair of Lucifer and Belial joined forces against YHVH and his angels, they made such a formidable pair that in the end they could only be brought down by YHVH's ultimate power. In fact, even the mighty warrior of Heaven, Archangel Michael, is quoted in the Book of Enoch as claiming that had it not been for the divine power of the intervening YHVH, the forces of Heaven could more than likely have been defeated.

Conjuring Words

The **Dead Sea Scrolls** is the title given to a collection of manuscripts found in a series of caves near the Dead Sea between 1947 and 1956. While considered apocryphal by mainstream Christianity, these scrolls shed light on many gaps in the canonical Judeo-Christian texts. They have been the subject of much debate among historians and religious scholars for decades.

After the fall, Belial was given domain as a King of Demons. He is the master of lies and the speaker of false promises. A very destructive and cleverly seductive entity, Belial would offer you anything in the world in order to secure your destruction because he never intends to live up to his end of any bargain he makes. Of all the fallen angels, Belial is the one most commonly encountered in cases of both human and localized demonic possessions (for more on this and rites of demon exorcism, see Chapter 7). And once he figures out how to charm his way into a human, object, or home, he is *extremely* difficult to cast out. Sometimes, he has even convinced the very people whose lives he has filled with torments that they actually *need* him.

Banished to Dudael

According to both the Book of Enoch and the Zohar, Azazel was leading the way at the front of the rebel line when the war in Heaven broke out. According to these texts, Azazel had a thing for human women and did not like that they were off limits. After the fall, however, Azazel finally had his wish to be among humans fulfilled when he was banished to the earth.

Azazel has been given credit for many of the things that have plagued humankind for many years. When he came to Earth, he reveled among humans and took many lovers. He also bestowed humans with a dangerous array of destructive knowledge. He taught human men the arts of metalworking and showed them how to construct weapons with which to wage war upon one another. To improve the beauty of his human female lovers, he taught women how to use cosmetics.

Conjuring Words

Azazel is probably the demon responsible for the eventual association of the goat-head with the satanic/demonic, as he is often described as having the head or horns of a goat. Originally, Azazel may have been the name of a goat-headed sex/fertility god that was identified as a demon by ancient Judaism. For example, it is written in 2 Chronicles that Jeroboam had a number of goat idols constructed to non-Judaic gods.

After a while, YHVH saw the trouble Azazel was causing on Earth and reconsidered the original conditions of his banishment. YHVH sent the Archangel Raphael to deal with Azazel, instructing him to bind the rather troublesome fallen angel in the dark depths beneath the desert called Dudael, meaning "Despair/Desolation." For his further sins against YHVH's creation, Azazel will remain bound beneath the vast sands of Dudael until the coming of the Final Judgment.

Sons of the Fallen (The Nephilim)

The Enoch text sheds light on the mysterious passage in Genesis 6:4 that says "The Sons of Heaven/God (depending on translation) lied down with the daughters of men." The Genesis passage has caused some to interpret this to mean that the angels had sex with human women. However, the Enoch text specifically claims it was the fallen angels who did this. The most frequent one to do this was Azazel, who seemed to have been lusting after human women even before the fall from Heaven.

Of course, where there is sex there are often children, and such was the case here. The result was a race of giant and powerful beings, the off-spring born from the unions of the fallen angels with human women. These giants were called the *Nephilim*.

Apparently, the gigantic Nephilim, sons of the fallen, turned out to be the epitomes of "Like father, like son." They ran rampant across the earth, fornicating with and raping human women, murder-ing humans, and waging wars. According to the Enoch text, their evil deeds contributed greatly to YHVH's decision to flood the world in order to wipe them out.

Conjuring Words

Nephilim, plural for *Nephil*, refers to an ancient race of powerful giants who were the offspring of fallen angels and human women ... although some religious scholars contest this interpretation and believe the passage refers to either angels in general or some long-extinct race of giant (or at least extremely tall) humanoids.

The Least You Need to Know

♦ The only complete extant account of the war in Heaven is found in the Book of Enoch.

♦ Some fragments from the Enoch text have been found in the Dead Sea Scrolls, written in either Aramaic or Hebrew.

♦ While there are differing versions of what caused the uprising in Heaven, all accounts agree that the rebel angels lost.

♦ Beelzebub is often mistaken for Lucifer, since both demons are referred to by the title Satan, which means "enemy/adversary."

Chapter 7

Demons and Exorcisms

In This Chapter

- The relationships between demons and fallen angels
- The different types of demonic possession
- Prayers of protection against demonic forces
- Objects used as protection against demonic forces
- The basic elements of demonic exorcism
- Documented cases of demonic possessions and exorcisms

Where there is light, there is also darkness. Some say that in order for there to be good, there must also be evil. In the realm of the spiritual and paranormal, agents of darkness and evil are referred to as demons. These wicked spirits seek the ruination of all humankind. They thrive on fear and chaos, and exist to spread both across creation. While they can be powerful, demons are in no way all-powerful. As long as humans have been aware of the demonic, they've also been aware of the means to battle them.

Demons vs. Fallen Angels

Sometimes the difference between demons and fallen angels can be confusing, so the best way to understand this is to remember that while all fallen angels are labeled as demons, not all demons are fallen angels. In fact, in Judeo-Christian lore many demons existed long before the war in Heaven that led to the expulsion of Lucifer and his rebel angels.

While many of the known demons are found in Judeo-Christian lore, some are not. Nearly every civilization that's ever existed has had its own malevolent spiritual entities, often credited with destructive forces such as disease, famine, etc. From the Native American tribes to Africa to Europe, demons (or evil spirits) exist in every society's mythic lore. Therefore, it's important to understand that every demon one might encounter cannot necessarily be identified as, or by the name of, a fallen angel.

Demon Possession

There are two primary forms of demonic presence, *area possession* and *personal possession*. Area possession is somewhat less dangerous (though no less troublesome) and often is a case of one or more demons occupying a physical space (usually a home) and tormenting the inhabitants in an attempt to spiritually or mentally weaken them. This is done in order to open a path by which one or more of the inhabitants can become personally possessed. So one might view area possession as a common precursor to personal possession. However, sometimes demons occupy an area due to a past event or some preexisting *binding*. Area possessions can also occur in places where humans regularly engage (or once engaged) in negative, violent, or overly selfish activities, as these are thought to attract demonic presences.

Personal possession is when a demon succeeds in invading the body of an individual human being. This is commonly believed to occur in three stages, which are achieved more or less quickly depending on the disposition and will of the possessed person. The three main stages of demonic possession are as follows:

- ◆ Stage 1: Demonization

- ◆ Stage 2: Personal possession

- ◆ Stage 3: Perfect possession

Conjuring Words

Area possession is when one or more demons occupy a physical space, often a home, building, or other structure. Sometimes this includes the possession of certain objects. A number of potential factors can lead to area possessions.

Personal possession is when a demon successfully infiltrates the body of a human being and gradually exercises influence or control over his or her behavior or actions. This is also the second stage of demonic possession of humans.

Binding refers to a spell, ritual, prayer, or other ceremony by which a spirit or demon is bound from certain actions (such as doing harm), then usually imprisoned in, permanently barred from, or attached to a place, structure, object, or animal.

In the first stage, called *demonization*, the demon succeeds in infiltrating the individual (sometimes after first wearing the person down during an area possession). The demon's control over the person is erratic but still identifiable as the possessed person's behavior begins to undergo extreme and often uncharacteristic changes. For example, the person may become unreasonably irritable or display an unexplained or irrational aversion to anything having to do with faith or religion (such as prayers, relics, churches, temples, and even sacred/biblical names). Demons in general have often been known to experience extreme discomfort in the presence of any and all spiritual practices of just about *any* nondemonic religion. At this stage, something as simple as a blessing by a holy man or a cleansing ceremony can usually expel the demon.

Conjuring Words

Demonization is the primary stage of demonic possession in humans, characterized by the demon infiltrating and occupying the person's body. At this stage, removing the demon remains somewhat simple as long as the possessed person honestly desires the demon's removal.

In the second stage of personal possession, the will of the possessed becomes less and less their own as the demon begins to sporadically demonstrate an influence over the person's speech or behavior. The possessed may begin to exhibit knowledge or abilities that are not a part of their experiences. For example, one very common behavioral trait of the possessed is spontaneously and fluently speaking in languages that are unknown/foreign to them. They may also know the details of events they did not witness and of which they could not possibly have any previous knowledge. However, at this stage there is still hope for the possessed person. While the more extreme step of an *exorcism* may be necessary in order to expel the demon, the possessed still has some control of his or her own will and can assist in his or her own exorcism.

Once a person reaches the third stage, *perfect possession*, the situation gets much more serious. At this point, little of the possessed person's original personality remains. In fact, those who are unfortunate enough to experience perfect possession usually appear and behave as though they have accepted the evil spirit within them. They have developed a spiritual attachment to it, leading them to fear the demon's expulsion.

Conjuring Words _____

An **exorcism** is any spiritual rite, ritual, or ceremony meant to expel demons or other malevolent spirits that have successfully occupied a physical space or human body. We can find specific methods for carrying out exorcisms in the spiritual practices of almost every culture in the world.

Perfect possession is the ultimate form of demonic possession in humans. By this stage, those possessed have surrendered to the will of the demon (or demons) within them. This is the most dangerous and difficult type of possession to exorcise, because the possessed have often developed a dependency upon the demon(s) and are usually uncooperative in the removal process.

Cases of perfect possession are considered the most dangerous. For any exorcist, an encounter with a demon that has achieved perfect possession involves detailed planning. Such exorcisms are approached with extreme caution as they can prove to be fatal, for both the exorcist and the possessed.

Protection Prayers

To ward off evil or demonic forces or entities, protection prayers are recited. These prayers are not necessarily considered to remove demons that are already present. Instead, they are meant to prevent demonic entities from entering into or otherwise influencing a person, home, property, or object.

Paranormal investigators and professional exorcists often use the repetitive recitation of protection prayers as a chant to shield themselves from harm or fear whenever engaging malevolent spirits or demons. Since demons cannot really be destroyed, so to speak, but only banished from one individual or space to another, these prayers also prevent demons from "jumping."

When demons jump, they shift from a currently possessed individual or space to a new one. Demons have been known to do this in order to temporarily fool exorcists into believing they have successfully cast them out, when in fact the targeted demons have only moved to a new space (more details on exorcisms later). In extreme cases, when serious mistakes are made by an exorcist, demons have even been known to attempt jumping from the possessed person or space to the body of the acting exorcist. Reciting prayers of protection can offer a protective shield against the demon being engaged.

The Circle of Light

The "Circle of Light" prayer is a very good, spiritually universal, non-denominational protection prayer. Sometimes, this prayer is recited after lighting a blessed (or just a normal) candle. The individual, before reciting the prayer, first envisions that he or she is completely surrounded by a strong circle of protective light.

Some alternate versions of the prayer are available (some only recite the first four or five lines), but the majority of them are similar to the following:

> The light of God surrounds us (me).
> The love of God enfolds us (me).
> The power of God protects us (me).

The presence of God watches over us (me).
Wherever we are (I am), God is.
And all is well.

The Prayer to the Archangel Michael

One of the most powerful prayers of protection against demonic forces
is the "Prayer to St. Michael the Archangel" (for more on Michael and
other archangels, see Chapter 5). There are several known alternate
versions of this prayer. The longest version is also the original, which
Pope Leo XIII issued and ordered to be used as a protective exorcism
prayer against Satan and other demonic forces.

Three primary versions are most commonly used by today's exorcists,
mediums, and paranormal investigators. Those who regularly deal with
demons and malevolent spirits usually memorize the shortest version
and believe they gain strength when a group recites the prayer in uni-
son. This short version is as follows:

> Saint Michael the Archangel, defend us in battle.
> Be our protection against the wickedness and snares of the devil.
>
> May God rebuke him, we humbly pray.
>
> And do thou, Oh Prince of the Heavenly Host, by God's power,
> thrust into hell Satan and all evil spirits who wander the world
> seeking the ruin of souls.
>
> Amen.

The second known version, only slightly longer, integrates the short
version with certain important passages from the original Roman
Catholic version. This second, middle-length version is as follows:

> Glorious Prince of Heaven's armies, Saint Michael the Archangel,
> defend us in battle against the principalities and powers, against
> the rulers of darkness, against the wicked spirits in the high places.
>
> Be our protection against the wickedness and snares of the devil.
>
> May God rebuke him, we humbly pray.

And do thou, Oh Prince of the heavenly host, by the power of God, thrust into hell Satan and all evil spirits who wander throughout the world seeking the ruin of souls.

In the name of the Father,
And of the Son,
And of the Holy Spirit.

Amen.

The Bermuda Triangle

Since direct (memorized) recitations are thought to be more powerful than those done through visual readings, priest exorcists who are trained by the Roman Catholic Church use almost exclusively the original long version of this prayer. In addition, it is important to note that some sources state that the original version of this prayer should be recited *only by a priest.*

The original, Catholic version of this prayer is rather lengthy and integrates long citations of biblical passages from Ephesians and Revelations. Because of its length, memorization of this version can be slightly more difficult, and so it sometimes must be recited by reading from a written piece. This original version is as follows:

In the Name of the Father, and of the Son, and of the Holy Spirit.

Oh Glorious Prince of the Heavenly Armies, Saint Michael the Archangel, defend us in "our battle against the principalities and powers, against the rulers of this world of darkness, against the spirits of wickedness in the high places" (Ephesians 6:12).

Come to the assistance of those God has created to His likeness, and whom He has redeemed at a great price from the tyranny of the devil.

The Holy Church venerates you as her guardian and protector; to you, the Lord has entrusted the souls of the redeemed to be led into heaven. Pray, therefore, to the God of Peace to crush Satan beneath our feet, that he may no longer retain men captive and do injury to the Church.

Offer our prayers to the Most High, that without delay they may draw His mercy down upon us; take hold of "the dragon, the serpent of old, which is the devil and Satan," bind him and cast him into the bottomless pit "that he may no longer seduce the nations" (Revelations 20:2–3).

In the Name of the Father, and of the Son, and of the Holy Spirit.

Amen.

The Twenty-Third Psalm

The Twenty-Third Psalm, from the Old Testament *Book of Psalms*, can be recited for a variety of purposes. Therefore, some consider it a multipurpose prayer. As a prayer for those in mourning, it is often recited at funerals of both the Judaic and Christian faiths. It also gives courage to the fearful and hope to those who suffer from despair. Additionally, it is considered a prayer of protection against evil or demonic forces.

There are various English translations of the Twenty-Third Psalm, but almost all of them basically contain the following:

> The Lord is my shepherd: I shall not want. He makes me lie down in green pastures; He leads me beside the still waters. He restores my soul. He leads me in the paths of righteousness for his name's sake, and though I walk through the valley of the shadow of death, I will fear no evil for thou art with me. Thy rod and thy staff, they comfort me. You prepare a table before me in the presence of mine enemies; you anoint my head with oil; my cup overflows. Surely goodness and mercy will follow me all of the days of my life, and I will dwell in the house of the Lord forever.
>
> Amen.

Jabez's Prayer

In 1 Chronicles 4:10 in the Christian Bible, we find the "Prayer of Jabez." Jabez was one of Israel's most righteous and faithful men during a rather unremarkable time in its history. However, Jabez is known for offering one simple prayer to the god of the Israelites, YHVH … and for his piety and faith, his prayer was granted. Again, many translations are available. One translation is as follows:

> Oh, Lord that you would bless me indeed, and enlarge my territory, and that your hand might be with me, and that you would keep me from evil so that it may not grieve me.

St. Benedict Medals and Sacred Objects

The practice of wearing or using protective charms, amulets, or objects in order to ward off evil has been around since ancient times. Sometimes the wearing of blessed medals or the use of certain sacred objects, a practice that still remains very common in Catholicism, is believed to offer protection against evil spirits and demonic entities.

Many believe special medals referred to as the "Medals of St. Benedict" are the most potent objects in the barring of malevolent or demonic entities. St. Benedict was the founder of the Benedictine monastic order, and many stories involving the barring or thwarting of evil or demonic forces are credited to him.

The front of a St. Benedict medal portrays him holding a cross in his right hand and an unfurled scroll on which he wrote the rules of behavior for the Benedictine monks in his left. Behind him is a cup of poison, which symbolizes a specific story regarding one of his miracles. According to the story, when a servant of evil offered St. Benedict a poisoned goblet, the man of God made the sign of the cross, and the goblet immediately shattered. A loaf of poisoned bread that the man had also offered to Benedict was then set upon by a raven that flew away with it, thwarting the man's plan to kill the monk.

The back of a St. Benedict medal shows a cross along with a specific series of letters, VRS-NSMV-SMQL-IVB. These letters were first discovered written on crosses hung throughout the interior of the Benedictine Abbey of Metten. The discovery was made after several women who were being tried for witchcraft claimed to have been quite unable to work their spells near that building.

For some time, the meaning of the letters remained a mystery until a manuscript from 1417 was discovered. These letters, which stand for the words Benedict supposedly spoke when the agent of the devil attempted to poison him, were later used to form the following prayer of protection and exorcism:

> *Vade retro Satana* (Step back Satan)
> *Numquam suade mihi vana* (Tempt me not with vain things)
> *Sunt mala quae libas* (What you offer is evil)
> *Ipse venena bibas* (Drink the poison yourself)

Many other objects are considered effective in protecting oneself against malevolent spiritual influences. For the most part, any sacred religious object in which the wearer/holder has faith can offer protection against demonic forces.

Some of the most commonly used objects for protection against evil or demonic forces are as follows:

- Holy water

- Blessed salts

- Anointment oils

- Crosses, crucifixes, or rosaries

- A pentagram, pointing upward (for Wiccans)

Exorcisms

Once a demon has successfully taken hold of a physical space or entered into the body of a human being, it must be removed by the cleansing rite of an exorcism. The business of conducting exorcisms is no laughing matter. The conduction of exorcisms often results in serious long-term ramifications for the exorcist, including permanent physical, psychological, or spiritual damage.

Laymen or paranormal dabblers should never attempt an exorcism. Only a properly trained and appropriately experienced individual should try to perform an exorcism because once an exorcist has named and engaged a demon, there is no way to stop or call off the battle until the demon has been successfully expelled.

Trained exorcists do not consider failure to complete an exorcism a valid option, and it's not uncommon for this to create a permanent bond, a spiritual or psychological connection, between the exorcist and the demon(s) he or she engaged. This connection will torment the failed exorcist, in mind and body, for the rest of his or her days and can sometimes still occur even if another exorcist succeeds in completing the exorcism. Therefore, it is important to note that engaging a demon (especially if calling it by name) should be done at one's own risk.

The Legion Exorcism

Perhaps the most well-known tale of a demon exorcism can be found in the New Testament of the Christian Bible. Commonly referred to as the "Legion Exorcism," it involves an encounter between the Christian messiah, Jesus Christ, and a demon-possessed man in the country of the Gergesenes (sometimes spelled Garsenes) people. The Gospels of Matthew, Mark, and Luke all contain accounts of this encounter. While the accounts found in Mark and Luke are nearly identical, the one in Matthew is somewhat different.

The story generally says that when Jesus arrived on the Gergesenes coast, a man possessed by demons approached him. The man had abandoned his human dwelling and now lived among the tombs of the dead. On many occasions, the people of the city had attempted to subdue him with metal shackles and chains. However, the demons possessing him gave him the inhuman strength to break the chains, shatter his shackles, and escape. Upon seeing Jesus and knowing his true nature, the demons in the man grew fearful and pled for mercy.

The demons, speaking through the man, knelt before Jesus and begged him not to expel them from the land. Jesus demanded to know the name(s) of the demons, to which they replied, "My name is Legion, for we are many."

The Bermuda Triangle

The account of Jesus' expulsion of Legion found in the Gospel of Matthew is unique in comparison to those found in Mark and Luke. For example, the Matthew account claims there were two demon-possessed men, not just one. In addition, the demon's self-identification by the specific name of Legion is entirely absent from this account.

This reply is believed to reveal one important aspect in the nature of demonic entities—they exist outside the normally accepted rules regarding physical space, meaning they're able to be both one and separate at the same time, and multiple demons can occupy the same space at the same time. The demon(s) first says "*My* name," suggesting singularity, but then says "*We* are many," which implies plurality. Jesus' demand for a name is also of important note, and many rites of exorcism claim that a demonic entity must be identified by a name before it can be successfully engaged and expelled.

Having identified the demon, Jesus demanded that Legion leave the man. Legion, however, begged that it be allowed to enter into the bodies of a nearby herd of pigs. Jesus granted the request, casting Legion out of the man and into the pigs, all of whom immediately ran into the ocean and drowned. This illustrates another aspect of demons—they cannot be destroyed, only cast out from the possessed space or person. Some claim this is because demons and fallen angels were granted domain over the physical realm until God's final judgment of the earth.

The swineherd shepherds rushed to tell people what Jesus had done. When the people of the nearby city heard of what happened, they came running and found the formerly possessed man clothed and in his right mind. However, the simple people became fearful of Jesus' abilities (which, to them, may have appeared to be nothing more than the power to command demons … an ability they may have associated with dark magic) and implored him to leave their land. As Jesus prepared to leave, the man he had exorcized begged Jesus to let him become one of his followers. Jesus refused but told the man to go back to the city and tell others of what he had experienced. The man spent the rest of his days traveling the *Decapolis* (Ten Cities), telling all who would listen about what Jesus had done for him.

Recent Possession Case Files

Demonic possession is not new, and episodes are still said to occur. However, in today's world cases of possession are only identified after all other medical or psychological methods of explanation have been exhausted. In ancient and medieval times, demon possession was often diagnosed in cases of unknown mental or physical ailments. For example, people suffering from Tourette Syndrome, a condition that causes a person to involuntarily act on certain impulses (such as ticking, jerking, writhing, screaming, or shouting obscenities), were commonly labeled as possessed in past ages. Also, before schizophrenia—a psychiatric condition that usually causes a person to hallucinate, hear voices, and have paranoid delusions—was identified, the label of possession was frequently given to those suffering from it.

Today, when a person is suspected of being demon-possessed, the first thing a properly trained exorcist does is have that individual undergo a series of medical and psychological examinations. This is done in order to rule out mental illness or physical defect as the cause of the person's odd or unexplained behavior. Usually, suspected cases of demon possession don't make it past these initial tests, as a rational explanation is usually uncovered and treated. In the rare circumstances when these tests fail to discover another cause, however, the exorcist prepares to engage the person in order to bring out, identify, and expel the demons hidden within. The following are two examples of some of the more extreme exorcisms that have occurred in recent times—one example of a mistakenly undertaken exorcism and another of a valid series of exorcisms.

The Mistaken Exorcism of Anneliese Michel

When a case of extreme mental illness is mislabeled as demonic possession, the outcome can be catastrophic and even fatal. Perhaps the best modern example of such a case is the attempted exorcism of a German girl named Anneliese Michel. When the teenage girl began to suffer increasingly frequent episodes of extreme thrashing through the early 1970s, her concerned parents took her to doctors. She was examined and diagnosed as suffering from grand mal epilepsy, a neurological condition that causes spastic seizures and can even damage the brain. The girl was also given a psychiatric evaluation and found to suffer from multiple mental disorders (thought to have been linked to her neurological defect). These mental ailments led her to exhibit psychotic, sometimes violent, behaviors. Anneliese's parents, who were extremely religious, soon came to their own conclusion that their daughter was acting this way because she was demon-possessed.

The Michels contacted the church about their suspicions, and the appropriate church authorities conducted their own investigation and ultimately concluded that the initial diagnoses of the doctors were sound. They found no evidence of any of the usual unexplainable phenomenon associated with demonic possession, such as levitation, abnormal strength, precognition, etc. They refused to conduct an exorcism, explaining to the Michels that their daughter suffered from nonspiritual issues. An exorcism, the church officials explained repeatedly, would be of no use. Anneliese's family was told that prayer and psychological treatment were the best avenues for healing their daughter.

However, Anneliese's parents vehemently refused to accept this answer to their daughter's behavior and, for years, implored the church to perform an exorcism on their violently deranged daughter. Sometime in 1975, they managed to convince a small group of priests to perform an unauthorized rite of exorcism. Since the girl was mentally ill and not demon-possessed, the ritual only made things worse. In her deranged and delusional state, Anneliese was only reinforced in her belief that demons were inside of her. However, no amount of exorcizing rites (performed multiple times a day, several days a week, and for an unknown number of weeks) did her any good.

As the unnecessary exorcism continued, Anneliese's physical health suffered along with her deteriorating mental state. Obsessed with the idea of ridding herself of demons, she began performing roughly 600 *genuflections* every day. Eventually, this caused the fluid sacs in her knees to rupture (an excruciatingly painful and crippling condition).

The Scary Truth

The tragic case of Anneliese Michel is believed to have inspired the 2005 film *The Exorcism of Emily Rose*. However, unlike the true-life case, the film seems to suggest a true demon possession was being conducted but led to the possessed character's unfortunate death.

Conjuring Words

Genuflection is a practice performed in the Roman Catholic and Anglican churches, involving touching one or both knees to the ground as a sign of worship or a gesture of respect to God.

The mistakenly undertaken exorcism finally came to a tragic end on July 30, 1976. Deprived of food as part of the exorcism rites, Anneliese Michel died of starvation. The acting priests and her parents were brought up on charges of negligent homicide and were all found guilty of needlessly causing the poor girl's death. While everyone involved appeared to be convinced that she was demon-possessed, belief does not trump the truth. This case now stands as an example to modern exorcists for why it is so imperative that human exorcisms only be conducted after the proper authorities have deemed a case as valid and in need of exorcism.

The Last Exorcism of Father Peter

In 1965, a Roman Catholic exorcist referred to simply as "Father Peter" performed his third and final exorcism on a New York girl recorded by the name Marianne K. The account of this case was first published in 1987 in Malachi Martin's book *Hostage to the Devil*. The Irish-born Father Peter had been an exorcist of the Roman Catholic Church for many years and had already acted as a lead exorcist on two previous occasions (and had assisted in many others).

During the very first exorcism in which Father Peter had acted as lead exorcist, at the *breakpoint* of the exorcism, the demon had made a foreboding announcement. As the 13-hour ceremony finally came to a head, the demon screamed out through the possessed man's clenched teeth, "Third strike and you're out, pig! Remember us!" This statement would haunt Father Peter for the rest of his days as an exorcist.

 **Conjuring Words**

In exorcisms, the **breakpoint** is the moment when the demon is the closest to expulsion. As possessed individuals begin to regain control of their will, the demon exhausts itself trying to retain its hold. Eventually, the demon has no choice but to release the person and vacate.

In 1952, when he was called to perform as lead in his second exorcism, Father Peter jokingly said something along the lines of "Well, it isn't the third time yet." The ceremony went off without a hitch. However, it is said to have gone on for an unusually long period of time—three days and nights—which is recorded as being a point of concern for Father Peter. He would later claim to have viewed this exorcism as a warm-up for his third.

Father Peter's third exorcism, which took place in August of 1965, was his most difficult. A girl in New York named Marianne had reached the point of perfect possession, and by her own personal account admitted that she had totally surrendered to the will of the demonic entity residing within her. The demon is named in the account as "The Smiler," for the way it had caused the possessed girl to assume an almost constant (and rather disconcerting) smiling expression.

Father Peter temporarily made an error during the exorcism and entered into a philosophical debate with the demon. This is a common pitfall exorcists encounter, as contradicting the false ideas of a demon is tempting. However, doing so also opens the exorcist's mind to attack and can result in a loss of the will to fight. Luckily, Father Peter caught it and recovered.

At the breakpoint, it took two good-size men (one a former police officer) to subdue the violent thrashing of Marianne's body. The demon locked eyes with Father Peter and addressed him as "Peter the Eater," a private nickname he'd been called only once by a girl he'd loved (and to whom he'd lost his virginity) back in the days of his youth (long before he had joined the priesthood … the girl had died of a ruptured spleen in 1929). At that moment, Father Peter experienced an aching pressure in his head, but with the help of his assistant, he was able to complete the ceremony and cast the demon out of Marianne.

Father Peter was never the same after his encounter with "The Smiler," and less than a year later, Father Peter died in 1966. The official cause of death was coronary thrombosis, but after his last exorcism, colleagues claimed that Peter had entered into a state of extreme depression from which he never recovered. His eyes often seemed blank, and his voice had lost the air of strength that had once made him such an imposing figure. Despite once being capable of knocking a pipe out of a man's mouth by kicking a soccer ball from 30 yards away, his physical strength had simply left him. While the physical cause of his death had been his heart, many believed his death was the result of his third and final exorcism. He was never again called up to participate in exorcisms, fulfilling the ominous words of the demon he'd first exorcized—"Third strike and you're out."

The Least You Need to Know

♦ While all fallen angels are considered demons, not all demons are fallen angels.

♦ There are a number of prayers of protection believed to shield people from demonic forces.

♦ Certain objects of faith are also said to offer protection against malevolent spirits and demons.

♦ Only a properly trained and experienced exorcist should ever attempt to cast out demonic entities.

♦ Cases of demon possession must first be properly verified through medical and psychiatric examinations.

Chapter 8

Necromancy

In This Chapter

- ◆ The dark art of conjuring the dead
- ◆ Spirit necromancy vs. physical/traditional necromancy
- ◆ King Saul's experience with the Witch of Endor
- ◆ The relationship of séances and Ouija boards to spirit necromancy
- ◆ The truth about the *Necronomicon* manuscript
- ◆ The relationship between physical necromancy and the practice of anthropomancy

The dark art of conjuring forth the spirits of the dead has been around since ancient times. Almost all currently practiced religious/spiritual traditions strictly forbid any attempts to conjure dead spirits (or even to resurrect the dead physically) in order to communicate with them or gain special knowledge through them. It is almost universally understood that forcing open doors between our world and the realm of the dead comes at a terrible price.

Bringing Up the Dead

Originally, *necromancy* specifically referred to the art of conjuring or communicating with the dead (in spiritual or physical forms). Later, the term came to have a broader meaning, and by medieval times it was used as an umbrella term to refer to all forms of "black magic." This may have occurred due to its confusion with the phonetically similar term *nigromancy*, which first appeared in medieval texts. Nigromancy refers to those malevolent magical arts that involve conjurations of the demonic. In this text, however, I do not use necromancy to mean all dark arts, but instead its original specific definition as the art of conjuring the dead. Necromancy spells do commonly involve the invocations of demons, of course, but primarily as tools to retrieve the spirits with which the necromancer wishes to consult.

Conjuring Words _____

Necromancy comes from the Greek *necros* (death/corpse) and *manteia* (prophecy/divination), and refers to the art of conjuring or actively communicating with the dead (in spiritual or physical form) by way of rituals, spells, or incantations.

Nigromancy comes from an improper combination of the Latin *nigero* (black) with the Greek *manteia*, and it is sometimes seen being used interchangeably with necromancy. However, nigromancy is a much broader term that refers to all mystical or magical arts that are dark, malevolent, or demonic in nature.

One common misperception confuses the concept of a necromancer (one who practices necromancy) with that of a spiritual *medium* (one who has an innate awareness of spirits). However, they are not the same thing by any stretch of the imagination. The primary difference between them is that a necromancer conjures up spirits by the use of spells or incantations and sometimes will bring forth a desired spirit by force if necessary. In addition, necromancers often disturb spirits already peacefully at rest. Doing such a thing, as any true spirit medium would tell

Conjuring Words _____

A spirit **medium** is one who is endowed with a natural awareness of spirit activity and, therefore, does not use necromantic rituals in order to communicate with the spirits of the deceased.

you, will usually result in terrible consequences. Most people, mediums or not, seem to know already what necromancers ignore: it's just not a good idea to go messing with the dead.

A spirit medium would never voluntarily disturb a spirit that has already found rest, and instead would commonly seek to help any wayward spirits find their way to peace in the afterlife. Additionally, necromancers are not naturally endowed with the ability to communicate with spirits, while spirit mediums are usually born with their gifts (and therefore do not require the use of spells, incantations, or special objects/symbols).

Remember that attempting necromancy (or any arts that involve the dead) without proper training and experience can have dire consequences. Just by attempting a necromantic ritual, you risk sending out an open invitation to the nonphysical realms. Without the proper training, you cannot control the exact nature of whatever entity, if any, chooses to answer your call. The range of such potentially contacted entities can run the gamut of danger from playfully innocent to harmlessly mischievous to frighteningly hostile to downright deadly. Simply put, if you consider dabbling in the arts of necromancy … consider yourself warned.

Spirit Necromancy

Spirit necromancy is the longest-standing form of divination by way of the dead. Necromancers commonly refer to the resurrected soul as a *shade*, as one is commonly said to resemble a shadow or silhouette when rendered visible. Sometimes called psychic necromancy in modern times, this form of divination seeks to call forth dead spirits in order to gain knowledge or power. Many of the earliest forms of this dark art were born from ancient cultures that practiced *ancestor worship* and were employed in order to communicate with the spirits of deceased ancestors. This is usually done through the employment of mystic symbols or ritualistic incantations. The important thing to note about spirit necromancy is that the physical bodies of the deceased spirits are not disturbed.

> **Conjuring Words** _____
>
> **Spirit necromancy,** also called psychic necromancy in modern times, seeks to conjure forth the spirits of the dead in order to gain special knowledge or power.
>
> A conjured soul/spirit is called a **shade** in necromancy.
>
> **Ancestor worship** was a religious practice very common in the ancient world, in which one's deceased ancestors were believed to reach the status of deities after death. Sometimes, rituals of spirit necromancy would be performed in order to consult with the spirits of these deified ancestors for purposes of guidance or receiving blessings.

In some spiritual necromantic ceremonies, a special box is used. Once the spirit has been raised, it is then bound through the necromancer's incantations to the interior of the box, acting as a type of vessel for the spirit. These vessels are sometimes referred to as *spirit boxes*, and it is believed that one or more spirits may be kept in them until needed. Most necromancers ensure that the spirit's binding to the box is only temporary. Bolder necromancers, however, have been known to bind a spirit to its vessel for all eternity.

> **Conjuring Words** _____
>
> **Spirit boxes** are special boxes used in spirit necromancy, into which a spirit may be bound through a necromancer's incantations, acting as a vessel for the invoked spirit(s).

Séances and Ouija Boards

Probably the most well-known modern forms of spirit necromancy are the *séance* and the use of *Ouija boards*. A séance is a group ritual, often led by a spirit medium, that seeks to communicate with spirits. Sometimes these rituals are passive and seek only to communicate with spirits that are already present (passive séances are also relatively harmless as long as they are conducted under the supervision of a competent medium).

On the other hand, some séances are invocative. These séances seek to draw forth spirits already at rest. These types of séances are more volatile and can very easily grow dangerously out of hand. Unfortunately, many of today's untrained, amateur, would-be spirit mediums have come to view the leading of invocative séances almost as a form of group entertainment, which it is not.

⊚ Conjuring Words

A **séance** is a group ritual, usually led by some form of spirit medium, meant to open communication with spirits. These rituals may be done in either a passive or invocative manner.

A **Ouija board,** also called a talking board, is a flat board with the letters of the alphabet written upon it, along with the options of "yes" and "no."

The word *Ouija* (pronounced *wee-JAH*) literally translates into English as "yes-yes." It is a combination of the French word for yes, *oui*, and the German word for yes, *ja*. Also referred to as a "talking board," a Ouija board is a flat board of wood with the letters of the alphabet written upon it, as well as the answers "yes" and "no." (Sometimes they have in-between options such as "maybe" or "perhaps.") The user lightly allows his or her fingers to rest upon a teardrop-shape pointer, which usually has a small glass window in the center.

In all honesty, Ouija boards in and of themselves are not commonly considered specifically designed as necromantic devices. Sometimes, mediums simply use them as a convenient tool for communicating with disembodied spirit entities that are already present. When used to invoke the specific spirits of those who have already crossed over, however, the Ouija board can be turned into a somewhat necromantic tool.

The current understanding of the Ouija board was first introduced into mainstream Western society in the form of a spooky "board-game-like" device that was commonly used for nothing more than freaking one's guests out at social gatherings. The first novelty Ouija boards were patented and released by the Kennard Ouija Novelty Company in the late nineteenth century. Later, the Hasbro toymaker corporation adapted and released a Ouija board model as a board game.

Today, many people view the idea of Ouija boards as rather comical. And many see them as little more than a fun way to spook everyone out at a party, not as a way to attempt contact with the spirit realm. Ninety-nine percent of the time, of course, their assumptions are correct.

However, there is always that 1 percent chance that using a Ouija board will result in actual spirit contact.

As with anything that deals with the nonphysical realm, using a Ouija board in a sincere attempt to communicate with spirit entities carries with it a certain amount of risk. This risk is further compounded if the tool is being used by a layman. This doesn't mean that Ouija boards are dangerous, as long as their use is reserved for lighthearted entertainment. It is unlikely that any self-respecting spirit entities would be willing to waste their time talking to a roomful of panicking, squealing teenagers or a candlelit table manned by a bunch of inebriated partygoers. If you are using a Ouija board with the sincere intention of contacting something from the other side, however, be warned that you have no control over exactly what kind of "something" will answer you.

Physical Necromancy

Unlike spiritual necromancy, *physical necromancy* is, well, quite icky in nature. Also referred to as traditional necromancy, physical necromancy seeks to divine special knowledge from the dead by employing some form of physical manipulation that involves the deceased spirit's actual corpse. Also, whereas ancestor worshippers used spirit necromancy, they certainly did *not* use physical necromancy (because defiling a corpse was considered an unforgivable act of blasphemous disrespect to one's divine ancestors). Also, physical necromancers seek to enslave spirits (temporarily or permanently), forcing them to do their bidding. Putting it bluntly, a physical necromancer works his or her craft through the dismemberment or mutilation of dead bodies.

 **Conjuring Words**

Physical necromancy, also called traditional necromancy, seeks to divine special knowledge from the dead by employing some form of physical manipulation that involves the use/mutilation of a deceased spirit's actual corpse.

A physical necromancer is fond of frequenting graveyards, as this is where he acquires the tools of his craft. Certain pieces of a corpse were considered more valuable than others. The skull, which necromancers preferred with the brain still inside, was considered the most valuable.

Secondary to this were sensory organs, such as the ears and eyeballs, which were believed useful in forcing the spirit to convey memories of sensory data (sights, sounds, etc.). Last but certainly not least, pieces of a corpse such as the hair, teeth, skin, and fingernails were considered useful for both conjuring and binding a spirit.

Whereas spirit necromancy can be either passive or invocative, physical necromancy is a purely aggressive form of spirit conjuring ... and far more dangerous by comparison. A physical necromancer, for example, gathers the bones or certain organs from a corpse and uses them to first call forth and then bind the spirit. Once this has been done, the necromancer uses the spell to inflict torturous pain upon the spirit until it agrees to comply with his or her demands. As a result, these spirits are usually extremely hostile toward the responsible necromancer and will take any opportunity to bring them harm.

In order to secure themselves from the spirit's wrath, physical necro- mancers are usually required to stand within protective circles inscribed on the floor (in chalk, wax, or even blood). The most well-known of these protective circles is called the "Seal of Solomon," which consists of a six-pointed star (made by two overlapping triangles) inside a circle, inscribed with mystical writings. Legends say the sagely King Solomon (yes, the one from the Bible) knew how to command demons, angels, and disembodied spirits to his will. Available lore claims that Solomon was able to successfully command such entities (many of which were as evil as they were powerful) by using this seal as a magical, protective barrier against any malevolent entity that might try to do him harm.

The *Necronomicon*

The question of whether or not a book called the *Necronomicon* exists really depends on the details of what you're asking. If you're asking whether a book has ever been written under the title of *Necronomicon*, then the answer is yes. However, if you are asking whether an ancient mystical text ever existed that contains secret necromantic rites, referred to as the *Necronomicon*, then the answer is a clear, loud, and resounding no. There is no real ancient necromantic text called the *Necronomicon*. It will forever and always exist solely as a figment of the human imagination.

The first mention of a book called the *Necronomicon* was an alleged citation from the text, which appeared in H. P. Lovecraft's fictional story, *The Nameless City*, published in 1923. In 1927, Lovecraft expounded on the book when he wrote and published a full (but still entirely fictional) background story for the imaginary text, which he titled *History of the Necronomicon.*

According to Lovecraft's "history," the *Necronomicon* was first written under the Arabic title of *Al Azif.* His tale claims the text was originally compiled and written sometime around 700 C.E. by the hand of a lapsed Muslim and mentally unstable poet/philosopher from Sana'a, Yemen, named Abdul Alhazred, commonly referred to as the "Mad Arab." He claimed that Alhazred had journeyed down into the lost catacombs of the great ancient cities of Babylon and Memphis and uncovered their secrets for conjuring the dead, as well as their specific incantations for invoking ancient and powerful demons.

The Scary Truth

While H. P. Lovecraft's use of the *Necronomicon* certainly lent a mood of believable creepiness to his stories, it is important to understand that no such book exists. Even Abdul Alhazred, "The Mad Arab," was entirely a creation of Lovecraft's imagination; no such man ever existed.

According to Lovecraft's tale, Alhazred's necromantic rituals eventually brought him into direct contact with two ancient gods named Cthulhu and Yog-Sothoth. They granted him increased powers, and in return he worshipped them. However, he also drew the attention of many angry and malevolent entities that sought his destruction. He grew paranoid of the outside world and spent his final days in his estate in Damascus. Believing his end was drawing near, he used his time in seclusion to write down all he had learned.

Alhazred's ominous feelings about his own demise weren't without merit, and Lovecraft explained how, sometime in 738 C.E., Alhazred met with a horrifically gruesome end … though Lovecraft claimed he had encountered two conflicting versions of his death. One version claimed that Alhazred was dragged away by an unseen force, never to be seen or heard from again. The other, more fantastic version claimed he was seized by some invisible monster and eaten alive by the beast in broad daylight and in the presence of many witnesses.

In recent years, a number of fraudulent attempts have been made to write and publish texts that claim to be the real *Necronomicon*. In fact, Avon Publishing is still selling a book edited by an unknown individual using the simple pseudonym of "Simon" who claims to be privy to the original manuscript. And Llewellyn Publications is currently offering a number of similar texts that have been translated and/or edited by Donald Tyson, who also claims to have access to Alhazred's lost original writings. The authenticities of both authors' claims have long been debunked as nothing more than pure fiction.

Perhaps we shouldn't be surprised that H. P. Lovecraft's creation has lived on in the form of a modern myth. Lovecraft himself was once quoted as saying that "no weird story can truly produce terror unless it is devised with all the care and verisimilitude of an actual hoax. The author must … build up a stark, simple account, full of homely corroborative details, just as if he were actually trying to 'put across' a deception in real life—a deception clever enough to make adults believe it." And, apparently, many adults still believe in Lovecraft's well-crafted and clever literary deception.

Saul's Dance with the Dead

In the Western world, perhaps the most well-known account of spirit necromancy comes from the Old Testament's first *Book of Samuel*, 28:3–25 in a story that involves the Israelite King Saul. Shortly after the death and burial rites of the great Hebrew prophet Samuel, Saul found himself facing overwhelming odds against the vast military forces of the Philistines who were already marching their way straight into his territories. In the past, Saul had always relied on the counsel of the prophet to acquire divine guidance (although he was also prone to ignoring the prophet's instructions when they did not suit him). With Samuel dead, Saul now had no choice but to make his appeals to YHVH/God himself. However, YHVH's reply was nothing but silence.

Per the words of the Hebrew book of law, Deuteronomy, King Saul had already expelled all diviners, spellcasters, and necromancers from Israel. In Deuteronomy 18:11, Israel was ordered to drive out any individual "who is a spirit medium or who consults with the dead." So those people had little choice but to either leave Israel or go into hiding, lest they be put to death.

Finding himself on what would most certainly be the losing end of a bloody battle and still having received no reply to his prayers, Saul decided to ignore the law. He summoned his advisors and inquired if any person who communicated with spirits could still be found in the area. They informed him of a woman who practiced such arts by use of a special *talisman*. King Saul disguised himself and traveled out to meet with the woman necromancer, hoping she would be able to conjure the dead spirit of Samuel the prophet so he could consult with him from beyond the grave.

Conjuring Words

A talisman is quite simply any relic, amulet, or similar trinket that is worn on the body (usually about the neck) and believed to provide the wearer with magical protection or abilities.

Stranger Than Fiction

Although the biblical story of Saul's necromantic encounter does not give the Witch of Endor a specific name, the Midrash texts of the Jewish rabbis claim her true name was Zephaniah. They also claim that she was the mother of Abner.

This woman was never specifically named in the canonical texts but was commonly referred to as simply the "Witch of Endor." And she appeared to have been little more than a clever con artist in all truth. At first, she refused to do anything because she feared she was being led into a trap by her Israelite visitors. Saul assured her he would not trap her or expose her (although he did not go so far as to reveal his true identity). As she began to go through the theatrical motions of summoning the dead and actually saw the real spirit of Saul rising up from the ground, she went absolutely spastic.

The Witch of Endor realized that this was a real spirit, with real spiritual power, in the tent with her (in fact, she initially mistook Samuel for a god that was rising up out of the earth). To make matters worse, she also realized that the man in front of her was none other than King Saul who was rather well known for having people such as herself put to death for practicing the forbidden arts of necromancy and divination. King Saul reassured her that he would allow no harm to befall her if she acted as a medium for him. Saul was thrilled that Samuel's spirit had come to him and fell prostrate on the ground before the invisible spirit. The prophet Samuel, however, was not all that happy to see what King Saul had done.

Stranger Than Fiction

Some rabbinical texts have explained that God allowed the spirit of Samuel to appear before Saul because 12 months had not yet passed since his death. During these first 12 months, it was believed that the deceased spirit still lingered relatively close to its physical corpse. They also claim it's evident that it was YHVH, and *not* the Witch of Endor, who brought Samuel's spirit forth. As support, it is pointed out that only Saul could hear Samuel's voice clearly (though he could not see him). The Witch of Endor could see Samuel but did not understand his words. Of course, one might be able to use this situation to argue either way.

The first phrase out of Samuel's mouth was a bitter complaint: "Why have you disturbed me by bringing me forth in this way?" When Saul explained the great desperation of his current situation against the Philistines, Samuel remained less than sympathetic. He replied, "Why do you summon me after YHVH has abandoned you and become your enemy?" From here on, Saul got nothing but a laundry list of bad news from the resurrected spirit of Samuel. Saul did not receive the counsel he was seeking, but instead got a prophecy of his own (and all of Israel's) imminent doom.

Reading the Living

Like physical necromancy, *anthropomancy* involves the physical manipulation or mutilation of a human body but with one very big difference. Whereas physical necromancers use corpses, the human bodies used in anthropomantic rituals are *not dead*. While physical necromancy is indeed icky, anthropomancy is absolutely ghastly in its level of cruelty.

The human subject of an anthropomantic ritual does not experience a pleasant death. The most common form of such rituals was performed by disemboweling a living person, one of the slowest and most painful ways to die. Once the

Conjuring Words

Anthropomancy is a term that comes from the Greek *anthropos* (man/human) and *manteia* (prophecy/divination) and refers to the ritualistic disembowelment of live human sacrifices for purposes of divination. A practitioner of this art is called an anthropomancer.

bowels had been properly strewn about, the anthropomancer attempted to divine certain signs/omens by observing specific aspects of the person's slow and agonizing death.

The first and most important observation for an anthropomancer came from the examination of the arrangement in which the person's entrails spilled out from the abdomen. Once the signs were read and carefully noted, the anthropomancer moved on to observing the person's circumstances and behavior as he or she died. Observations were made of the number of times the person had screamed out, as well as in what ways; the amount that the person did or did not bleed, and the path the blood had traveled before hitting the ground; the way the person's body had writhed and jerked, especially when it came to the final position of the body at the exact moment of death; and, finally, the exact length of time it had taken the person to die.

While the idea of anthropomancy sounds quite unbelievable to the modern mind, it was practiced all over the globe at one time or another. The Aztecs and Incas of America did it, as did a number of ancient European civilizations. Certain civilizations in ancient Mesopotamia were avid anthropomancers, as were the inhabitants of ancient Japan.

The two most frequently practiced, specialized types of anthropomantic rituals in the ancient world are as follows:

♦ **Antinopomancy:** Perhaps the most terrible to consider, this form of anthropomancy dealt specifically with using children as ritual sacrifices for divination by reading entrails.

♦ **Splanchomancy:** Commonly seen in the civilizations of the ancient Greeks, this form of anthropomancy involved the specific use of live female virgins as ritual sacrifices for human divination.

Similar to anthropomancy is the ancient practice of haruspicy, which involved the ritualistic sacrifice of an animal followed by the reading of its entrails. This practice was frequently used in the religious orders of the ancient Babylonians, Etruscans, and Anatolians. A priest who carried out such rituals was called a Haruspex.

These practices have one thing in common: they all involved inflicting a slow, excruciating, and gruesome death upon a living entity (whether it was human or animal). Today, such practices have been deemed completely forbidden in the modern pagan/nature religions that are still being practiced all over the world. It is important to note that modern pagans *do not* practice any form of live sacrifice (not of animals, and certainly not of humans). Most human beings would agree that the practice of anthropomancy is nothing more than a negative example of humanity's barbaric past—and one we have gladly left behind.

The Least You Need to Know

♦ Necromancers are not the same as spirit mediums because they forcibly conjure forth the dead.

♦ Necromancers must rely on spells, rituals, and incantations to communicate with the dead.

♦ There are two primary types of necromancy: spirit/psychic and physical/traditional.

♦ The *Necronomicon* is a work of fiction, a clever creation of H. P. Lovecraft's imagination.

♦ Anthropomancy is a forbidden practice in today's pagan/nature religions.

Chapter 9

Faith Magic

In This Chapter

- ◆ Faith magic's unique combination of religion and superstition
- ◆ The "protection deception" of certain faith magic practitioners
- ◆ The integrated nature of Voodoo
- ◆ Santeria's sacrificial and ritualistic tradition
- ◆ Espiritismo and its tradition of manipulating the spirit world

Even the most hard-nosed of modern scientists agree that human beliefs are powerful. Often, what we believe in has a significant effect on our lives. Most of us know at least one person (or we are that person) who avoids walking under ladders or laments a broken mirror because he or she believes that such things have the power to bring misfortune. Faith magic seeks to harness the power of human beliefs, faiths, and superstitions. After all, power perceived is often power achieved.

The Integrated Origins of Faith Magic

What if … just what if … actions such as breaking a mirror or spilling salt do not bring about ill luck, in and of themselves? What if our own beliefs about these "bad luck" actions cause them to come true? This "faith power," the psychosomatic power of human beliefs, is what faith magic practitioners seek to manipulate and exploit.

The signature trait of any faith magic practice is a unique integration of faith, belief, and superstition. Such practices are by no means new, though no one can say for certain just how long they've been around. Faith magic has likely existed since someone discovered that the beliefs of the many could be used to increase the power of the few. In truth, the priest/priestess of faith magic can only exercise the power others give them. For example, a faith magic curse or blessing won't have the power to work unless the person upon whom it is placed believes it will.

The "Protection Deception" of Faith Magic

This perceived weakness in faith magic (that it didn't work if one didn't believe in it) led practitioners to develop one of the cleverest deceptions ever conceived. They began to spread rumors about the ways in which the uninitiated could protect themselves from the magical powers of the initiated (those learned in faith magic). For example, Voodoo priests/priestesses spread a rumor that drawing a salt line across a doorway would bar them from entry. When people heard these rumors about special protective methods, they began to use them, and simply by using these supposed protection methods, these individuals unknowingly sealed their fates.

You see, because these individuals chose to believe in the power of these protective methods, this also meant they believed in the powers of the faith magic they wished to avoid. As you might imagine, dealing with such faith magicians (especially if you get on the bad side of a practitioner) could become a slippery situation if one is not properly prepared.

Voodoo

What we commonly refer to as "Voodoo" in Western culture actually comes from the African term *Vodun*, which roughly translates as "spirit." However, in context it means the practice of engaging spiritual beings. No one knows exactly when the original African practice of *Vodun* began, but most scholars believe it was definitely well over 5,000 years ago. *Vodun* practices are thought to have originally involved a type of ancestor worship, and its rituals were meant to invoke the influential power of ancestral spirits. However, at some point it also came to be used to invoke additional entities, such as divine forces or malevolent spirits.

The most well-known form of what we now call Voodoo originated on the Caribbean island of Haiti during the 1800s. At that time, the island was one of many sugar plantation islands. As African slaves were brought to the island, they were indoctrinated into the Roman Catholic religion. However, they continued to practice their native religions in secret. As time passed, the various indigenous religions of the Haitian slaves became heavily integrated with one another and came to include many of the symbols and ritualistic aspects of Catholicism.

Voodoo priests are called by the title *houngan,* and priestesses are referred to as *mambo.* They are the keepers of Voodoo temples and shrines, called *humforts,* which can be as large as a building or as small as a shelf-top. Sometimes the priest's own home, even if a small apartment, is arranged in the proper design of a *humfort.*

At the center of every *humfort,* you will find a sacred pole, called a *poteau-mitan,* which is used to draw in and bind spirits during certain rituals. Divine, spiritual, angelic, and demonic voices are supposed to come through these poles to the acting *houngan* or *mambo.* Aside from the central pole, the temple will also have a shrine. These shrines are often unique to each temple, but generally involve a mesh of symbolic items from Catholicism, superstition, and other faiths. It's not uncommon for a Voodoo shrine to be adorned with pictures of various Catholic saints, crosses/rosaries, special candles, coins of different metals, and other such faith amulets.

As in most magical practices, Voodoo practitioners believe in the idea of cosmic balance (similar to the idea of Karma). Basically, what one creates will influence what one receives. This means that performing white magic rituals/spells for healings and other beneficial purposes will result in good things. In contrast, performing dark magic, malevolent or destructive rituals, will ultimately result in a return of bad things. Because of this, nearly all *houngan* and *mambo* restrict themselves to beneficial, white magic rituals.

However, some dare to delve into the dangerous methods of dark magic; these Voodoo priests, often called *caplatas*, are said to practice "left-handed *Vodun*." A group of Haitian *caplatas*, for example, were responsible for a despicable practice they long passed off as the power to create zombies (see Chapter 13). The vast majority of *Vodun* believers, including the *houngan* and *mambo*, do not look kindly upon such practitioners.

Santeria

The practice of Santeria is very closely related to Voodoo/*Vodun* as many elements of it are believed to have been brought by slaves from Africa sometime during the 1800s. Also like Voodoo, Santeria is an integration of indigenous African beliefs, Catholicism, and various common superstitions. However, since it was developed on the island of Cuba rather than Haiti, it has certain unique elements. When brought to Cuba, the slaves were (like their *Vodun* counterparts) forcibly indoctrinated into the religious practices of Catholicism. Though they attended Mass and openly pretended to be happy converts, they secretly retained their native spiritual beliefs and practices, which they cleverly hid by integrating symbols from the beliefs of their Christian slavers. First and foremost, they symbolically replaced the visual images of their native deities and ancestral spirits with depictions of the Catholic saints (who usually served rather well as equivalents in nature and role).

In general, Voodoo and Santeria practitioners consider themselves to be of the same brethren. Despite the cultural differences between them, which resulted from their differing geographical locations, they view themselves as united in one religion.

Espiritismo

Similar to the word *Vodun*, the Spanish term *Espiritismo* literally means "spiritism." While Espiritismo shares common African elements with Voodoo and Santeria, it is markedly different from these practices. Unlike these other faith magic practices, Espiritismo includes additional rituals and elements from various Native American traditions. This is not surprising, since the practice arose in Latin America. Also, the primary focus of Espiritismo is the invocation and manipulation of the spirit world for beneficial (but sometimes destructive) purposes.

Unlike Voodoo and Santeria, the practice of Espiritismo was not originally restricted to slaves. In fact, it was closely related to a similar nineteenth-century European movement called Spiritualism, which also focused on engaging the spirit realms. Espiritismo was founded on the basic monotheistic belief of one supreme entity. However, they believe that the physical world exists simultaneously with a nonphysical/spirit world, which cannot be seen or engaged by most people. Through initiation into the practice of Espiritismo, however, one is supposedly able to discover how to see, understand, and even control the disembodied entities that inhabit this unseen realm.

The Least You Need to Know

◆ In the majority of cases, most faith magic spells or curses will not affect someone who does not believe in them.

◆ Voodoo/*Vodun*, the most well-known form of faith magic, was developed in Haiti by African slaves.

◆ Santeria is nearly identical in form and practice to Voodoo but was developed in Cuba and has certain unique cultural traits.

◆ Espiritismo has some things in common with Voodoo and Santeria but is a markedly different practice.

Part 3

Monsters, Shapeshifters, and the Undead

Where does one find the blurry line between what is an animal and what is a monster? An introduction to the new science of cryptozoology will help you better understand how to draw it. You'll learn about the natures of werewolves and other shape-shifters, as well as the many faces of the undead, from blood-sucking vampires to flesh-eating zombies.

Chapter 10

Cryptozoology

In This Chapter

- An explanation of cryptids and the study of cryptozoology
- Cryptozoological theories regarding humanoid cryptids
- A discussion of sea monsters
- A look into the chupacabra
- An overview of several confirmed cryptids

Are there monsters among us? Are there strange creatures that, even to this day, remain unknown to the scientific community? The answer to both of these questions is quite possibly yes. We know of true animal behemoths such as elephants and giant whales. And, indeed, we have seen a number of unusual animals, such as tree sloths and the Chimaera fish that washed up during the Indonesian Tsunami of 2004. But we don't think of these animals as monsters because the human mind has come to accept and understand their existences. In ancient times, however, such large or strange creatures were often described as mythical, man-eating monsters. Perhaps humans still have this tendency and still mistakenly label as monsters any unusual animals they don't recognize. Welcome to the world of cryptozoology.

What Are Cryptids?

The line between monster and animal is drawn heavily by human perception. Often, the human mind sees what it expects to see. For example, imagine you were to encounter a gorilla in the forests of North America. Since your mind tells you gorillas do not live in North America, your eyes do not see the gorilla for what it is. Instead, you interpret what your eyes see as a monster. Perhaps your mind conjures up images of a werewolf or sasquatch or recollections of some local legend. And this becomes, in your mind, what you have seen.

> **Conjuring Words**
>
> **Cryptids** are hidden animals or creatures thought by many to be either extinct or restricted to the realms of legends.
>
> **Cryptozoology** is basically the study and research of animals that are considered cryptids.

Bringing the truth of such encounters to scientific light is the main focus of a fairly new area of study called *cryptozoology*, which is the study of *cryptids*. Cryptids are, quite literally, hidden animals. Cryptozoologists seek to either debunk or confirm the existence of animals generally thought to be mythical, imagined, or extinct.

Many members of the mainstream scientific community refuse to recognize cryptozoology as a valid area of animal research. But this hasn't stopped cryptozoologists from pursuing the hidden truth about legendary creatures. They soldier on, and in recent years their work has produced some very impressive findings (as you will see later in this chapter).

Many people mistakenly think that cryptozoologists initially believe in the creatures they seek to uncover. In actuality, belief has nothing to do with it. The vast majority of legitimate cryptozoologists pursue their research with the highest levels of scientific rigor. When presented with potential evidence, any true cryptozoologist will be the first person to start looking for holes.

True cryptozoologists first seek out rational explanations for any potential pieces of evidence (and, most of the time, debunk the evidence at this point as being falsified or misinterpreted). They painstakingly analyze photos and videos for possible fraud or alternate causes long before they even consider them for examination as evidence of a cryptid.

They even submit physical evidence, which may be visually impressive, to DNA tests before they accept it. Often, suspected corpses of cryptids are actually normal animals that have somehow been deformed, manipulated, or mutilated, giving them the visual appearance of certain cryptids.

Cryptids are commonly classified by one of the following labels:

◆ **Hoax**—Investigations uncovered solid evidence that falsified the evidence of the proposed cryptid.

◆ **Discredited**—Investigations uncovered solid evidence that proved the proposed cryptid did not exist.

◆ **Extinct**—The species of proposed cryptid has died out.

◆ **Proposed explanation**—The proposed cryptid, upon investigation, turned out to have a rational explanation. (Usually, they turn out to be nonindigenous animals that have escaped from zoos or other such facilities.)

◆ **Unconfirmed**—While there may be eyewitness accounts, no solid evidence confirms the cryptid's existence.

◆ **Confirmed**—During an investigation, irrefutable evidence confirmed the proposed cryptid's existence.

Humanoids, Apes, or "Other"?

Unless you've been living in a cave for the last few decades, you are probably well aware of the North American sightings of the so-called "Bigfoot" or *sasquatch*. This is but one of many hairy *humanoid* creatures that are on the cryptozoology watch list.

Among cryptozoologists, four primary theories exist when it comes to explaining the multitude of hairy humanoid sightings in North America. In order of plausibility, these theories are as follows.

> **Conjuring Words**
>
> **Sasquatch** is an anglicization of the Indian word *Sesquac*, which roughly translates as "wild man." In modern times, it has become interchangeable with "Bigfoot."
>
> **Humanoid** means something that resembles a human.

- **Missing links**—A small minority of cryptozoologists believe hairy humanoids are the undiscovered "missing link" between humans and primates.

- **Neanderthals**—Some believe that hairy humanoids are the few surviving Neanderthal ancestors of the current human race.

- **Giant apes**—Some believe that hairy humanoid sightings are of the *Gigantopithecus* genus of giant ape, believed to have been extinct for the last million years or so.

- **Unidentified primate species**—The most popular explanation for hairy humanoid sightings is that they are an undiscovered species of large primates, perhaps some unknown North American gorilla.

Aquatic Cryptids

Perhaps the most well-known cryptids are those of the aquatic variety. All over the globe, many lakes have their own "lake monster." Unfortunately, sightings of these cryptids often occur in lakes with exceedingly poor underwater visibility. While it cannot be denied that witnesses of such creatures have at least seen *something*, what they have seen may or may not turn out to be a lake monster.

The available photographic and video evidence of aquatic cryptids is often sketchy, distant, or of poor quality. This could be evidence of a large creature, but then again, it could just be fuzzy photos or video of drifting wood or indigenous fish. Let's take a look at three of the most well-known aquatic cryptids in the modern world.

Loch Ness Monster

Almost everyone on the planet knows the legend of old "Nessie," as she is sometimes called. This large aquatic cryptid is believed to inhabit the murky depths of Loch Ness in the Scottish Highlands. Since at least 1871 C.E., people have seen something large rising from the surface of the lake. Exactly what they've seen, however, remains a matter of debate.

Some claim that the first sighting of the Loch Ness Monster occurred in 565 C.E. during the travels of Saint Columba. The Christian missionary's boat had not been moored down properly and had wandered out into Loch Ness, which he needed to cross in his mission of spreading the Gospel. As one of his assistants swam out to retrieve the vessel, suddenly a giant beast is said to have risen from the surface and towered over the helpless man as if to eat him. The missionary ordered the monster back in the name of Christ, according to the legend, and it again submerged into the depths of the lake as the assistant frantically swam to the safety of the shore.

Over the years, an estimated 10,000 to 11,000 people have laid eyes on the creature that inhabits Scotland's Loch Ness. Theories abound as to what it is. Some more superstitious people believe it's a demon, which was bound to the lake during ancient times. Some cryptozoologists speculate it is perhaps a plesiosaur that somehow survived the last ice age. Others believe it's not a species of dinosaur, but perhaps some as yet unidentified species of giant amphibian or aquatic reptile. These theories are based on the fact that several sightings of the lake creature have claimed it was resting (at least partially) on the shores of Loch Ness.

Champ

Over the last century, nearly 300 sightings of a giant creature have been reported in Lake Champlain, which is located on the border of Vermont and New York. The first reported sighting of the creature is commonly believed to have occurred in 1609, when Samuel de Champlain (for whom the lake is named) reported seeing a strange monster rise out of the water.

Today, belief in "Champ," as the creature has come to be called, continues, especially among those who live near the lake. Like the creature of Scotland's Loch Ness, some cryptozoologists believe the Lake Champlain creature is a surviving plesiosaur. Also like Loch Ness, some assert that Champ is a species of unidentified large amphibian or aquatic reptile. While photo and video evidence exists that seems to support the existence of Champ, none of it has proven to be definitive.

Lake Van Monster

Lake Van is the largest lake in the Middle Eastern country of Turkey and is also one of the world's saltiest inland lakes. In 1995, the first report came in that a large creature had been seen rising from the salt lake's surface. However, witnesses had not secured any video or photo evidence of what they had seen.

Video evidence of the creature did not appear until 1997, when a teaching assistant at Van University named Unal Kozak presented what he claimed to be a video clip of the actual Lake Van monster. This short video, which remains the strongest evidence of the creature's existence, shows the bulbous head of an unidentified creature rising from the lake, moving to the left, and then submerging once again. One eye and a soft, cartilaginous skinned head can be seen, which has led some cryptozoologists to speculate that this may be some species of unidentified large amphibian or giant squid.

However, some would point out certain issues with Kozak's video. First of all, the camera never moves to the left. Some claim this is because the alleged creature was, in fact, a latex dummy being hauled behind a boat. Others point out that the creature only moved in a straight line, whereas most aquatic organisms move back and forth in order to create propulsion. However, this "back-and-forth" rule does not apply to squids (they use a contraction of their tentacles to push themselves straight forward).

Japanese Frilled Shark

Until recently, many marine biologists believed the Japanese frilled shark was extinct despite a few rare purported sightings of them. They were proven wrong, however, when in 2007 a living specimen turned up in Japan. This remains one of the most astounding cases of a species believed extinct turning out to have survived. Up until this point, remains of the creature were said to have turned up in fishing nets from time to time, but scientists refused to accept this as evidence that living frilled sharks still existed.

On January 21, 2007, experts at Japan's Awashima Marine Park in Southeast Tokyo received a wave of reports that some strange creature was swimming offshore. In initial reports, the creature was said to be an extremely large eel; but when marine park experts arrived, they found something far more astounding—a living, swimming frilled shark. On top of that, it was a female. And what's more, she was pregnant. They quickly retrieved and tanked the creature. Unfortunately, despite their best efforts, she died shortly thereafter.

Chupacabra

The chupacabra is often referred to as the "Hispanic vampire," but it doesn't quite fit the criteria. In the world of cryptozoology, it's classified as an as-yet-undocumented (or at least nondebunked) cryptid. Above all, the chupacabra would appear to be a voracious blood-drinking creature. In fact, the word chupacabra comes from the Spanish *chupa* (to suck) and *cabra* (goat), which roughly translates as "goat-sucker." This name stemmed from the first reports of the creature, where it killed domesticated goats by way of *exsanguination*.

> **Conjuring Words**
>
> **Exsanguination** refers to an extreme and fatal loss of blood. More or less, it is just a fancy way of saying "bleeding to death."

Chupacabras are said to be between 3½ and 4½ feet tall. However, the available descriptions don't explain whether these estimates are for a bipedal or four-legged creature. As far as mass is concerned, they can be between the size of a large-breed dog and a bear. Unfortunately, available descriptions don't specify what kind of bear, so they might be as large as a grizzly or as small as a koala. The only way to settle this is to see one with your own eyes. Have fun pulling that one off, since few have.

Two Sides to the Chupacabra

As you may have already noticed, descriptions of the chupacabra vary, and this is further complicated because it's never been captured in a photo or video (real or fake). As a result, we have no single description of what a chupacabra looks like. Commonly, there are two primary descriptions, Type A and Type B.

The Type A chupacabra looks like a cross between a kangaroo and an iguana. The Type B chupacabra looks more like a cross between a coyote and a hybrid. Sightings of the Type A chupacabra are more common in Mexico and South America, while reports of the Type B chupacabra have occurred in North America and Russia.

Whether it's Type A or B, one thing remains the same: chupacabras are amazing jumpers. This would explain why many eyewitness accounts claim they have the hind quarters of kangaroos. The powerful rear legs allow chupacabras to leap well over 20 feet.

> **The Scary Truth**
>
> A large number of crypto-zoologists, zoologists, and other scientists believe that reports of the Type B chupacabra are actually the result of hysterical accounts of encounters with inbred coyotes. Inbreeding among coyotes can result in terrible mange and deformities. Others believe the Type B chupacabra may be some unidentified species of wild dog.

The Chupacabra's Defenses

If a chupacabra finds itself trapped, startled, or threatened, its eyes supposedly glow bright red. Looking into the eyes of a chupacabra, you should know, is not a good idea. If you are unfortunate enough to see one, you'll probably notice that you feel sick, as the glowing eyes of a chupacabra are said to induce extreme nausea and vomiting.

If the glowing eyes defense doesn't work, the chupacabra will fall back on his secondary form of defense. According to accounts, the chupacabra first lets out a long, loud hiss, which some speculate is the sound of it inhaling. Take note—if you hear the creature hiss, plug your ears. After hissing, a cornered chupacabra will unleash a terrible scream loud enough to deafen almost any organism in earshot. While you are stunned, it will slip away into the surrounding vegetation.

Extinct Confirmed Cryptids

Despite the assertions of many zoologists and scientists, cryptozoology has produced some impressive results in recent decades. For example, many animals once thought nonexistent, mythical, or extinct have been proven otherwise. In cases where witnesses claim to have seen known species that are assumed to be extinct, cryptozoologists usually categorize these as "extinct" or "proposed explanation."

In cryptozoology, researchers seek to confirm these sightings of creatures once thought extinct. However, these animals are still considered to be confirmed, since it is known that they certainly once existed. And no matter what science says, their existences can no longer be denied. The following examples are a sampling of some of the cryptids that have been shown to exist.

The Tasmanian Tiger

It was widely believed that the last living *thylacine*, or Tasmanian Tiger, died in captivity in 1937. In past centuries, the animal had flourished on the islands of Australia, New Zealand, and Tasmania. Eventually, the last few groups of the species existed only in Tasmania. When bounties were put on their heads, the animals were hunted into extinction. At least, that's what everyone thought.

In recent years, eyewitness reports have begun to surface of Tasmanian Tiger sightings. A number of photos and videos have been presented but none clear enough to offer definitive proof. However, these photos have been enough to renew interest in the possibility that the animal still exists in Australia and Tasmania.

A Horse Is a ... Zebra? (Quagga)

The horse-zebra animal called the *Quagga* was, like the Tasmanian Tiger, long believed to be extinct. The hindquarters of the animal are striped like a zebra's, while the front end looks somewhat like a horse or donkey. For many years, the scientific community had asserted that no living specimens of the animal could be found. In 2006, however, a frantic search was undertaken when a man came forward to claim that he had once possessed the last remaining member of the species. According to him, someone stole the animal from his property in Canada.

To this day, the animal the man claimed to own has never been found, but the search continues. Some have been quick to accuse the man of orchestrating a hoax. Others, however, believe his story and fear that the last member of this endangered species is now in the possession of people who do not understand how precious it truly is.

The Least You Need to Know

◆ The line between monster and animal is largely based on human perception.

◆ Just because a photo or video appears to prove that something exists, it doesn't necessarily do so.

◆ Despite numerous sightings of chupacabras, the animal has never been caught on video or in photos.

◆ Aquatic cryptids are popular, but not one of them has ever been confirmed.

Chapter 11

Japan's Monstrous Plethora

In This Chapter

- The many faces of the frightening *bakemono* monsters
- The unique mermaid known as the *ningyo*
- The two sides of the story regarding the winged dog called *Ha-Inu*
- The mildly annoying *kama-itachi* flying weasels
- The man-eating *oni* and the legendary *oni* slayer of feudal Japan
- The various (and very creepy) female members of the *bakemono*

If you've ever seen such legendary films as *Godzilla*, *Mothra*, or *Gamera*, you may have noticed that the Japanese are all about the monsters. However, monsters are nothing new to Japanese culture. From Japan's feudal eras to the streets of modern-day Tokyo, the Japanese have dealt with more monsters than you could shake a stick at. (But why in the world would you shake a stick at monsters? Just start running!) Some do little more than revel in the fear they cause, while others are relentless murderers or voracious human-eaters who show no mercy to those unlucky enough to become their helpless victims.

The *Bakemono*

The word *bakemono* literally translates as "a changed thing," meaning these creatures have assumed disfigured or perverse forms. Sometimes, they are referred to as *O-bake* or *O-bakemono*. The *O-* prefix is used as a form of respect in the Japanese language, and is often roughly translated as "great" or "honorable." However, these aren't exact equivalents, especially in this case. When used with *bakemono*, the *O-* prefix mainly denotes strength/power. The *bakemono* are nothing if not powerful, and this (potentially, at least) makes dealing with them extremely dangerous for any humans who might, for their own insane reasons, attempt such a thing.

To truly grasp the nature of *bakemono*, you first need to understand that in the beliefs of Japanese culture, the line between the supernatural and physical realms is not a clear one. *Bakemono* are certainly viewed as supernatural creatures. Although many of them were at one time human beings, and some even assumed their *bakemono* forms after their human deaths, we can't exactly classify them as ghosts. So, basically, they don't fit into the Western concept of monsters, but they don't qualify as ghosts either … yet they have many characteristics of both. *Bakemono* are generally thought of as cursed beings, turned to hideous physical representations of their own evil natures.

The *bakemono* can usually choose to be invisible or visible (and are often able to change back and forth at will), and many can also choose whether or not to have physical substance (sometimes they can change this at will, but sometimes the form is permanent). This is similar to the Western concept of transubstantiation (moving across substances), which is often applied (especially in Catholicism) to situations where either the substance of something is changed (such as water to wine) or a being shifts back and forth from spirit to physical form (such as angels or demons, who sometimes disguise themselves as human beings and interact in the physical realm). While the *bakemono* are certainly not angels and are somewhat demonic in nature, they don't really fit the Western definition of demons because a vast majority of them were originally human beings, whereas demons are not thought to have previously been human beings.

Ningyo: The Monkey-Faced Mermaid

In the Western world, the words "mermaid" and "merman" conjure up images of beautiful beings that have the glistening, scaled tails of fish. Well, not this time, buddy! The Japanese version of a mer-creature, called a *ningyo*, doesn't have any real human features to speak of and isn't exactly what most people would call beautiful. The good news, however, is that they taste delicious! According to legend, the fishlike flesh of a *Ningyo* is tastier than you can imagine.

According to Japanese folklore, a *ningyo* resembles a big fish with a somewhat monkeylike head or face. From the top and back of its head sprouts a tuft of thick hair, but the rest of its skin is covered in shiny (sometimes golden) scales. It does have arms, which are also scale-covered, and a pair of humanoid but webbed hands. If you see one, don't be too worried about it. They tend to steer clear of humans and won't try to harm anyone who does the same for them. When cornered or provoked, however, they can heavily damage any seagoing vessel. And if that doesn't work, they have another, seldom-used option—their voice.

One element of the *ningyo* is somewhat of a twist on the Western mermaid. It is said that they don't speak, but that they are blessed with voices so beautiful that if humans were to hear them, they'd be immediately spellbound by the angelic sound. Some stories, which are similar to the Greek myths of the seductive sirens, even claim that a human who hears the voice of a *ningyo* will immediately swim after it, often until he or she is overcome by exhaustion and drowns. If you think about it, this might explain why they don't speak. Either they do so to protect us from our own frail human natures, or they are sick of being chased around the ocean by spellbound, love-crazed humans.

Ha-Inu: Toyotomi's Winged Dog

In the Japanese city of Chikugo, located in the Fukuoka prefecture (on the island of Kyushu), an interesting stone monument stands near the city's railroad station. This rather oddly named monument is called *Ha-inu-tsuka*, which roughly translates as "Flying/Winged Dog's Burial Mound." There are two stories about this burial monument, both of which claim to explain the true reason behind its construction.

The city's local newspaper published the earlier story about the monument sometime around 1777 C.E. This article explained that the burial mound under the stone monument contained the remains of a monstrous *ha-inu* (basically "flying/winged dog") that had terrified the people of the region for much of the 1500s. The *ha-inu*'s reign of terror continued until the great samurai warlord Hideyoshi Toyotomi, of the Japanese Imperial Court, began his 1587 conquest of the island of Kyushu. When Toyotomi led his forces into the Chikugo area, the troublesome beast became a serious issue. He assembled his best warriors, and together they slew the beast (though some stories credit Toyotomi with killing the creature on his own). Despite the trouble the beast had caused, Toyotomi had grown to respect the animal's courage, skill, and tenacity. As a gesture of this respect, he had the creature properly buried and ordered the stone monument placed over the mound.

The Scary Truth

In all honesty, the more spectacular story about the *Ha-inutsuka* monument was probably based on local folklore that had become exaggerated over time. Nonetheless, these stories were likely originally based on Toyotomi's very real dog (some historical evidence supports this was his dog). While the real dog likely did not fly or have wings, its unbelievable courage and skill turned it into a local legend.

The second, far more believable, version of this story claims that Hideyoshi Toyotomi kept a canine companion that was one of the most amazing dogs one could ever hope to see in action. Some even say that the brave *inu* ("dog") accompanied his master on the field of battle and proved itself a formidable combatant.

Kama-Itachi: The Blade Wielding Weasel

Have you ever been walking along and suddenly found a cut on your body you could not explain? Well, according to Japanese folklore, you may have just had a brush with the *kama-itachi* (which roughly translates as "sickle weasel/creature"). These small, weasel-like *bakemono* are said to travel on the wind and swirl together in small but powerful whirlwinds. Their furry little hands are equipped with small, curved, and extremely sharp blades/steel claws, although sometimes they are depicted as simply holding a pair of little *kama*.

Kama-itachi are said to travel in groups of three, and each has a specific job in the synchronized nature of their attacks. The first weasel temporarily stuns or just incapacitates the human target; the second weasel immediately rushes in and delivers the cut; and the third weasel masks their presence by quickly applying a special medicinal/magical salve that eliminates the pain caused by the cut before it is detected. This all happens so quickly that the cut human doesn't feel a thing, aside from maybe a sudden gust of wind. Only later, when the numbing effects of the special salve wear off, does the human even notice that he or she has been cut. By the time the victim realizes what has happened, the responsible trio of *kama-itachi* is already long gone.

> **Conjuring Words**
>
> A *kama* is a short, hand-held sickle that Japanese farmers have long used to harvest grain and rice. From the side of the handle's "business end," a sharp curved blade extends. The tool was eventually developed into a martial arts weapon by Karate *Shuri-Te* founders on the island of Okinawa.

> **Stranger Than Fiction**
>
> In the popular Japanese *manga/anime* series *Naruto*, a *kunoichi* (female ninja) named Temari wields a giant folding fan that she uses to employ *kaze-no-jitsu* (wind techniques). One of her special techniques involves summoning a trio of *kama-itachi*, which she then blows toward her opponent with the wind of her large fan. Since *kama-itachi* move so quickly and in synch, they are hard to keep in sight, making this technique very difficult to counter.

The Ravenous *Oni*

The *oni* are giant, human-eating, ogrelike monsters from Japanese folklore. While some *oni* are born that way, the majority of them were originally human. For example, any humans who killed too many people, killed needlessly or for pleasure, or killed children or other such helpless victims could find themselves transformed into an *oni*. Basically, any humans who allow their hearts to be consumed by hate, violence, or bloodlust have the potential of becoming an *oni*.

Oni have a number of different descriptions and a vast array of stories about them. The one common element in *oni* descriptions is that they all have long teeth of some sort. Some have long, straight, felinelike fangs, while others have long, curved tusks like those of wild boars. Most of the time, they have horns protruding from their foreheads and upturned, piglike noses. There are two main types of *oni*, called by the colors of their hidelike skins—*Ao-Oni* ("Blue Oni") and *Aka-Oni* ("Red Oni").

Once in a while, you might see an *oni* depicted wielding a sword. This, however, is not a common occurrence because 9 times out of 10, *oni* prefer more barbaric instruments of death. For example, *oni* are most frequently shown holding the *kanobo*, a very large, macelike weapon. The *kanobo* is extremely heavy, made from strong Japanese oak, and adorned with spikes or steel studs at the club end. Needless to say, it is a rather imposing weapon … fitting for an *oni*.

Japan's Legendary *Oni* Slayer

The legendary (and very real) samurai warrior, Minamoto Yorimitsu, was one of the greatest heroes of the Heian Period (tenth-century Japan). He is well known in Japanese culture as the "Slayer of the *Oni*." According to one story, a murderous gang of *oni* in service to the Shuten Doji (the demonic *oni* king), had taken up residence on *Oe-yama* (pronounced *Oh-ay-ya-ma*) mountain and had, for a good many years, been making violent raids throughout Kyoto. Finally, the emperor summoned the greatest warrior he knew, Yorimitsu, and ordered

Conjuring Words

The Japanese term *yama* means "mountain." So the name *Oe-yama* actually means "Oe Mountain."

him to bring an end to the violent chaos. Even before this, Yorimitsu had already become a living legend for his sword skills.

Believe it or not, historical and very official Japanese records still exist regarding this event. They outline the emperor's orders as well as the events that transpired during Yorimitsu's quest. According to these records, the bloody battle between Minamoto Yorimitsu and the *oni* of Shuten Doji took place on January 25, 990 C.E.

The Bermuda Triangle

Don't confuse Minamoto Yorimitsu with another legendary hero from the Heian Period named Minamoto Yoshitsune, whose rather tragic yet heroic adventures occurred during the twelfth century (roughly 200 years after Yorimitsu's).

According to the legends, Shuten Doji had once been a human being—a murdering, heartless criminal, but a human one nonetheless. As punishment for having killed an astonishing number of people during his life, the *kami* had turned him and his followers into *oni*.

Realizing the task before him was daunting, Yorimitsu decided not to go alone and assembled a small group of his very best warriors, a legendary group of four known to the Japanese as *Shitennou*. Before Yorimitsu and his *Shitennou* warriors set out for *Oe-yama*, they disguised themselves in the robes of *Yamabushi* (mountain-dwelling warrior monks). As they began making their way up the mountain, they came upon three rather unusual old men who gave Yorimitsu a magical helmet and an enchanted elixir called *Shinbenkidokushu*. In actuality, these old men were three powerful *kami* in disguise—Sumiyoshi, Iwashimizu, and Kumano.

In their monk disguises, Yorimitsu and the *Shitennou* approached the entrance to Shuten Doji's mountain fortress. They claimed to be fallen priests, evil men who pretended to be righteous in order to commit atrocious crimes. They must have put on a convincing performance because they were invited inside and presented with a feast of cooked human flesh. In order to keep up their deception, the warriors had no choice but to eat these horrific dishes. As the feast commenced, Yorimitsu succeeded in pouring the *Shinbenkidokushu* elixir into Shuten Doji's goblet. Shortly after downing all of the elixir, the *oni* king fell asleep.

Seeing their chance, the warriors drew their weapons and charged Shuten Doji. Yorimitsu slashed at his head with his sword, and his *Shitennou* colleagues went after his legs with their spears. Despite being drugged, Shuten Doji was roused by the pain and, though weakened, began to put up a fight. Yorimitsu, seeing the *oni* king was coming to, quickly slashed through his throat and took off his head. Unfortunately, the head flew into the air, came right for Yorimitsu, and bit down on his head with his immense jaws. Luckily, Yorimitsu was wearing the magical helmet given him by the *kami*, which shielded him from the attack. With the protection of this helmet (which from that time on was referred to as *Yorimitsu-no-Men*, or "Yorimitsu's Helmet"), he and the *Shitennou* succeeded in slaying Shuten Doji and his band of *oni*, saving Kyoto from their bloody rampages.

The Creepiness of *Bakemono* Women

Often, male-gendered *bakemono* are portrayed as being more terrifying than their female counterparts. What these ladies lack in intimidation, however, they more than make up for in creepiness. Female *bakemono* are the masters of turning beauty into horror, and seduction into terror.

Like their spectral *yurei/onryo* counterparts (see Chapter 3), these "monster women" are fueled by anger, often from events that happened in their human lives. Unlike the *onryo*, however, these femme fatales were not always all that nice during their human lives and are even worse as *bakemono*. Usually, deceptive appearance and seduction are their primary weapons. Unfortunately, identifying one is very difficult. In all likelihood, if you ever encounter one, by the time you realize what is happening, it'll be too late.

Yuki-Onna: The Snow Women

Yuki-Onna are cold-hearted ladies or "Snow Women" who've assumed this form in a number of ways. Some are said to be wives who were abandoned in snowstorms by cowardly or hateful husbands. Others are young mothers who've run into snowstorms in search of a lost child and become lost themselves and freeze to death. While they are usually thought to be rather pretty, looks can often be deceiving, especially when dealing with the paranormal. Most of the time, they use their "damsels in distress" appearances to lure humans to their deaths, so usually, it's best to ignore a *Yuki-Onna*. But this is not always the best advice, as one *Yuki-Onna* who dwells in Ibaraki Prefecture is said to push anyone who ignores her into a ravine.

A *Yuki-Onna* kills in numerous, terrifying methods. Some *Yuki-Onna*, especially those who prefer to attack children, will tear the livers out of their (still-living) victims and eat them. Sometimes, they can freeze a person solid with just a single touch of their icy fingers. Others are said to be able to pull a person's very soul from his or her living body. Last but certainly not least, they are said to walk around with what appears to be a baby. They incessantly beg people to hold their babies until someone finally agrees to do so. When the person takes it, however, it suddenly transforms into a gigantic boulder that crushes them to death.

Futa-Kuchi-Onna

Futa-Kuchi-Onna, or a "Two-Mouthed Woman," is a female *bakemono* with a second mouth on the back of her head. These *bakemono* can wind up assuming this monster form in one of two ways. Most of the time, they are evil stepmothers who (sometimes after the death of their husbands) allowed their stepchildren to starve to death while keeping their own children well-fed. In other cases, they are women who starved themselves in order to make their bodies attractive to a suitor and then gained weight once they were married. In some (less frequent) cases, they are women who were struck in the back of the head with axes when their husbands were carelessly chopping wood (thus causing the gash that becomes the second mouth).

The mouth on the back of a *Futa-Kuchi-Onna*'s head, strangely enough, often torments her more than other people. Unless it is being fed, the mouth constantly insults and berates her with demands for food thrown in between. If unfed for too long, the mouth will let forth an ear-piercing wail that causes the *Futa-Kuchi-Onna* unbearable pain. Having been in this form for a time, the woman's hair will begin to transform into serpents (or at least begin to move and behave like snakes). When a *Futa-Kuchi-Onna* tries to feed herself, these "snake-hairs" snatch the food from her hands and feed it to the mouth on the back of her head.

However, this does not satiate her hunger, and she is rarely able to eat anything herself unless she does so while the mouth and "snake hairs" are already occupied.

Rokuri-Kubi

Rokuri-Kubi, or "Long/Pulled Necks," are often caused by curses, which are not always deserved. This affliction almost exclusively affects women. When the woman sleeps, her neck begins to stretch, and her head travels away from her body. Weirdly enough, the afflicted woman isn't always aware that this is happening to her.

While the woman sleeps, her head apparently runs off and does its own thing. Some of these roaming, stretchy-necked heads' favorite activities include sucking the blood/life out of sleeping people and animals, drinking lamp oil, and scaring the crap out of people. One of the favorite tricks of a *Rokuri-Kubi* head is to wind its way up and rest its head against a window until some passersby (or peeping toms) come along and peer inside. When they do, they see a body on the floor and a head against the window, which, needless to say, usually sends them running and screaming. In many stories, women who are afflicted with *Rokuri-Kubi* cannot break the spell unless they marry. Unfortunately, however, they often have a hard time keeping a lid on the fact that they have necks that stretch while they sleep and heads that roam around sucking the blood or life-force out of people and livestock.

Kuchisake-Onna

The story of the *Kuchisake-Onna*, or "Slit-Mouthed Woman," began in feudal Japan. However, in modern times the story has been altered and modernized into an urban legend. No matter what time period the story comes from, one element remains the same—her mouth has been sliced open at both corners, giving her a grotesque "ear-to-ear" smile.

According to the original folktale, the *Kuchisake-Onna* was a beautiful woman. After she got married (usually to a young samurai), she found it hard to remain faithful. She was lustful and had a number of torrid affairs. When her samurai husband learned of her affairs (or, some stories say, caught her with another man), he went into a fit of jealous rage. He took his *tanto* (knife) and slit her mouth open at both corners. He then barked this question at her—"Who will think you're beautiful now?" From that day on, she became a *bakemono* and wandered the countryside with a veiled face, asking unsuspecting men, "Do you think I am beautiful?" If they said yes, she would remove the veil that concealed her deformed mouth and ask, "Even if I look like this?" If the man answered no, she killed him on the spot. If he answered yes, she followed him home and then killed him. Talk about a lose-lose situation.

Stranger Than Fiction

Among the youth of modern Tokyo, there is a new answer said to give someone a chance at surviving an encounter with a *Kuchisake-Onna*. Instead of saying yes or no, just answer "Your looks are average" or "You look so-so." These answers are said to baffle her long enough for you to escape. Another, less reliable, new part of the legend states that she can be temporarily stunned if you throw candy at her. However, it is more likely that this originated after some easily spooked kid threw candy at the face of a girl who was dressed up for Halloween in a *Kuchisake-Onna* (or nurse) costume and then ran away.

Today, the legend remains a part of Japanese culture, but certain elements of the story have changed. For example, the woman's face was cut up not by a jealous husband but by a plastic surgeon. (Sometimes she is said to have had an affair with the surgeon.) Instead of a veil, she now wanders the streets of Tokyo wearing a surgical mask. From here the story is about the same: she asks the same question, with the same outcomes.

The Least You Need to Know

- *Bakemono* often pass back and forth between physical and spirit forms.

- There are two main types of *oni*—*Ao-Oni* (Red Oni) and *Aka-Oni* (Blue Oni).

- The warriors who slew the *oni* king Shuten Doji were Minamoto Yorimitsu and the *Shitennou*.

- *Bakemono* women may often be less gross-looking, but they make up for it in creepiness.

◆ If you ever encounter a woman in a snowstorm, try to steer clear because it might be a *Yuki-Onna*.

◆ If a creepy woman in a surgical mask ever asks you if she is pretty, say "You look so-so," throw some candy, and run for your life.

Chapter 12

Vampires

In This Chapter

- Supernatural and viral vampire lore
- The abilities and pitfalls of psychic vampirism
- The relationship between vampires and revenants
- The frightening truth about Vlad Tepes, the real-life model for Bram Stoker's Count Dracula
- Possible real-life cases of vampirism
- The do's and don'ts when going toe-to-toe with a vampire

They are the immortal, nocturnal predators … and we are their prey. They hunt us with sharp fangs, sharp senses, and superhuman strength. One might think we don't stand a chance. While the weapons we have to fight against them may be few—stakes, garlic, and sunlight—they are highly effective. No one knows how long the vampires have lurked in the shadows. Some believe they've been here since before the days of humans, while others say they came here from a doomed planet or alternate dimension. Regardless of where they came from, the vampires are among us.

The Supernatural Vampire

The early concepts of the *nosferatu* were supernatural and superstitious in nature. Vampires were viewed as demonic beings, demon-possessed immortals, or the resurrected corpses of cursed humans. The original vampire was considered an unholy and condemned creature. In short, the vampires of old were portrayed as unclean abominations, agents of the devil that were vulnerable to the holy power of the Christian Church.

Conjuring Words

Literal translations of the German word *nosferatu* are conflicting, mainly because no one can say for certain where it originated. One translation is "carrier of disease," and another, more common one is "night creature." Regardless of *nosferatu*'s literal definition, the word now has the connotation of "vampire." This is likely because *Nosferatu* was the title of a 1922 silent film in Germany that portrayed the nocturnal exploits of a hideously grotesque vampire. This is widely considered the first (and many would say the most creepy) vampire film ever made.

The supernatural vampire had many unbelievable abilities and was thought to be able to shapeshift into almost anything. They could assume the forms of wolves and bats, and it was said they could even turn into mist. In addition, people commonly believed supernatural vampires could fly, either by supernatural power or by shapeshifting into the form of a flying creature.

In the past, most tools and weapons thought to be effective against vampires were supernatural, superstitious, or religious in nature. For example, a cross or crucifix was the primary object for warding off the vampires of old. Of course, people also believed they were held at bay by strings of garlic cloves, which were believed to have magical or healing properties. Holy water, and sometimes garlic, was said to scorch the skin of (or even kill) supernatural vampires and is often portrayed by today's special effects as similar to the reaction of hydrochloric acid on human skin.

Physical weapons also could bring down vampires. The most popular, of course, was the old standby of a wooden or silver stake, which had to be pierced through the creature's heart. Some lore claimed this killed a vampire, while other legends stated it would only paralyze or incapacitate it. After the vampire was staked, it had to be beheaded and/or immediately cremated.

The supernatural vampire had powers that could cause its resurrection, sometimes even after it had been staked and beheaded. For example, some of the lore surrounding supernatural vampires claimed they would be resurrected if exposed to the light of a full moon or just moonlight in general. This was said, for unknown reasons, to somehow cause the stake to be expelled from the corpse, allowing the wounded vampire to regenerate.

The old lore even claimed certain woods could not be used for stakes. For example, the wood of evergreen trees was said to be completely ineffective against these undead bloodsuckers. This is because evergreens were associated with immortality in the old European lore, as the trees didn't lose their greenery during the winter season. Therefore, it was reasoned that a stake cut from an evergreen (a wood of immortality) would not work against a vampire (an immortal being).

The Scary Truth

In truth, it is very possible that supernatural vampires were frequently used as scapegoats and were credited with the very real crimes of mortal men. In other cases, they may have been used to explain away certain phenomenon that science and medicine could not. Remember that the decision between reality and superstition, between a monster and an animal, is frequently only a matter of the available knowledge of witnesses.

And in the old days of vampire lore, especially in Europe, there were a variety of odd beliefs regarding how one could identify a vampire. The most well known of these is the belief that vampires did not cast a reflection, which stems from the old superstition that one's soul actually casts one's reflection. Since vampires were undead, they were thought to be soulless, so they did not have reflections. Also, supernatural vampires could not enter a residence if they hadn't been invited and could not cross the threshold of a church or tread upon holy or sanctified ground.

The Viral Vampire

As time passed and advancements continued in the realms of science, medicine, and technology, the concept of the vampire evolved. Because these advancements revealed the truth behind the mysteries of illnesses and naturally occurring phenomenon, the superstitions of the past were increasingly debunked. As a result, the vampires of today are not viewed as demon-possessed creatures, but as beings infected with viral vampirism.

Since the transference of vampirism, even in its supernatural form, is achieved through a bite or through exposure to a vampire's blood, it greatly mimics the behavior of a virus. In today's world, viruses are the new "boogey man." For proof, one need only consider the widespread panic caused by the recent anthrax and swine flu outbreak scares. Humans of today have learned to fear the power of viruses, especially fatal and incurable ones such as HIV/AIDS.

Stranger Than Fiction

One interesting aspect that vampire enthusiasts have long and hotly debated deals with whether or not vampires can procreate (or even have sex). The supernatural vampire was said to have a voracious sexual appetite but was sterile. Modern lore often claims there are "true-blood" vampires, born of two vampire parents. A new addition to this myth is that of the *Damphir*, the "half-blood" offspring of a human and vampire. Since vampires are now seen as infected with a mutating virus, instead of actually dead, this idea (albeit in a rather weird way) makes sense.

In the modern lore of viral vampires, their strengths, abilities, and weaknesses have changed dramatically. For example, viral vampires are rarely portrayed as having shapeshifting abilities, especially when it comes to more extreme forms such as bats and mist. The idea that vampires cannot tolerate sunlight remains. However, this is usually shown as an allergic reaction to UV rays caused by the virus. Stakes still work just fine, and garlic is still an effective weapon (which is also explained as an allergic reaction to the virus). Viral vampires still have supernatural strength, but are almost *never* shown as being able to fly (though sometimes they are portrayed as jumping across great distances).

Psychic Vampires

Psychic vampires, sometimes called "energy vampires" or "life-force vampires," do not feed on human blood, but instead feed upon the psychic energy or life-force of other humans. Technically, psychic vampires are not undead or immortal, but just human beings with the ability to draw the energy of others into themselves. However, these vampires can be just as dangerous as the ones that feed upon blood … especially if they have not yet learned how to properly control their powers.

You see, psychic vampires are said to be born with their abilities, so as a result, not all of them are even aware they are feeding. They enjoy being with lots of people because of the available energy. Usually, unaware psychic vampires just think of themselves as social people because they feel happy and energized when around other people. However, if their powers are not properly developed, they can involuntarily begin feeding on the wrong people (such as family members and loved ones) and at the wrong times (when sitting next to someone on a park bench, for example).

Stranger Than Fiction

In pop culture, the concept of psychic vampirism first came to the silver screen in the 1985 film *Lifeforce*. Based on the novel *Space Vampires* by Colin Wilson and directed by Tobe Hooper, the film tells the story of a man who discovers that the woman he has fallen in love with is from a race of "space vampires" who have come to Earth in order to feed upon the life energies of human beings.

We can compare an unaware psychic vampire to a baby cobra. When a venomous snake is young, it will release all its venom in a single bite. As it grows, the snake learns to reserve its venom so as not to render itself venomless. An unaware psychic vampire runs the risk of drawing in energy from everyone around them all the time and can do serious physical and psychological damage (which can be permanent in extreme cases) to those around them, especially in situations where only one person is accidentally being fed upon.

Psychic vampires who are aware of their abilities usually learn to feed responsibly, being careful to do no harm to those they feed upon. Sometimes however, they become aware of their abilities on their own. This can also be dangerous, because they can develop a kind of addiction to the energies of certain people. At other times, a more malevolently inclined person might even come to enjoy the knowledge that he or she can drain a person of energy.

Revenants

The word *revenant* comes from the French *revenir*, "to return," and literally means "one who returns." In the terminology of vampire lore, however, the word refers to "one who returns from death." Revenants, technically speaking, are not exactly vampires. Some believe, especially in modern times, that revenants are cases where the vampire virus encounters some unknown physical anomaly within a host. The result is usually said to be an abomination that surpasses vampirism.

Whereas vampires regenerate and therefore retain their eternal appearances, revenants begin to decay. Revenants' teeth become jagged and deformed, instead of being the straight, sharp fangs usually given to vampires. They also stink ... very pungently. The putrid odor of a revenant can be smelled from a good distance, especially if one is unfortunate enough to be standing downwind.

In medieval lore, revenants were believed to be the reanimated corpses of evil men, criminals, or those who died violently or of disease (especially if they died from a fever). The lore that claimed they fed upon human blood or flesh is now believed to have been added at a later time. Originally, revenants were not thought to actually feed upon the living in any way, shape, or form.

Best-case scenario, a revenant will only carry out a physical attack when it encounters someone during its nocturnal wanderings, usually delivering quite a beating to its victim. Worst-case scenario (and the most likely, unfortunately), the revenant will infect the person with a mysterious and often fatal illness. In the early lore, it was sometimes said the revenant would bite or scratch its victims to spread disease, which may have led to the creation of additional vampiric elements.

The Scary Truth

The concept of revenants likely stemmed from cases where people were mistakenly declared dead, causing them to be buried alive. A minority of lucky (if you can call it that) individuals, still infected by illness, may have managed to dig themselves out. When they returned to their villages, however, the superstitious villagers barred them from returning. This likely caused anger toward their neighbors, which would explain why they beat up anyone they encountered. The bites and scratches may have simply been the result of these scuffles. The spread of disease may have been nothing more than the result of coming into close contact with the infected (and terribly unwashed, which explains the smell) person.

Vlad the Impaler

The most well-known vampiric figure in Western culture is known to history as Vlad III. However, as the evil often are, he's been called by many names—Vlad Tepes, Vlad *Dracula*, and Vlad the Impaler. While this man is believed to have been the inspiration for Bram Stoker's vampire character Count Dracula, the real details surrounding his life are perhaps even more frightening than the fiction.

Conjuring Words

Dracula/Dracul was a hereditary title given to Vlad Tepes III. The word translates in multiple ways. Dracul, the title of Vlad II (his father), means "dragon" if taken from its root *drako*. In Romanian, however, the word has the secondary meaning of "devil/demon." Therefore, Vlad III's title name of *Dracula* can mean "Little Dragon" or "Son of the Dragon." However, in Romanian it can also mean "Son of the Devil/Demon." In either case, this title served as a powerful psychological weapon against enemies of the Tepes clan.

Vlad II, Vlad III's father, was forced to live in exile in the Romanian land of Wallachia. Sometime during the last two months of 1431, his second son was born—Vlad Tepes III, who would eventually be the middle sibling of Vlad II's three sons. His older brother was named Mircea, and his younger brother, said to have been amazingly fair-faced, was often called Radu "The Handsome."

When Vlad III was five years old, his father had succeeded in eliminating almost all of his rivals, the most powerful being a group of nobles called the Danesti. He assumed the throne and declared himself the ruler of Wallachia. Having achieved this high status, his sons received the education of the nobility. From a very young age, Vlad III was educated in the arts of warfare and the details of administration, as well as the usual combative instruction given to all Christian knights of the period—horseback riding, swordplay, archery, etc.

Soon enough, Vlad's father learned there was a downside to the elimination of his rivals (most of whom were Christian nobility), as he had made enemies of most potential allies on the Christian side of the ongoing conflict between Western Christianity and Eastern Islam. In order to survive, and to make sure his lands were not invaded from the east, he had no choice but to secure several pacts with the Muslim Sultan. One such pact involved handing over his two youngest sons, Vlad III and Radu, as hostages. The oldest son, Mircea, was probably not included in the deal because he was already of the accepted adult/ fighting age for male nobles, which meant he was bound to the service of his father's kingdom.

Strangers in a Strange Land

Now 13 years old, Vlad III and his younger brother were sent to live in the palace home of the Sultan in Adrianople, Turkey. While the boys were, technically speaking, hostages of the Sultan, this didn't mean they were ill-treated. The practice of exchanging hostages to secure agreements was not uncommon at the time, and the boys were merely kept to ensure that their father kept up his side of the pact with the Sultan. Any attempt to betray the Sultan would result in the immediate execution of his two sons.

In 1448, the Sultan finally released Vlad III at the age of 17. Since Vlad had received at least half of his education among the Muslims in Turkey, the Sultan saw it fitting to endorse Vlad III as successor to his father's throne. Vlad's little brother, Radu, who had been a little boy when he arrived in Adrianople, stayed behind (since he'd spent more of his life there than in Wallachia, it is believed he probably came to consider Turkey his homeland).

The Bermuda Triangle

Though it cannot be verified, it is commonly believed that Vlad Tepes III was first introduced to the practice of impalement during his time in Turkey. There is much evidence that, from a very young age, Vlad displayed a special fascination with methods of execution and torture. He excelled in all weapons of warfare, both physical and psychological. Since impalement was very effective for both, it is not surprising that he brought the practice back to Wallachia with him.

Betrayal by the *Boyars*

Vlad returned home to assume his father's throne, but was almost immediately usurped by an attack from his fellow Wallachia nobles, the *boyars*. To add insult to injury, Vlad soon learned the truth about the fate of his father and older brother. During the final months of his absence, these same *boyars* had ambushed them. Vlad's father had been killed in the ambush, but his older brother had not been so lucky. Mircea had surrendered to the *boyars*, only to suffer a cruel death. They dragged him to an open grave and buried him alive. Unable to assemble a sizeable force of troops, Vlad turned to both the Hungarian Empire and his long-time ally the Sultan for assistance. He spent the better part of eight years carefully plotting his vengeful return.

In 1456, with the collective forces of the Sultan and the Hungarians behind him, Vlad returned to Wallachia. It would appear that the *boyars'* act of betrayal and the defeat he had suffered by them had turned Vlad's heart to darkness. He had not forgotten, and he would not forgive. He had a plan for those who had opposed him, one that involved deception, cruelty, pain, and death.

The Rise of the Impaler

Vlad soon assumed his rightful place on his father's throne, and the *boyars* had not put up much of a fight because they knew they couldn't stand against the combined might of Vlad Tepes, Hungary, and Turkey. In short, they knew they were powerless, and most feared retribution. Vlad took advantage of this situation to stage one of the most cunning set-ups of all time. He had notices of amnesty sent to every *boyar* in the region. These notices claimed that Vlad wished to usher in a new period of peace and prosperity in Wallachia. They also included beautiful invitations, asking the nobles and their entire families to attend a grand feast and celebration at a castle in Tirgoviste, Wallachia, which Vlad was holding in honor of the newly established peace. Every single one of the nobles attended ... a decision every single one of them would regret.

When entering a feast, it was common for everyone to disarm at the door. (You can imagine how a room full of armed and intoxicated warrior-nobles might prove to be a very bad combination.) While everyone was being seated and disarmed, Vlad had concealed a large contingent of troops outside the banquet hall. At the doors of the banquet hall, however, only the usual formal guards were seen, which would not appear out of the ordinary. Once everyone had been assembled, Vlad gave a subtle predetermined gesture to the door guards, who immediately stepped outside, shutting and barring all but one door to the banquet hall. The waiting troops now poured in through the only open door. Before any of the guests could even react (though, since they were disarmed, this wouldn't have made much of a difference), every man, woman, and child within the hall was his prisoner. Anyone who resisted or even spoke out was immediately killed.

Now that his enemies were at his mercy, Vlad informed them that he was seizing all their properties and even stripped them of any valuables they were wearing. He then had them all bound and forced them to make an exhausting march to the peak of a mountain near the Arges River. Any who proved to be too old, weak, feeble, or ill were faced with the choice of either being executed by way of impalement or dying slowly in transit. However, many of those who survived the march probably grew to wish they had not. Almost all these nobles spent the remainder of their short and miserable lives constructing Castle Dracula for Vlad Tepes.

Most of the atrocities with which Vlad Tepes is credited took place during his cruel supervision of Castle Dracula's construction. Vlad was cruelly vigilant in making sure he made the nobles' lives hell. Anyone who spoke out against him, anyone who attempted to escape, or just anyone he felt wasn't working hard enough was publicly tortured, impaled, or executed by the cruelest methods he knew (which were as diverse as they were gruesome).

A Legacy of Impalement

You have likely already concluded that Vlad Tepes was especially fond of using impalement for executions. But exactly what is involved in the process of impalement? While there were multiple methods, they all followed the same basic steps. Simply put, it involved skewering a victim's body with a long, sharp pole, usually made of wood.

Vlad Tepes' favorite method for impalement appears to have involved having one horse tied with a strap to each of the victim's ankles. The blunt end of the pole was anchored with the sharp end pointed directly between the victim's legs. The horses would then forcibly pull the person in the direction of the sharp tip. Needless to say, impalement was a terribly slow and excruciatingly painful way to die.

There were other, simpler methods of impalement as well. The easiest was to simply stab the long stake into the back or abdomen of the victim, then raise him up and plant the blunt end into the ground until the person was suspended by it. This would allow gravity to slowly and very painfully drag the writhing victim's body down along the shaft. One was considered lucky if the stake accidentally pierced a vital organ, as this might speed up one's death before the stake was raised.

The horrific nature of impalement also made it a powerful psychological weapon, which Vlad Tepes frequently used to his advantage. At one point during his reign, a Turkish army attempted to invade Wallachia. When they reached the banks of the Danube River, thousands of impaled corpses greeted them. The sight demoralized the invading force to such a degree that they turned around and went home. In 1461, Mohammed II, the legendary "Conqueror of Constantinople," led another force into Wallachia. However, he was so sickened and horrified when he came upon a veritable forest of 20,000 impaled victims that he marched his army straight back to Constantinople and never again dared to lead a force into Wallachia. This event came to be referred to as the "Forest of the Impaled."

Was Vlad Tepes a Vampire?

There are many theories as to why Vlad Tepes III came to be thought of as a vampire, most of which are heavily based on speculation. The simplest explanation is to point to Bram Stoker's novel as the cause. The problem with this lies in the fact that Stoker used very little historical fact in his novel. In all honesty, Vlad Tepes simply served as a template for his creation of the Count Dracula character.

One theory points to references to Vlad Tepes in written correspondence from the period, calling him a vampire (but mostly just suggesting it). However, this could easily be an error caused by linguistic confusions as the title Dracula can be interpreted with at least two alternate translations. A hastily translated or mistranslated letter could have referred to Vlad Dracula as "Vlad, the Son of the Devil" in its translation. Concluding that a man who is called "the Son of the Devil" is a vampire would not be much of a stretch.

Another theory that attempts to explain how Vlad Tepes came to be thought of as a vampire also deals with correspondence, namely how they are dated. Letters allegedly written by, to, or about Vlad Tepes have some rather unusual dating. If one were to check the dates of these letters, it certainly could appear that he had an abnormally long life span of roughly 200 years. However, this could be nothing more than a series of typographical errors. Additionally, names were often passed down, just as Vlad "Dracul" Tepes passed his name on to his son, Vlad "Dracula" Tepes. It is not at all impossible that Vlad Tepes III had a son or heir who assumed a name similar to his, which ultimately led to this misunderstanding.

Perhaps the most reasonable explanation for Vlad Tepes' association with vampirism comes from the fact that he was known to have collected blood from the recently impaled into a chalice, from which he then drank. Evidence also suggests he practiced cannibalism, eating the cooked flesh of the recently executed. Anyone from that period, after witnessing Vlad performing such acts, would have immediately associated this with vampire lore.

Then again, maybe labeling Vlad Tepes III as a vampire was the only way people could make sense of how any human being could be so terrible and cruel. Maybe this was the only way people could fathom how a man could be capable of doing something as inhumane as impaling 20,000 people, then arranging them into a forest of death, just to make a point. Some cultures believe men who kill too many people risk being transformed into bloodthirsty monsters; perhaps Vlad Tepes III finally reached his limit.

The Plogojowitz Incident

The 1725 event referred to as "The Plogojowitz Incident" is either one of the first real-life accounts of vampirism or a record of one of the most extreme cases of mass hysteria ever. During the early 1700s, renewed interest in vampires spread throughout Europe, especially in England. So perhaps it only makes sense that this event took place during this period of time.

The Bermuda Triangle

Geographically speaking, the Plogojowitz Incident occurred in a village called Kisilova. At the time it was located in Serbia, although it is not uncommon to find sources that place it elsewhere. This is because some of the older summarizations and translations mistakenly claimed it took place in Hungary. This mistake usually stemmed from either geographical error or a general lack of familiarity with the political history of the region. In 1725, the region was in a state of political chaos, with several ruling bodies claiming ownership. The resulting confusion may have led to this common error.

According to the official records of the event, which were written down in the log of a German official sent to investigate, everything started when a villager from Kisilova named Peter Plogojowitz died from an unknown illness. Ten weeks after he was buried, however, Peter began to appear at night to people in the village. He appeared to a total of 10 people, the first being his recently widowed wife. Adding to the suspicious situation was the fact that 9 of the 10 people who reported having encountered the deceased man died within roughly 24 hours from an unidentified or mysterious illness.

The only person to ever encounter the reanimated man and *not* die was his wife. According to the villagers, she told people that her deceased husband had come knocking on her door late one night and, strangely enough, had demanded she give him his *opanki* (shoes worn in the region). Bewildered, she handed over the shoes. The next day, after conveying her story to some of the other villagers, Mrs. Plogojowitz apparently packed up her belongings and left town. As you might imagine, having the reanimated corpse of one's deceased spouse show up at the door in the middle of the night asking for his shoes would probably be enough to make anyone want to pack up and move.

Stranger Than Fiction

At one point in the history of Northern and Eastern Europe, belief in vampires reached such an extreme degree that caskets were constructed in a special design meant to prevent the dead from rising. The lid was fitted with a sharp stake that, once it was closed, would impale the heart of the corpse within. Some casket lids were even equipped with the secondary measure of a sharp blade positioned at neck level, which would decapitate the corpse when closed. So if people weren't dead before being put in these caskets, they definitely would be once the lid closed. The upside (sort of) to this practice was that no one was buried alive, which happened a lot back then.

Since the belief in vampires was a strong part of the local folklore, it didn't take long for the villagers to conclude they had a vampire on their hands. They were certain that Peter Plogojowitz had joined the ranks of the undead, which meant they'd all be doomed if they didn't do something soon. Since the only way to make sure was to inspect his corpse for specific signs of vampirism—a lack of decomposition and new growth of the hair, beard, and nails—the villagers decided to dig the fellow up. Perhaps not wanting to get themselves into legal trouble, they first sent word of their intentions to the acting Imperial Official who resided in the neighboring district of Gradisk.

Unsure what to make of the situation, the German Imperial Official implored the villagers to wait until he could secure the proper authorization for an exhumation of the corpse from his superiors in Belgrade (which would take weeks, at best). The villagers, however, could not have cared less about his authorization. In their opinion, they'd all be dead by the time his request made its way through the Belgrade office's miles of bureaucratic red tape. Realizing they were going to dig up the body with or without his consent, he decided to go to Kisilova to witness the exhumation himself. Just in case, he brought the Pope of Gradisk along for the ride. If this turned out to be a real vampire, he probably figured having a holy man on hand would be a good idea.

By the time the Imperial Official got to the village, the villagers had just finished digging up the casket that held Peter Plogojowitz's (possibly reanimated) corpse. They then pried free the lid and began inspecting the corpse within for the signs of vampirism. This is where things got even weirder.

According to the Imperial Official's record of the inspection, Plogojowitz's corpse did not have even the faintest odor of decomposition. The only visible sign of decay was that the man's nose had collapsed in on itself. His hair and beard exhibited signs of new growth. His nails had fallen away, and new ones had already grown in their place. What's more, the corpse's pale-white skin appeared to be peeling away, revealing a new layer of pink, flush skin.

Having found Plogojowitz's body in this condition, the villagers were confident they'd been correct in their suspicions: Peter Plogojowitz had most certainly become a vampire. So they did what most reasonable people would do in that situation. They used a mallet to drive a sharp wooden stake right through old Peter's heart. According to the Imperial Official's account, when the stake pierced Plogojowitz's chest, he let out a bloodcurdling shriek. Just to make sure Peter didn't somehow manage to get back up, the villagers dragged him onto a pyre and burned his body to ashes.

The Scary Truth

While it is easy to get caught up in the amazing nature of the Plogojowitz accounts, modern medical science can now easily explain all of the supposed "vampire signs" the body displayed. But what about the shriek he is said to have let out? This, too, has a rational explanation. A dead body accumulates gases in the chest cavity during decomposition. When suddenly compressed by the forced entry of the stake, these gases were shoved into the throat, which stimulated the vocal cords, producing a sound that resembled a shriek. Then again, maybe he did scream.

The Highgate Vampire Incident

In the Highgate area of London, England, Highgate Cemetery is the most famous historical landmark. It was first constructed in 1839, but due to financial difficulties it had fallen into a state of neglect and decay by the mid-twentieth century. In the 1960s, the cemetery was most known for being the final resting place of Karl Marx, author of the *Communist Manifesto*, and it received worldwide attention in 1970 when Scotland Yard thwarted an attempt to bomb his tomb. However, it soon became known for a far darker reason. According to a team who claimed to have been investigating paranormal activity in the cemetery for many years, Highgate Cemetery was home to a real-life, honest-to-goodness, bloodsucking vampire.

The self-styled Vampire Research Society (VRS), headed by a rather grandiose young man by the name of Sean Manchester, carried out the Highgate Vampire incident investigation, the details of which had been kept secret for years. In 1970, however, Manchester and another man named David Farrant, who claimed to be a psychic investigator, both went public with their findings. These two men later passionately disagreed on the details of the phenomenon and eventually went their separate ways. However, in the beginning, they agreed on at least one thing—some kind of supernatural entity was at work in Highgate Cemetery, which needed to be dealt with and removed.

According to Manchester's account, his case began several years before, in 1967. In the early months of that year, he'd received a report from two 16-year-old girls who had recently had a strange experience while walking by the cemetery at night. They claimed that, as they passed the cemetery, they witnessed what appeared to be people walking out of tombs. Soon after, one of the girls began to experience terrible nocturnal terrors as well as an increasing, and unexplainable, loss of blood. Manchester immediately began to investigate.

Manchester went public with his investigation in a letter to the *Hampstead and Highgate Express* on February 27, 1970, which it later published. According to him, Highgate Cemetery was home to a "King Vampire of the Undead." He claimed that this "King Vampire" was a nobleman from medieval Wallachia (which, incidentally, was the home of Vlad Tepes III) who had practiced demonic magic. He explained that a group of the nobleman-turned-vampire's most devoted followers had brought his reanimated body to Highgate in the early nineteenth century (which would roughly match up with the years just before the cemetery was constructed). They had purchased a home where they placed their vampire lord's coffin, which had been located on the site of what was now Highgate Cemetery. The vampire had remained dormant in his coffin for quite some time, but had been disturbed from his slumber by the activities of Satanists who held dark rituals in the abandoned sections of Highgate Cemetery. He now firmly believed that this "King Vampire" had somehow relocated his coffin to a nearby location and would continue to torment (and eventually kill) the girl if not found in time.

The Bermuda Triangle

One popular rumor claims that Highgate Cemetery was the inspiration for the graveyard scene of Bram Stoker's novel *Dracula*. While this is not entirely impossible (after all, he did fashion the villain after a historical figure), most authorities on the subject consider this an urban legend. There is no solid evidence (aside from comparisons) to support the claim that Stoker used the real Highgate Cemetery as inspiration for his work.

Around the same time, a local student named David Farrant claimed to have spent an entire night in Highgate Cemetery on December 21, 1969. During his experience, he reported witnessing a grey figure that he believed was a supernatural entity of some sort. A few days later, on December 24, 1969, Farrant was walking past the cemetery and again briefly caught sight of the same grey figure. He went public with his findings to see if any other people had experienced similar sightings. Eventually, only two of the resulting accounts even came close to matching up with his.

The immediate result of Manchester's and Farrant's public declarations was absolute pandemonium, and the rivalry between these two men seemed to only add fuel to the fire. Manchester finally issued a public challenge for Farrant to prove his claims. In the same television interview, Manchester claimed he would enter Highgate Cemetery and hunt down the vampire once and for all on March 13, 1970 (which, of course, just happened to be Friday the 13th). An ITV television crew interviewed Manchester on the eve of the hunt. Within two hours, the cemetery was thrown into a state of absolute chaos when a mob of hundreds of curiosity seekers and would-be vampire hunters overran Highgate.

The police were called in to bring things under control, and the entire area was cleared and cordoned off.

In an account Manchester published many years later, he claimed that he did, in fact, locate the coffins of at least two vampires that night. He claimed he and his VRS team had eluded the police and managed to locate a suspicious tomb by following the young girl being victimized by the vampire as she walked the cemetery in a psychic trance. The team had been unable to open the door to the tomb, no matter how hard they tried. He claimed that, eventually, they found an opening in the tomb's roof and he had himself lowered inside by a rope. Once inside, Manchester reported that he'd found a pair of empty coffins, which he believed had been temporarily abandoned by vampires. He dumped garlic and a cross into the empty coffins and then sprinkled the tomb's sealed door with holy water before having himself lifted back out. The burned remains of a dead woman were found in the cemetery several months later, on August 1, 1970. Manchester and his supporters believed these were the charred remains of a vampire that had been exposed to the sun when it could not reenter the tomb that Manchester had treated with garlic and holy water. While police suspected that occult activities were involved in the unidentified woman's death, they didn't openly endorse the whole "vampire angle."

Not long after this, police arrested David Farrant when they found him on the grounds of a church next to Highgate Cemetery in possession of a stake and crucifix. The case against him, however, was later dismissed when it went to the courts. To this day, Farrant claims to know the truth about what was really going on in Highgate, which he says (in his own words on a video he posted on his YouTube channel, "DFTVX") was simply a haunting caused by a "harmless ghost."

The Scary Truth

Many skeptics of Manchester's firsthand accounts with the Highgate Vampire have pointed out that many elements of his story mirror events from Bram Stoker's *Dracula* almost to the letter. But some supporters of Manchester have gone so far as to claim that this is because Stoker's story was based on true events. You decide for yourself what you would like to believe.

In a later, rather more sensational account, Manchester claimed to have finally brought down the "King Vampire of the Undead." According to his own writings, he finally located the vampire's coffin in the catacombs of an abandoned house near the cemetery, the exact address/location of which he refused to divulge. Supposedly, it was then that he was finally able to drive a stake through the vampire's heart and burn the remains. We can say at least one thing to his credit, however. Since that time, no further reports of vampiric activity have come from the areas in or around Highgate Cemetery.

Poor Man's Guide to Killing a Vampire

Regardless of lore, time period, or belief system, all sources agree on four primary weapons that are effective against vampires. The kit of any vampire hunter should be equipped with the following:

♦ Six to 10 stakes, made from either silver or wood (but not from an evergreen)

♦ A sharp sword with a blade of either silver or combat-ready steel (aluminum alloy blades are definitely not recommended)

♦ Some form of fire-producing tool (Zippo lighters are durable and fairly reliable if properly maintained)

♦ At least one clove of garlic (just in case; some modern lore does not endorse its effectiveness)

First and foremost is the method of driving a stake (constructed either from wood or silver) through the vampire's heart. However, according to some lore, this method may only incapacitate the vampire. Even though a vampire has been staked, don't consider it permanently down until you've carried out the proper secondary measures.

The Scary Truth

This instructional section has been included solely for the purpose of entertainment. Please don't go out and start staking people. That would definitely be a bad thing and would more than likely end with you in prison. Just keep it real and remember: this is all in good fun.

Second is the sword. It should have a silver blade, which will allow it to still be effective if you drive it through the vampire's heart. Since a silver-bladed sword would likely be very expensive (not to mention *very* hard to find), you may want to go with a sword with a regular steel blade, but test its durability exhaustively before putting it into use. However, a steel sword will only be effective if used to either decapitate the vampire or cut its heart out (however, you won't have much luck getting a vampire to sit still while you do the latter).

Once you've staked and/or decapitated the vampire, it still might not be down for good. To ensure that it stays dead this time, burn the vampire's corpse. However, fire does not destroy bone even under the extreme heat of a crematorium. Therefore, separate any skeletal remains into multiple groups and bury them apart from each other.

The Least You Need to Know

◆ The earliest lore about vampires was primarily either supernatural or religious in nature.

◆ Later, as superstition gave way to science, the lore evolved into the modern viral vampire.

◆ Psychic vampires do not feed on blood but on the psychic energies or life-forces of others.

◆ Revenants, while not technically vampires, were eventually credited with at least some vampiric attributes.

◆ Vlad Tepes III was the template for Bram Stoker's Count Dracula, but it is unlikely that he was a vampire.

◆ Don't go around staking people; it isn't nice.

Chapter 13

Zombies

In This Chapter

- ◆ The truth about the old hoax of the "Voodoo zombie"
- ◆ The Chinese creature referred to as the Chiang-Shih
- ◆ The films of George Romero and the rise of the viral zombie
- ◆ Ways to protect yourself in the event of a zombie virus outbreak

What happens when the dead no longer remain that way? How does the human race survive in a world swarming with flesh-eating, walking corpses? Better yet, how does one kill something that's already dead? Well, if you are looking for the answers to these questions, you've come to the right place. Rooted in the now-debunked myths of the Haitian Voodoo cult, zombies have become the very embodiment of humanity's widespread fear of viruses. A dehumanized reflection of our world, they call us to join them.

The Voodoo Zombie Hoax

The concept of *zombies* originated from Voodoo, namely from an elaborate practice of the *Vodun* priests of Haiti (for more on Haitian Voodoo, see Chapter 9). In recent years, however, some rather brave scientific researchers have brought the truth about these so-called "Voodoo zombies" into the light of day. The real power of Voodoo, and of similar faith magic practices, is dependent on the beliefs and superstitions of others. As a result, practitioners react with hostility toward anyone who attempts to reveal their "magic" as nothing more than an elaborate hoax.

Wade Davis, a well-known Canadian researcher, learned firsthand just how hostile the Haitian Voodoo priests could be. Davis traveled to Haiti to investigate reports of a "zombie powder" the Voodoo priests of the island were said to use to resurrect the dead. His experience was as frightening as it was informative. While many of his findings have been hotly debated, it was Davis who first discovered the presence of a dangerous neurotoxin in the concoction.

Since Davis's initial claims, more researchers have traveled to Haiti to obtain (often at great personal risk) more samples of the Haitian zombie powder. Chemical analyses have revealed one common element, which existed in a majority of the samples, was tetrodotoxin or TTX. TTX is a powerful neurotoxin found in the poison of puffer fish (one species of which is indigenous to Haiti). Puffer fish poison is extremely potent, and human contact with the substance is often fatal. However, in recent years, the substance has been used in proper doses for certain medical procedures. You see, at just the right dose, TTX can cause a person to go into a state of paralytic suspended animation, similar to how some animals go into hibernation. To most observers, even doctors, the person appears to be dead. So the zombie powder was meant to make a person seem dead, although vital functions often remained operating at almost undetectable rates.

The idea of this zombie powder becomes even more terrifying when you consider how the Voodoo priests employ it. Imagine, if you will, what it would be like to be the victim of this substance. First, the powder would be thrown into your face or sprinkled onto your skin—often on your left arm, due to its close proximity to the heart. Suddenly, you find yourself completely paralyzed: you can't speak; you can't move. Everyone around you thinks you've dropped dead. Then the ambulance or coroner van comes and takes you away. In your mind, you are screaming out to them, "I'm not dead!" However, your body does not respond. You are completely aware of everything as they wheel you into the hospital. You even hear the doctor declare you dead. Later, you can only lie there helplessly as the medical examiner or mortician begins to perform an autopsy or embalming procedure on you—and you can still see, hear, and (most horrifically) *feel everything*. Luckily (some might say) for the Haitian victims, autopsies and embalming are rarely performed, and burials are performed very soon after death.

Conjuring Words

The root for the anglicized **zombie** comes from the Haitian Creole word *zombi*, which refers to a now debunked practice of the Haitian *Vodun* cult. The initial belief stated that a *zombi* was one who, through the dark powers of Voodoo, had his or her soul stolen by a priest/priestess (causing a "temporary death") and later was brought back to life. After being resurrected, a *zombi* was said to be bound into the service of the acting Voodoo priest/priestess.

In Haitian cases, the victim, who is believed dead, is soon buried. Later, often that very night, the priest/priestess will dig up the victim and claim he/she has brought the individual back to life with dark Voodoo magic, to serve him/her as a zombie. Often, such Voodoo zombies move clumsily, speak with slurred speech, and exhibit somewhat "spacey" behavior. We now believe these symptoms are the result of permanent brain damage caused by a combination of prolonged oxygen deprivation during the time they are buried alive and exposure to the neurotoxin TTX. In all honesty, many researchers claim it is a miracle that anyone has ever survived being victimized by the Voodoo zombie hoax.

In truth, research shows that the use of zombie powder has a ridiculously low success rate. A Voodoo priest would likely only succeed in creating 1 "zombie" in as many as 100 attempts (the others would likely end in death for the victims). That means that as many as 99 people could be killed just so one of these "priests" could have a brain-damaged servant.

The Chiang-Shih

Many refer to the Chiang-Shih as the "Chinese Vampire," but it has far more traits in common with zombies than vampires. The term Chiang-Shih roughly translates as "Hopping Corpse." Chinese lore explains that the Chiang-Shih are reanimated corpses of people whose souls were unable to pass on to the afterlife, usually because of the ways in which they died. For example, the Chinese lore claims that anyone who commits suicide is at high risk for coming back as a Chiang-Shih.

The Chiang-Shih, like a zombie, does not initially possess any super-natural powers. Also like a zombie, they are not very agile. In fact, a Chiang-Shih is called a Hopping Corpse because it is unable to walk or move very efficiently. This is probably due to the occurrence of *rigor mortis*, which causes the undead corpse to become stiff as a board. Because of this, the Chiang-Shih must hop in order to pursue its victims ... but are said to be *very* good at it.

In the early stages following *reanimation*, a Chiang-Shih is physically weak and awkward but makes up for this with serrated teeth, a long tongue, and clawlike fingernails. Its skin is green from decomposition and is sometimes said to give off a strange glow. While one is not all that difficult to deal with at first, a Chiang-Shih can grow more power-ful as time goes on. This increase in power is measured by the amount of white hair a Chiang-Shih has on its head. Once all its hair has gone white, you better steer clear. This means it has reached the highest stage of power and now has the ability to fly (which means it doesn't have to hop anymore), has superhuman strength, and can change shape (usually into a wolf).

Conjuring Words

In terms of zombies, **reanimation** refers to the resumed movement of dead tissue/organisms. Literally, the word means "to return to move-ment" or "made to move again."

The good news about a Chiang-Shih is that it doesn't appear to be dif-ficult to ward off. Often, any extremely loud noise is enough to scare one away, especially if the noise sounds anything like thunder. Chiang-Shih are terrified by thunder because one of the only ways they can be killed is by a hit from a bolt of lightning. Another way is to shoot one with a bullet (which, oddly enough, works on normal people as well). You can hold off a Chiang-Shih with little or no white hair with a broom. Also, these weaker Chiang-Shih cannot cross any border made from rice, red peas, or iron filings. If you manage to kill even a weaker Chiang-Shih, however, you still need to burn the corpse to ashes as soon as possible.

If you find yourself dealing with a powerful white-haired Chiang-Shih, then you need to employ the services of a specially trained *Tao* priest to get rid of it (if you can find one). Depending on how powerful it has become, the priest will first subdue the monster by tacking one or more small slips of paper to its forehead. These have special prayers or incantations on them, often written in either red ink or blood. Once the Chang-Shih has been subdued, the priest will ring a special bell that forces it to go back to its grave. Unfortunately, the lore is kind of vague about exactly what the priest does to keep the subdued Chiang-Shih from coming back out again. Perhaps the power of the slips of paper remains permanent.

Conjuring Words

Tao (pronounced *dow*) literally translates as "the way/path." This is the Chinese root word for the Japanese term *Do*, which has the same basic meaning (though usually without a religious connotation). The *Tao* religion is based on a search for hidden spiritual truths and walking a righteous "path" in one's life. *Tao* priests dedicate their lives to serving good and combating evil, which explains why they would train to fight something as evil as a Chiang-Shih.

Sometimes, when the special slips of paper are not enough to seal the powers of an extremely powerful Chiang-Shih, the priest must go toe-to-toe with the undead creature. These priests are trained to wield special weapons, the most common being a sword with a blade constructed from a series of overlapping copper coins bound together by a long interwoven thread of strong red string. In some cases, though, they just use a wooden sword (which is probably just as effective, but doesn't sound nearly as cool).

Rise of the Viral Zombie

Today, the viral zombie is the most common type that comes to mind when we think of reanimated corpses. The viral zombie was first introduced by the films of legendary horror director George Romero, such as his 1978 classic *Dawn of the Dead* and his most recent film *Diary of the Dead*. As often happens with the paranormal, the explanations/beliefs about zombies have changed with the times. People are no longer willing to believe that zombies could be caused by some Voodoo curse. The fear of the virus, however, has become the new "bogey man" of the modern world.

Stranger Than Fiction

George Romero's films have made him an icon in the world of zombie filmmaking. Over the last few decades, his classic films *Night of the Living Dead* and *Dawn of the Dead* have been adapted into updated remake films. Also, the widely popular British horror-comedy *Shaun of the Dead* was inspired by Romero's works, and a number of lines in the movie were written as honorific quotes from his films. For example, in one scene the character Patrick says, "We're coming to get you, Barbara." This is homage to a famous line from Romero's first *Dead* film, "They're coming to get you, Barbara."

Viral zombies are believed to be caused by the infection and spread of a lethal virus that initially kills its victims and soon after reanimates their dead bodies. There are two basic schools of thought regarding how a zombie virus would behave. One believes the virus reanimates anyone who has died (whether or not that person has been bitten by a zombie). The other side of this debate believes the virus only affects those who have been infected with it (usually by being bitten by a zombie).

Whereas Voodoo zombies are creepy but relatively harmless, viral zombies are far more dangerous. This is because, unlike the easily manipulated, brain-damaged Voodoo zombies, viral zombies feed on humans. We cannot stress this enough: once a viral zombie reanimates, it will immediately attack any living human being who happens to cross its path. This includes family members, friends, and spouses.

While just about everyone agrees that these zombies feed on humans, exactly what body parts they feed on has become a matter of debate. Once again, we have multiple sides to this hypothetical argument. One side believes zombies will eat any living thing, including humans (but also animals, bugs, etc.). Another side claims zombies eat only human flesh. The final side claims zombies specifically eat human brains. No matter which side turns out to be right, none of these hypotheses bodes well for the human race if a zombie virus ever breaks out.

The Modern Zombie Virus Concept

The viral zombie, first and foremost, possesses absolutely no supernatural powers of any kind. In fact, one zombie isn't really all that dangerous. Viral zombies are weak, clumsy, slow, and about as dumb as a bag of hammers. In all honesty, most able-bodied people could handle a group of several viral zombies without too much difficulty. So why are they considered so dangerous?

Simply put, the virus that causes the reanimation of zombies (often referred to by enthusiasts as the "Z-Virus") is extremely contagious. All it takes is one bite for a person to be infected. As the risen dead bite their first, unsuspecting victims, they quickly double their numbers. So before humankind even becomes aware of what is happening and wraps its collective head around it, it will likely be far too late to contain the outbreak. In short, the living will quickly become overwhelmingly outnumbered by the walking dead. Some estimates see this high level of infection happening in a matter of one to three days, while more conservative estimates see it taking at least a week or two.

Think about ants for a moment. One ant, if cornered by a larger insect, will likely be killed. However, a horde of ants can overtake, kill, and devour insects significantly larger in size and strength. In regions where ant colonies are larger than normal, hordes of them have been known to kill and devour animals, livestock, and even human beings! Zombies are very similar to ants in this way: both creatures become more dangerous as their numbers increase.

Viral zombies are commonly thought to be primarily attracted by sound and movement, which is where the real danger lies. A zombie, once locked onto a living human presence, lets out a wail that attracts others. One zombie soon becomes several; in a single day, several can become dozens. This fact nullifies the usefulness of any structure, no matter how well it is fortified or supplied. In a week, you will find that your fortress has become completely surrounded, and you will likely no longer have any avenue by which to escape.

How to "Re-Dead" the Reanimated

Killing a viral zombie is fairly simple. You only have to do one thing—destroy its brain. Viral zombies are nothing more than reanimated corpses driven by the central regions of the decaying brain. Take out the brain, and you take out the zombie. Some believe chopping off the head is also effective. However, others claim this only severs the brain's connection to the body, and that even a severed head will continue to wail and bite until it has been destroyed.

The best zombie fighting weapons are durable, blunt objects. Hammers, baseball bats, crowbars, and axes are just a handful of potential tools that can be used to crush the skull of an advancing zombie.

There is, of course, the option of using firearms. However, these are often not helpful to those not apt enough in marksmanship to fire them with accuracy (headshots are very difficult to make, especially consistently, with most firearms). Shotguns work very well at mid-range, as they don't require as much ability, but are not effective at longer ranges. No matter what firearm you use, almost any zombie survival enthusiast will give you the same piece of advice: always save the last round of ammunition for yourself. Better that than to be eaten alive or worse … forced to join the shambling ranks of the flesh-eating undead.

The Least You Need to Know

- Voodoo zombies are not reanimated corpses but poisoned, fooled, and brain-damaged victims of an elaborate scam.

- Chiang-Shih, often called "Chinese Vampires," actually have much in common with zombies.

- To take down a Chiang Shih that has a lot of white hair, you probably need help from a *Tao* priest.

- The viral zombie is now the only example of an actual (though still hypothetical) reanimated corpse.

- The true threat of viral zombies comes not from their strength but from their overwhelming numbers.

- Destroy the brain, and you destroy the zombie.

Chapter 14

Werewolves

In This Chapter

- ◆ The ancient myth of Lycoan, considered by some to be the first werewolf
- ◆ The different types of werewolves, and how they are created
- ◆ The evolution of human perceptions of werewolves from superstition to virus
- ◆ The strange modern case of Bill Ramsey, the "Werewolf of Southend"
- ◆ The available lore on how to protect yourself against a werewolf

When humans cross the line into the realm of the wolf, they are commonly referred to as werewolves. Mythologically, they often represent the subconscious human fear of having our reason overtaken by bestial savagery. Whether the result of magic, curses, or charms, werewolves stand as the most universal form of the union between man and beast.

Lycoan's Curse

In ancient times, King Lycoan was the king of the Greek Arcadians. Today, many werewolf enthusiasts believe Lycoan was the first werewolf whose curse spawned the entire bloodline of *lycanthropy*. Whether or not this claim is true, the story of Lycoan is certainly significant to the origins of werewolf lore. His story is of a king so evil that the gods strip him of his very humanity because of his savage behavior.

According to the ancient Greek myth, long ago when the earliest race of humans populated the world, the gods largely ignored the physical realm. So left to their own devices, the human race entered a period of darkness. Some held to their faith and continued to make altar sacrifices in the hopes that the gods would answer their appeals. But other, far more evil humans saw the absence of the gods as an opportunity to commit the most atrocious and blasphemous of crimes.

> **Conjuring Words**
>
> *Lycanthropy* is an integration of the Greeks words *lykoi* (meaning "wolf") and *anthropos* (meaning "man/human"). The term refers to the state of being a werewolf, a human who assumes the form or attributes of a wolf.

> **The Bermuda Triangle**
>
> The name Lycoan (also spelled Lykoan, Laocan, or Lycan) is often mistakenly thought to be the origin of the term *lycanthropy*, which refers to a human who transforms into a wolf (commonly called a werewolf). His name does, however, survive in the classification of the grey eastern timber wolf species, called *canis lupius Lycoan*.

The Arcadian king Lycoan, a tyrant who ruled his people with unspeakable cruelty, was perhaps the worst of these evil opportunists. He cared nothing about the sanctity of human lives and was a bloodthirsty, psychotic, and immoral man. But Lycoan's worst, and ultimately final, offense was believing he was somehow above the will of the Olympian gods.

After years of hellish torments, the multitude of sacrificial appeals made by the pious finally caught the attention of the thunder god Zeus, the powerful lord of the Olympians. Hearing of the atrocities being committed in the human realm, Zeus decided to go down to Earth in the guise of a human form to learn the truth for himself.

As Zeus traveled, he quickly heard of the savage deeds of King Lycoan, so he headed straight for Arcadia to see if this man was as terrible as the rumors claimed. Once there, Zeus revealed his true form to the Arcadians, who all bowed to him in worship. Even King Lycoan pretended to humble himself to Zeus. In his arrogance, however, the cruel ruler actually doubted Zeus' power and soon devised a plot against him. Lycoan invited Zeus to stay in his palace and attend a feast in his honor, planning to slit the thunder god's throat that night as he slept.

Stranger Than Fiction

According to one traveler's guide manuscript written in the second century C.E. by Pausanias, a Greek travel writer, Lycoan supposedly brought a baby as a sacrifice to the altar of Zeus. As a result, Zeus cursed him for his savagery by turning him into a wolf.

Once Zeus was shown to his guest quarters, Lycoan sent one of his men to his dungeon and had him bring up a prisoner to the palace kitchen. Lycoan then slit the helpless prisoner's throat, butchered his corpse, and cooked his flesh. At the banquet, when Lycoan served Zeus a plate of this human flesh, Zeus, with his divine insight, immediately knew what Lycoan had placed in front of him. Needless to say, the thunder god was more than a little displeased with the king. In a fit of indignant rage, Zeus brought Lycoan's entire palace crashing to the ground. Everyone inside was killed in the collapse … everyone but King Lycoan, who fled for his life. But, of course, no human feet were fast enough to escape the wrath of Zeus; Lycoan's fate would be even worse than death.

The Bermuda Triangle

Most versions of this myth state that Zeus transformed the cruel Lycoan into a large wolf. However, many artistic depictions of the myth portray the king during the middle of his transformation and show him as a man with a wolf's head or in some other half-man, half-wolf state. Such depictions probably have influenced the common portrayal of the man-wolf hybrid we now think of as a werewolf.

As King Lycoan fled from the overwhelming presence of mighty Zeus, grey hairs began to rapidly grow all over his body. Zeus cursed the terrible king and transformed him into a large wolf (though some later interpretations claim he became half man, half wolf). As punishment for his violence and savagery, Zeus cursed King Lycoan to remain a wolf for the rest of his miserable life.

Can Anyone Become a Werewolf?

Depending on what lore you're reading, there are two primary werewolf appearances. Some lore claims that a werewolf is a man who simply assumes the form of a normal (or large) wolf. Other tales, which have become the most popular in modern times, claim that a werewolf assumes an integrated form that looks something like a giant, bipedal human-wolf hybrid. Some modern werewolf stories claim they can be both.

In whatever form, just how does a person become a werewolf (or avoid becoming one)? Actually, more than one method exists for becoming a lycanthrope, but the most widely recognized methods are as follows:

- **Cursed lycanthropy:** Caused by a curse from a god, via a werewolf's bite, or through the spell of some form of dark sorcery.

- **Spirit lycanthropy:** Results from an invocation of the wolf spirit.

- **Enchanted lycanthropy:** Done by use of a special lycanthropic charm, spell, or enchantment (usually self-induced).

- **Viral lycanthropy:** The most modern accepted cause, this is thought of as a virus contracted by a werewolf's bite.

Of these, the easiest way to become a werewolf is to get bitten by one. There is, however, a catch to this—very few people have ever survived being attacked by a werewolf. So the bright side (if you can call it that) is that, in the rare chance you are attacked by a werewolf, you're far more likely to be torn to shreds and killed than to turn into a lycanthrope.

Supernatural Werewolf vs. Viral Werewolf

There are two main schools of thought—whose ideas are closely related to the beliefs, superstitions, and knowledge of the time periods in which they were created—as to why a werewolf's bite passes on the condition of lycanthropy. For example, in times long past, lycanthropy was thought to be caused by supernatural forces, like a curse, spell, or divine punishment. By the late middle ages, lycanthropy was believed to have spiritual or religious causes—that some illusion of the devil tricked such people into believing they could transform as werewolves.

As superstition became increasingly debunked and replaced by science and technology, the view of lycanthropy changed drastically. Over the last hundred years, for example, the cause of lycanthropy has come to be popularly viewed as some rare disease, strange virus, or some psychological or psychic phenomenon. Today, superstitions and curses are not widely accepted as valid. Viruses, however, have become the fear of the times. To find proof of this, one need only look back on the widespread panic that was caused by the anthrax and swine flu viral scares of recent years. In order for werewolf lore to remain within the boundaries of suspended disbelief, the viral lycanthropy view has become the most popular belief in modern times regarding the cause of lycanthropy.

Bill Ramsey: Werewolf of Southend

One of the most common true-life cases of lycanthropy is that of a man named Bill Ramsey. The official police case regarding this event began on July 22, 1987, though Bill's experiences with werewolflike behavior are thought to have begun long before this incident. For many years, Ramsey had worked as a carpenter in the Southend area of London, England. It is important to note that, before this incident, the 40-something Ramsey was considered a respectable member of his community, with no history of violence or even a criminal record to speak of. But on one eventful July evening, something wild was unleashed from Bill Ramsey.

That evening, Ramsey presented himself to the Southend police station. Upon encountering some officers in the parking lot who asked why he was there, Ramsey told them he could not remember but thought he really needed to be locked up. The officers thought the man was just having a laugh, until Ramsey suddenly went on a rampage.

First, Ramsey growled and bared his teeth at the officers. Then he attacked. According to reports, the nearly middle-age man lifted one officer (who was said to have been quite larger than Ramsey) over his head and tossed him to the tarmac, causing serious injuries to the man. Other officers, seeing the commotion, came to assist in subduing the snarling man. When all was said and done, it took about six officers to hold Ramsey down and restrain him in both wrist and leg irons.

The officers dragged Ramsey into a holding cell, which did little to calm him. Reports claim he tried to shove himself through the cell's dinner tray slot and managed to get one arm and his head through the slot before becoming trapped. Not phased a bit by this, Ramsey continued to snarl and growl, clawing and biting at anyone who came near.

The officers, fearing Ramsey would harm himself if left stuck in the tray slot as he was, called in the local fire department to find a way to free him. One look at the enraged Ramsey, however, and the firemen refused to go anywhere near him. They then called a local doctor to sedate Ramsey with drugs. It took another group of policemen to hold the wild man's arm still long enough for the doctor to inject the sedative. Reports indicate it took more than triple the average dose for the sedative to even have an effect on him.

The following day, when Ramsey recovered from the sedative, he claimed to have no memory of the event. He was referred to a mental health facility for evaluation. At first, the doctors diagnosed him with clinical lycanthropy and placed him on a treatment of anti-psychotic drugs. However, unlike in other cases of the condition, the drugs seemed to have no effect on Ramsey's bouts of wolflike behavior.

Some years later, news of Bill Ramsey's case came to the attention of the demonology/paranormal research team of Ed and Lorraine Warren, the couple who had made a name for themselves with their involvement in the "Amityville Horror," the well-known 1977 haunting case. The pair traveled to London, and after a few dead ends and being laughed out of a few police stations, managed to track down the Southend detective in charge of the initial case, who arranged for them to meet with Bill Ramsey. The detective himself was convinced that whatever was wrong with Bill was something beyond the scope of the many doctors who'd attempted to treat him. Ever since the initial incident, when Ramsey came to the police station on occasion, the officers immediately locked him up in a confinement cell. Some of the residents had begun to call Ramsey (much to the man's humiliation) the "Werewolf of Southend" or the "Werewolf of London." The detective hoped the Warrens could do something for Bill.

The Warrens conducted an initial interview with Ramsey, who informed them that he'd had bouts of wolf behavior since his childhood but until recently had not feared he might harm anyone. Afterward, they concluded that Ramsey suffered not from clinical lycanthropy but from a demonic possession by some kind of wolf-spirit. They arranged for an exorcism to be conducted on Bill Ramsey, with the assistance of a local bishop.

Regardless of what the truth of Ramsey's condition was, no one can argue with the results of the Warrens' exorcism. After the ceremony was performed, Bill Ramsey ceased to experience any further bouts of this uncontrollable werewolf behavior. Most of his fellow inhabitants from Southend have even learned to let bygones be bygones, and few refer to him as a werewolf any longer. In fact, most of his neighbors, while cautious of him, felt sympathy for him because aside from his bouts of werewolf behavior, all accounts of Bill Ramsey have portrayed him as a kind and generous man.

The Scary Truth

Despite the fact that all medications were ineffective in treating him, some people insist Bill Ramsey suffered from a psychiatric condition known as clinical lycanthropy and claim the exorcism only cured his condition because of psychosomatic reasons.

More Than One Way to Kill a Werewolf?

Contrary to what some might think, the available lore explains that there is, actually, more than one way to kill a werewolf. A silver bullet is not the only tool said to be effective in bringing down a lycanthrope (though it is one of them). Before one goes running after a werewolf, it is important to know what weapons and tools can (and cannot) be used against it.

Silver Weaponry

If you were to ask anyone today how to kill a werewolf, the first answer you'd receive is likely, "Shoot it with a silver bullet." Widely popularized by the creations of werewolf cinema, the silver bullet has long been mistakenly considered the only method for killing werewolves. However, this has led many to ask the question: "If it's true that a silver bullet is the only thing that can kill a werewolf, then what did people use before they had firearms?" The answer is simpler than you might think.

In truth, a good amount of werewolf lore explains that any weapon made from silver will do the trick—such as swords, knives, and stakes. Also note that most of these legends claim that only weapons of *pure silver* will work properly. In other words, a weapon only partially made from silver or made from an impure alloy may not have the desired effect. Of course, they may have at least some effect, but there's no way to know for sure. Needless to say, this isn't the kind of thing one wants to take a chance on.

The use of silver probably stems from the belief that silver is a magic or sacred/blessed element, as well as a symbol of purity. Today, pop culture werewolf lore suggests that silver, for whatever reason, prevents or at least delays a werewolf's wounds from regenerating until the weapons are removed. If this is true, then remember one little detail. If you are ever lucky enough to take down an actual werewolf, *never* pull out the blades, bullets, or whatever other silver weapon you may have used. Only after you have properly disposed of the werewolf should you retrieve your weapons.

It is universally understood that one of the greatest werewolf abilities is rapid regeneration, meaning they can heal from most wounds very quickly. To prematurely remove a weapon from a downed werewolf's wounds, you risk having it recover in as quickly as a few seconds, depending on the severity. For example, weapons only in the flesh may not affect the werewolf's revival, but those that have impaled vital organs likely will. To dispose of the werewolf, most lore explains that the downed beast must be beheaded and then immediately burned (though some just say to burn it to ashes without the whole beheading part).

Stranger Than Fiction

The most recent manifestation of silver's role in werewolf lore is believed to have originated with the Lycans from the *Underworld* films. In these films, Lycans who have been too mortally wounded by silver weapons cannot regenerate until the weapons are removed. If they are not removed in time, the Lycan dies. The werewolf-slaying "death-dealers" from the same films create bullets of liquid silver that enter the target's bloodstream, making them especially fatal to Lycans. In the films, this specially designed ammunition prevents the Lycans from being able to remove the projectiles in order to regenerate.

While silver-bladed weapons will work, do not attempt a toe-to-toe, close combat confrontation with a creature that is larger, faster, and incredibly stronger than any normal human. In this case, get yourself some silver bullets. But the trick is that not all bullets work with all firearms, so unless you have a specific one you plan to use, it'd be a good idea to have some made in the most commonly used calibers (such as 9mm, .38, and .45 caliber rounds). This will improve the possibility that you can use your silver bullets in any weapon you might happen to come across (though it probably wouldn't be smart to plan on this happening).

Stranger Than Fiction

The use of a silver bullet as a weapon against werewolves first appeared in the 1760s, with the lore surrounding the well-documented case of the Beast of Gevaudan. One story claims a local clergyman eventually killed the beast with a silver bullet. Another version claims a specially made silver bullet was blessed/enchanted by a priest/sorcerer and then given to a skilled hunter who took the beast down.

Though their use has never been recorded, it stands to reason that silver buckshot fired from a heavy-gauge shotgun would also be effective in battling werewolves. Since shotguns spray a wide grouping of shot pellets at the target, they require less experience, training, and accuracy to operate. Shotguns loaded with silver shot shells are what you might call "point and click" anti-werewolf weapons.

The Bermuda Triangle

Some of the older werewolf lore claims that mercury is also lethal to werewolves. However, it is now believed that this idea stemmed from the misconception in past ages that mercury and silver were two forms of the same element. This is why mercury was once called "quicksilver." Therefore, it is unlikely that mercury works against werewolves.

While movies often show silver bullets taking down werewolves with only one hit, most of the available lore does not agree. To kill the creature, you still must destroy or remove one or more vital organs needed to sustain life. A shot to a nonvital spot might slow down a charging lycanthrope, but probably won't kill it. Needless to say, the head and heart would be the primary targets.

Wooden Stakes?

You're probably familiar with the idea that impaling a vampire's heart with a wooden stake will kill it. Some werewolf lore, however, claims this method is also effective against werewolves. While the vampire version usually says any wood (except for evergreen types) can be used, for werewolves, only very specific types of wood will work. Most lore agrees the wood from three tree types—cinder, ash, and (wouldn't you know it?) silver—will work for making anti-werewolf stakes.

While silver weapons only require you to impale any vital organ, a wooden stake will only work if run through the werewolf's heart. To be completely honest, however, wooden stakes would not be a good bet if you plan to survive a fight with a werewolf. To hit your target, the heart, you'd have to get way too close to the werewolf. Doing this will likely get you mauled, killed, or infected with lycanthropy. However, if by some amazing stroke of luck you're able to stake down a werewolf in this way, the same rule about not removing the weapon still applies.

Wolf's Bane: Werewolf Repellent

Wolf's bane is kind of like werewolf repellant. However, you should know that it does not have the power to kill a werewolf (unless, of course, you can somehow manage to get the creature to eat the stuff … good luck with that). This method probably stems from the fact that wolf's bane is lethal to normal wolves if they ingest it (hence the name).

In the event you have to get close to a werewolf, however, wolf's bane might come in handy. So it might be a good idea to take some with you. Wolf's bane can be worn on a necklace to keep a werewolf at a distance. This might help you avoid being bitten long enough to hit the werewolf in a vital organ (or the heart, if you are using a stake).

Another issue with wolf's bane is that not all available lore agrees that it works against werewolves, even as a repellent. Therefore, even if you do bring some along, don't stake your life on its effectiveness. Never forget that most beliefs regarding anti-werewolf weaponry are extremely hypothetical.

Chop Him Up!

Some lore claims a werewolf can be killed in the same ways as any other living thing. However, since they regenerate so quickly, these methods are extremely difficult to use successfully. Some think the silver bullet theory only exists because the hunter who used it was just the first one lucky enough to hit a vital organ. If they're right, this means the entire "silver kills werewolves" theory is based purely on a coincidence.

This "conventional methods" theory suggests that the best way to bring down a werewolf is the same as for any other creature—by destroying or removing the heart or brain. Without one or both of these organs, most lore suggests a werewolf's ability to regenerate will be deactivated.

So, by the rationale that removal of the head or heart will work, the quickest thing to do would be to chop off its head. Even if you appear to have incapacitated a werewolf in any way, most lore says the head and heart should be removed anyway. Some lore claims other forms of dismemberment will work, though some of these sound a little fishy. For example, one proposed method is chopping off a werewolf's genitalia. However, the lore supporting this method offers no alternative method for what to do if the werewolf you're fighting is a female.

The Least You Need to Know

- Some werewolf enthusiasts believe that Lycoan was the original source of lycanthropy.
- There are many types of lycanthropy, the most common being cursed, spirit, enchanted, and viral.
- While conventional pharmaceuticals were ineffective in helping him, some still believe Bill Ramsey simply suffered from clinical lycanthropy.
- The only thing that succeeded in curing Bill Ramsey's lycanthropic behavior was an exorcism.
- Any pure silver weapons will work against werewolves.
- Some lore says wolf's bane works as a kind of werewolf repellent.

Chapter 15

Shapeshifters

In This Chapter

- ◆ The similarities and differences between therianthropy and lycanthropy
- ◆ The powers of the African were-hyenas
- ◆ The Japanese "monster cat" known as the *bakeneko*
- ◆ The mighty were-lions of Africa
- ◆ The Japanese *Tanuki*
- ◆ The nine-tailed fox spirits of Japanese and Korean folklore
- ◆ The *aitvaras*—strange, shapeshifting, fire-tailed roosters

Shapeshifters can prove to be a handful. After all, how does one track something when it can change its own form at will? From humans who become animals to spirits that can assume many forms, these are the shapeshifters of the paranormal world. Some are mischievous but relatively harmless. Others are violent and dangerous and should be avoided. Sometimes the behaviors of shapeshifters are as unpredictable as their appearances. No matter the form in which you find a shapeshifter, you can rest assured that the experience will never be a boring one.

Therianthropy

The ability to shift from human form to animal form, or vice versa, is called *therianthropy*. Whereas a werewolf has lycanthropy, which specifically means the ability to assume both wolf and human forms, *therianthropes* are shapeshifters that turn into any animal (sometimes even having the ability to take on the forms of multiple animals). So basically, all lycanthropes are therianthropes, but not all therianthropes are necessarily lycanthropes.

In addition, therianthropes are shapeshifters that have the specific ability of assuming both human and animal forms. However, not all shapeshifters are necessarily therianthropes. For example, a shapeshifter that is able to assume the appearance of an inanimate object (such as a tea-kettle or stone) would not be considered a therianthrope. Instead, this type of being would be a basic or universal shapeshifter. Throughout this chapter, we discuss a number of legendary shapeshifters. Some of these are therianthropes, while others are simply beings that possess the power to assume a variety of appearances.

> **Conjuring Words**
>
> **Therianthropy** comes from the Greek root words *therion* (wild/undomesticated animal) and *anthropos* (man/human), and refers to the condition of being able to assume the forms of both a human being and one or more animals. The true/original form of **therianthropes**, those who possess the powers of therianthropy, can be that of either a human or an animal.

Bakeneko

The creature known as the *bakeneko*, or "monster cat," comes from Japanese folklore. Unlike many shapeshifters, which originate as humans, the *bakeneko* started out as an everyday, run-of-the-mill house-cat. However, when a housecat is overfed for too long, the owners risk having it turn into a *bakeneko*. First, the cat becomes abnormally large in size. If the owners catch it at this stage, they still have a chance (though usually a slim one) of reversing the process if they restrict the feline's diet.

Symbolically, in Japanese culture cats have been closely associated with death. So it makes sense that nearly all the stories about humans who encounter *bakeneko* don't have happy endings. The *bakeneko* is one of many *bakemono*, or monsters, found in Japanese folklore.

Conjuring Words

The Japanese term **bakemono** refers to spirits or monsters with supernatural (and often frightening) powers. *Bakemono* can turn out to be a blessing or a curse for humans, depending on their natural dispositions, moods, or the condition under which they are encountered. These creatures are nearly all skilled, and often mischievous, deceivers. A good number of them are also known to eat humans.

One of the most popular Japanese *bakeneko* stories is about a poor country fellow named Takasu Genbei. According to the tale, Takasu kept a cat in his home to keep rodents out, a common practice at the time. One day, however, the cat inexplicably went missing. Not long after the cat's mysterious disappearance, Takasu began to notice strange changes in the behavior of his mother (who also lived in his home). She almost never said a word unless she had no other choice, and she refused to have any company, even the oldest of her friends. The most unusual change, however, was that she began to take all of her meals in the privacy of her room and refused to eat any other way.

Takasu became increasingly suspicious of these sudden changes. He decided to spy on her during one of her evening meals, hoping to uncover the cause of her odd behavior. That night, after she had shut herself in her room, Takasu peeked into the room through a small hole in the door. What he saw horrified him. Sitting there was a giant, furry cat, which looked just like his missing housecat, wearing his mother's kimono and gnawing on the carcasses of dead rats.

Takasu now had no doubt that a *bakeneko* had somehow replaced his beloved mother. He ran to his room, drew out the old *katana* he kept there, and rushed into his mother's room. In an attempt to fool him, the *bakeneko* had returned to the form of his mother. Knowing the truth, and with tears in his eyes, Takasu cut down the creature. By the time the sun rose the next morning, the creature had fully returned to the form of a normal housecat.

> **Conjuring Words** _____
>
> A *katana* is a long sword with a curved blade, which was often the secondary weapon of choice (the primary weapon being a spear or halberd) for the samurai warriors of feudal Japan.
>
> *Tatami* are thinly cushioned mats woven from bamboo and used in the floors and certain bedding materials of traditional Japanese homes.

Though the *bakeneko* had been slain, the question still remained of what had become of Takasu's mother. Everyone now realized, with much terror, that she had likely been missing for a rather long time. With a feeling of dread gripping his heart, Takasu pulled back the *tatami* on the floor of his mother's room. The poor man's heart sunk in his chest as, beneath the mats, he discovered the skeletal remains of his beloved mother. The *bakeneko* had killed her and fed upon her flesh, leaving little more behind than a pile of cleanly picked bones. Then it had assumed her appearance and cleverly taken her place. Though Takasu had discovered and slain the evil creature, most people would not call this a happy ending.

Africa's Were-Hyenas

A close relative of the European werewolf, were-hyenas are most commonly found in the regions of Africa. This is not surprising, since hyenas are a part of that continent's vast collection of wildlife. It would appear that this has led were-hyenas to become the signature canine therianthrope of the Africans, their equivalent to the European werewolf. African were-hyenas are usually referred to as *bouda*, a word that has spread into the many dialects and languages of Africa.

> **Conjuring Words** _____
>
> The African term **bouda** (sometimes spelled *buda*) has come to mean "were-hyena" in many of the continent's current languages. However, it likely could have had a different original meaning. In Ethiopia, Christians of that country sometimes use this term to refer to Ethiopian Jews, though in this use it is not always used with the "were-hyena" connotation.

The relationship between werewolves and were-hyenas doesn't end with their canine attributes. They do share other similarities. For example, the two main ways a person is believed to become a were-hyena is either by being bitten (which is the more common) or through powers of magic. Just as wolves run in packs, so do hyenas.

In contrast to the packs of wolves/werewolves, which are led by *alpha* males, hyena packs are matriarchal. Therefore, the alpha members of hyena/were-hyena packs are females. Some believe this matriarchal hierarchy causes hyena packs to have a higher ratio of females to males, though this belief has never been proven. As a result of this belief, some legends assert that were-hyena tribes can be identified because they have far more females than males.

> **Conjuring Words**
>
> In the animal world, **alpha** animals are those in charge of a social group, such as a lion pride or wolf/hyena pack. Sometimes there can be multiple alphas, but most frequently there is only one per social group.

The *Bultingin* of Borno

In the northeastern Borno state in Nigeria, a country on the African continent's western coast, the were-hyena legend is a popular part of the culture. In the dialects of this region, however, were-hyenas are called *bultingin*.

According to the legends of the Borno peoples, two powerful tribes of were-hyenas once existed until some mysterious catastrophe greatly diminished their numbers (or, according to some, completely wiped them out). Some legends say a war between the two tribes caused this, while others state that some kind of curse (from the gods or some dark sorcerer) was responsible.

> **Conjuring Words**
>
> The word *bultungin*, in the dialects of the Nigerian state of Borno, literally means "I become a hyena." In actual use, however, the term more generally refers to any person who shapeshifts into a hyena (meaning it doesn't have the same first-person connotation as it would in English).

The Sudanese Were-Hyena

In folklore from the northwestern African country of Sudan, the were-hyena is often portrayed in a very negative light. The Sudanese were-hyena is said to be a beast that prowls the night, hunting humans as prey. This version of the were-hyena supposedly has a particular taste for the flesh of young lovers, so during its nocturnal outings, it is most happy when it comes upon a pair of lovers and is able to tear them limb from limb.

The Sudanese were-hyenas, in human form, can still be identified by certain specific features. First of all, their skin remains abnormally hairy even when in their human forms. Also, the irises of their eyes are said to have a strange reddish tint (or their eyes are just red in general). Their voice is said to sound unusual, and legends frequently claim they sound nasally. Some descriptions claim they sound like a person with a plugged nose, while others explain they just sound like someone who talks through the nose.

The Ethiopian *Bouda*

Along the lower western border of Sudan is the country of Ethiopia, which has its own beliefs about were-hyenas. According to the Ethiopian lore, all blacksmiths are frequently believed to be were-hyenas. The occupation of blacksmith is almost exclusively a hereditary one in the culture of the Ethiopians.

In earlier times, blacksmiths had a close relationship with the elements of fire and earth/iron. This led people, namely those unfamiliar with the aspects of metalworking, to believe that blacksmiths possessed certain magical powers, most especially powers of healing. (A similar belief, interestingly enough, is also thought to have once existed in Europe.)

Ethiopian blacksmiths were also believed to have shapeshifting abilities, which likely stemmed from the misconception that they had the power to change the shapes of objects. For example, in the eyes of the unknowing, it seemed as if they took a piece of the earth (iron) and, by some mysterious power, turned it into the shape of a tool. Ethiopian blacksmiths have never been treated with disdain as a result of this.

Culturally, however, many Ethiopian folk beliefs say they should be regarded with a certain amount of caution and suspicion (which is likely a part of a larger belief that shapeshifters are always potentially troublesome figures).

A vast majority of those who first brought blacksmithing methods to Ethiopia were ethnically and spiritually Jewish. Today, most Ethiopian blacksmiths traditionally practice the religion of Judaism. Because of this, the term *bouda* has an additional meaning in the dialects of Ethiopian Christians and is sometimes used as an umbrella term for Ethiopian Jews (whether or not they are blacksmiths). But the term is not necessarily negative, because when used in this context, it is rarely meant to carry the connotation of "were-hyena." In actuality, the term (when used in this way) is really meant to imply that all Ethiopian Jews are descended from blacksmiths.

Tanuki

The *Tanuki* is a nature spirit from Japanese mythology. The word *Tanuki* is most commonly translated as meaning something like "raccoon dog." They are usually portrayed as standing upright and having masklike markings on their faces that somewhat resemble those of raccoons (hence the name). *Tanuki*, like many of the nature spirits in Japanese mythology, are tricksters. They love to have a little harmless fun at the expense of others every now and then. Unlike monsters like the *bakeneko*, however, *Tanuki* are usually nice to people (specifically, they certainly would not eat anyone), and in many stories they bring good fortune to those who encounter them as long as those people don't intentionally do anything that would harm them.

Stranger Than Fiction

In the popular Japanese animated series *Naruto*, the character Gaara is possessed by the spirit of a powerful *Tanuki* named Shukaku. The *Tanuki* had been sealed within him when he was only an infant, granting him great power but causing his young mind to be tormented by insomnia and psychotic tendencies.

One popular legend regarding the *Tanuki* tells of a Shinto priest's unusual experience near his mountain temple in Japan. This particular priest was rather fond of practicing *chanoyu*, or tea ceremonies, and his most beloved pastime was repairing and refurbishing old or broken tea-kettles. One day, while visiting a nearby village, he purchased a rusty old teakettle with the shape of a small *Tanuki*. The priest brought the teakettle back to his temple and spent the day scrubbing, shining, and repairing it.

Conjuring Words

The Japanese word *chanoyu* literally translates as meaning "hot water." However, the word eventually came to refer to the ritualistic practice of the special Japanese Tea Ceremony. This is one of the most honored traditions of Japanese culture and is viewed as a pursuit of perfection. When performed for someone else, the *chanoyu* is considered one of the highest gestures of respect and honor displayed in Japanese culture.

The next day, the priest took the refurbished teakettle to a lecture session with his pupils. He prepared the stove and tea leaves, filled the kettle with water, and then set it on a nearby stove to boil. A few moments later, the teakettle began to bounce, shake, and spin around. The kettle then shouted out in pain with the word *Ittai*, which is Japanese for "ouch." Suddenly, to the surprise of everyone in the room, it sprouted arms and legs, rushed off the stove's burner, and returned to its inanimate teakettle form. The priest and pupils all realized that this had been no ordinary teakettle, but a *Tanuki* in disguise.

The priest feared that the teakettle might be possessed or cursed, so he decided to take it far away from the temple grounds. When he reached the road, the priest encountered a traveling tile-maker, who commented on how nice the teakettle was. The priest offered it to him as a gift, conveniently leaving out the detail that the teakettle had only recently sprouted limbs, moved, and talked in front of a group of witnesses. The tile-maker could not have been more grateful and accepted the gift with a very deep bow before parting ways with the priest and taking it to his home.

That evening, when the tile-maker had finished his work, he returned home and placed his new teakettle on the stove to boil water for his tea. Once again, the teakettle began to move and raised a ruckus. The tile-maker was absolutely terrified by this, especially when the kettle spoke to him, saying, "Get me off of this fire, and I will gladly make a deal with you!" The man, not knowing what else to do, did as the teakettle asked. The *Tanuki*, relieved to be clear of the fire, now told the tile-maker he would make him rich just as long as he cared for him kindly—and absolutely, positively never again put him over a fire. The tile-maker agreed to the *Tanuki*'s terms, and this turned out to be the start of a beautiful friendship.

Stranger Than Fiction

Since the 1600s in Japan, tile-makers did not make floor tiles (as one might assume) because floors were covered by tatami. Rather, tile-makers created clay tiles to cover roofs. Before the use of these fireproof tiles, straw or similar materials were used (many of which were flammable), so any structure fire quickly jumped from roof to roof. This resulted in some catastrophic fires in some of feudal Japan's large cities. Roof tiles were a simple solution. Since all clay was not suitable for such use, tile-makers often had to travel around to locate and gather the proper clay for creating roof tiles.

The next day, the tile-maker went into the nearby town to buy supplies and sell his most recent batch of tiles. The *Tanuki* asked to be taken along, so the tile-maker packed him on the cart. When the tile-maker emerged from a shop, the *Tanuki* had disappeared from the cart. A large crowd had formed nearby, so the tile-maker went over and saw the *Tanuki* singing, dancing, and performing acrobatics, much to the crowd's delight. People began throwing coins to the dancing teakettle as reward for his performance, and by the end of the day, the *Tanuki* and the tile-maker had amassed quite a considerable sum.

Every day, for some time, they would travel to nearby towns and the *Tanuki* would perform. In a very short period of time, the tile-maker became very wealthy. He used his money to care for the *Tanuki*, as he'd promised, buying the creature its favorite food—sweet rice cakes. The tile-maker, however, was a good man and knew that to keep using the *Tanuki* would be a greedy thing to do, so he asked his little friend if he would like to go back to the temple priest who'd given him up as a gift. The *Tanuki* said that he certainly would like to return to the temple, as he much preferred to live in such a beautiful and holy place. However, the priest would have to agree to certain conditions.

In line with his little friend's wishes, the tile-maker gladly brought the *Tanuki* back to the Shinto temple. He explained to the priest that the *Tanuki* was not an evil spirit that wanted to harm people, but an enchanted and benevolent creature. The man told of his experiences with the creature and how it had so generously improved his life. He then set down the conditions for the *Tanuki*'s stay as told to him by the creature.

First and foremost, the *Tanuki* never wanted to be put on a stove or over a fire ever again. Next, it was always to be treated with respect and kindness. Last but not least, the *Tanuki* wanted a plate of his favorite sweetened rice cakes every day. The priest felt bad for how he had first treated the *Tanuki* and now graciously welcomed it into his temple. The *Tanuki* resumed his inanimate form as a teakettle, and the priest gave him a special place on a table (well away from the stove, of course). The *Tanuki* teakettle remains on the table to this very day, always next to a fresh stack of sweetened rice cakes.

Were-Lions of Africa

Stories about were-lions are found somewhat universally across the continent of Africa. Considering the lion is viewed as the most powerful predator in Africa, it isn't shocking that the concept of were-lions arose. Similar to the negative European view of the werewolf, the African were-lion is primarily perceived as an evil being. Usually, African were-lions are said to be dark sorcerers who assume the forms of lions so they can commit atrocious crimes against others … like eating them alive. Were-lions were also involved in at least one recent event in the modern history of Africa.

During the early twentieth century, in the western coastal African country of Tanzania, a mystical lion-rite cult rose to power by use of violence and the cultural fear surrounding the legends of the were-lions. The cult purchased mentally disabled children from the surrounding areas and held them in total isolation until adulthood. As a result of this isolated upbringing, these children grew up to display violently savage and sociopathic behaviors.

Once these children reached the proper age, they were dressed in lion skins from head-to-toe so as to give them the frightening appearances of were-lions. They soon came to be known all over Tanzania as "The Lion Men" and were regarded with fear by the warriors of nearly every tribe. The priests of the cult sold these adult Lion Men to local tribal leaders as war-slaves or assassins. They were often seen as valuable assets, especially in matters of assassinations. The savage nature of their killings (commonly done only with their filed teeth, sharpened nails, and bare hands) often caused the deaths of their victims to be dismissed as attacks by lions or other wild beasts.

The Bermuda Triangle

Some people attempt to draw parallels between the Lion Men of Tanzania and the wolf-skin wearing *ulfheðnar* warriors (the wolf equivalents of the famous *berserkers,* who wore bear skins). While both were formidable fighters and both wore animal skins, this is where the similarities between them end. The *ulfheðnar* were neither mentally disabled nor slaves, as were the Lion Men of Tanzania, but voluntary warriors who used the widespread fear of their wolf rites to gain fame and fortune for themselves on the battlefield. The Lion Men, sadly, were the involuntary victims of a cruel and greedy religious cult.

These Lion Men of Tanzania first came to the attention of the Western world in the early 1920s, when the country was still a British colony. The British colonial authorities had started to receive shocking reports that claimed that hundreds of people in the Tanzanian region of Singida appeared to have been killed in attacks by lions. However, lions were only suspected in the preliminary examinations of the corpses of these victims. Later, when more detailed autopsies were performed, it was deemed highly unlikely (much to the shock of colonial authorities, no doubt) that the bites and scratches on the corpses were from lions. No, the autopsies claimed it was far more likely that these bites had come from humans!

As the British colonial authorities pursued their investigation into these strange killings, they began to hear unbelievable stories about Lion Men.

They eventually found out that a powerful lion cult, which had long earned a hefty revenue by selling out the Lion Men as mercenaries, had begun to use them instead to extort the surrounding tribal villages— many of which could no longer afford to pay, especially in Singida. When many of the Singida villages had stopped making extortion payments, the cult had unleashed the Lion Men upon them. Hundreds of men, women, and children met violent ends at the hands of these mad warriors. Colonial authorities soon stepped in and brought an end to the atrocious acts of the Tanzanian lion cult.

Kitsune

The Japanese word *kitsune* has a double meaning, depending on the context of its use. First, it can refer to just a normal, completely unremarkable, plain old fox. In the context of Shinto myths, however, *kitsune* refers to a race of fox spirits/demons. These "demon fox" *kitsune* are said to be messengers for the Rice *Kami* Inari and have a number of supernatural abilities, not the least of which is the power of shapeshifting. A *kitsune* can use this shapeshifting ability to temporarily assume human form.

The Bermuda Triangle

While many sources often refer to *kitsune* as "demon foxes" or "monster foxes," such translations are not entirely accurate. Monsters or purely demonic beings are called *bakemono* in Japanese, and *kitsune* are not in this category. Usually, the best way for Westerners to think of *kitsune* is as a kind of demon-angel hybrid. *Kitsune* (and many other Japanese nature spirits) are viewed as having potential for being both good and evil (much like humans do). This means they can be beneficial or destructive in their dealings with humans.

Foxes often resided near human settlements in feudal Japan (and still do in more rural areas), attracted to such places by the presence of domesticated pheasants and the scent of discarded food waste. As a result, they were a frequent sight for the Japanese people. Since foxes are very apt at hiding, they often seemed to appear one moment and disappear the next, which likely led to at least some of the stories about the *kitsune*.

Kitsune have a special love for playing tricks on humans. However, they usually are not cruel in doing so. They are, by nature, playful beings. They like to make a little chaos but often only do so to teach people a lesson when they need it. *Kitsune* are often portrayed as spirit allies for humans. When treated with disrespect, however, this relationship can (and often will) easily go south.

Kitsune are often portrayed as being powerful, wise, clever, and stubborn. The number of tails a *kitsune* possesses (anywhere from one to nine) can be used to measure its power. Basically, the more tails a *kitsune* has, the wiser, older, and stronger it is. So if you were ever to encounter a *kitsune* that had nine tails, you'd be smart to give it a wide berth.

A nine-tailed *kitsune*, or *kyuubi* in Japanese, must be handled with extreme care because it can cause extreme destruction. A *kyuubi* can grow to the size of a mountain and, if provoked, can easily lay waste to an entire village without much effort. No matter how many tails they have, many Shinto myths warn people to always treat foxes with kindness and respect. Otherwise, one runs the risk of unintentionally offending a *kitsune* ... which is, in a word, *bad*. If there was ever a definitive list of things a person should *not* do, angering a *kitsune* would most definitely be found somewhere near the top, as a properly ticked-off *kitsune* (especially a *kyuubi*) can do some *serious* damage.

Stranger Than Fiction

In the popular Japanese anime (animated) series *Naruto*, the vengeful spirit of an angry nine-tailed *kitsune* is sealed within the body of the main character (Naruto) when he is only a baby. Because of the *kitsune* inside of him, the young ninja is treated with disdain by his fellow villagers. However, the stubborn young man struggles valiantly to prove himself as a strong ninja and for a time even succeeds in controlling the great power of the *kyuubi* by entering into an uneasy, symbiotic relationship in which the *kitsune* loans his *chakra* (energy) to Naruto in an attempt to eventually convince the boy to release him from his seal. But Naruto eventually comes to understand the danger of the *kyuubi* and learns to resist its attempts at temptation.

One popular story tells of one foolish samurai's encounter with a *kitsune*. One evening, the samurai warrior was riding his horse, returning from a visit to his *daimyo*'s (feudal lord) estate. While still a fair distance from home, he spied a fox stepping out onto the road. For sport, he drew out his bow and nocked a special flash-bang arrow (which had a tip loaded with gunpowder and a simple flint mechanism) to the bowstring, usually meant to frighten off wild dogs.

When he let the arrow fly, it struck the fox in the back of one leg. As the samurai began to nock a second arrow, this time a normal one (designed to kill), the fox disappeared into the shelter of a nearby bush. The warrior dismounted his horse and crept up to the bush with his bow drawn, planning to kill the fox. However, as soon as the fox came into view, it suddenly faded away and was gone. Somewhat unsettled, the samurai decided to retrieve his first arrow and continue on his way. As he picked it up, the fox suddenly reappeared before him. The samurai again attempted to draw his bow and kill the fox, and once again it vanished into thin air.

Now sufficiently spooked and wanting to get home before nightfall, the samurai got back on his horse and rode on. When he was less than a mile from his destination, the fox once again emerged onto the road, well ahead of the samurai. Much to the samurai's bewilderment, the fox had a lit torch in its jaws. Suddenly, the fox took off down the road in the direction of the samurai's home. In a panic, he spurred his horse to a full gallop.

When his home came into sight, the samurai could see the fox sitting calmly beside the front door with the torch still in its mouth. While the samurai was still well out of reach, the fox suddenly transformed into a human being right before his eyes. The samurai now realized, though far too late, that this fox was in fact a *kitsune*. This realization sent terror through the warrior's heart, even more so as he helplessly watched the transformed *kitsune* toss the lit torch onto the roof of the house.

As flames quickly engulfed the entire roof and poured into his home, the samurai finally found himself with the *kitsune* in range. He pulled out his bow once again but, before he could even nock an arrow, the *kitsune* returned to its fox form and vanished into the woods. The samurai now came to the horrifying realization that he had wasted precious seconds with his final attempt to kill the *kitsune*, and by now the heat had grown too intense for him to enter the house to salvage what he could. To make matters worse, he was much too far out to call for any kind of assistance. All he could do was stand and watch as the fire burned itself out. The home of this foolhardy samurai, as well as his worldly possessions within, were reduced to nothing but a pile of ashes.

Liver Hunter (Kumiho of Korea)

Many consider the kumiho, which literally translates as "nine-tailed fox," to be the Korean equivalent of the Japanese *kitsune/kyuubi*. Which culture first developed the concept cannot be confirmed, however, though both Koreans and Japanese authorities on the subject claim the original as their own.

According to the lore surrounding the kumiho, they begin their lives as regular foxes. Once they reach 1,000 years of age, however, these foxes transform into magical creatures, kumiho. They begin to quickly grow additional tails as the weeks pass until they eventually have a total of nine. Like the Japanese *kitsune*, the kumiho are talented shapeshifters. However, shapeshifting is usually shown to be the kumiho's primary skill, though not its only one.

In many of the stories about human-kumiho encounters, these magical foxes seem fond of assuming the forms of beautiful young women and then using these forms to seduce unsuspecting men. In contrast, at least one Korean folktale tells about a kumiho who assumed the form of a handsome young man and attempted to convince a beautiful maiden to marry him (it?). Kumiho are said to prefer to assume these seductive human forms during the nighttime hours, because (even though they look like beautiful girls/handsome men at first glance) their human forms are not completely perfect and they retain certain foxlike attributes and behaviors. They also seem to have trouble controlling their shapeshifting abilities, which can sometimes cause their disguises to become compromised. The cover provided by darkness, however, probably makes these fox elements and disguise flaws a bit less obvious. Interestingly, there is at least one frequently seen element of kumiho stories that is somewhat similar to certain tales about the Japanese *bakeneko*—they sometimes assume the appearances of certain people and attempt to take their places.

One popular Korean folktale tells about a certain kumiho that kidnapped a young bride, assumed her appearance, and then took her place at a wedding ceremony. Throughout the wedding, no one suspected a thing. The story claims that even the young bride's own mother was deceived by the kumiho's disguise. Later, when the bound (human) bride was found, no one could figure out which one was the real/human girl. The bride's parents even took a crack at it but were unable to say for certain which one was their true daughter.

In the end, the groom devised a way to find out which one was his true bride. Since the wedding had already been performed, he decided to take both brides (the kumiho and the girl) into the wedding chamber to disrobe them. As stated before, a kumiho's human appearance usually isn't perfect. When the groom disrobed his true bride, he saw she had the body of a normal female. When he pulled open the garments of the kumiho, however, he discovered its body was covered in gray and red fur. The kumiho was dealt with (this is an oral folktale, so some versions say the groom cut it down with his sword while others claim it ran off or disappeared once its deception failed), and everyone present greatly rejoiced that the bride had been discovered safe and sound.

A Rooster for a Soul (Lithuania)

In the folklore of the Lithuanians, there are special household spirits called *aitvarases*. These beings, depending on one's circumstances, can turn out to be either a blessing or a curse. According to the lore, any rooster more than seven years old can lay an *aitvaras* egg. Yes, you read that right—a rooster, as in the male equivalent of a chicken, which isn't supposed to be able to lay eggs.

Conjuring Words

In truth, no one has any idea where the word *aitvaras* originally came from. Not so much as a single record has ever been found to explain the roots of this word. Additionally, even the literal definition of the word is totally unknown, other than as a label for the creature in Lithuanian folklore.

Then again, maybe you don't feel like waiting around for seven or more years in the obscure hope that your rooster will grow up and turn out to be the *aitvaras*-egg-laying type; you have another option. However, this alternate method is kind of a good news/bad news situation. The good news is, you can just buy one. The bad news is that the only person who supposedly sells them is the devil … and the going price for an *aitvaras* is your immortal soul. So you may not want to go this route either.

While *aitvarases* can certainly be called shapeshifters, they don't exactly fall into the category of therianthropes because they never assume human form. An *aitvaras* begins its life as a white- or black-feathered rooster. This wouldn't seem all that unusual, if not for the appearance of its tail. The *aitvaras's* tail, according to some stories, is simply the color of fire. Other stories describe it as, quite literally, a tail of fire.

Once an *aitvaras* has hatched, if not already in one, it will immediately make its home in the nearest human abode (whether or not the inhabitants want it to). If you want an *aitvaras* to leave, you are plain out of luck. Once it has chosen a home, it never leaves, and the outcome is usually bad for those brave or foolish enough to try to make it leave. Once it leaves the interior of its chosen home, it immediately transforms into a dragon.

If you do manage to get your hands on an *aitvaras*, take extra special care of it because, depending on how an *aitvaras* is treated, it can bring either blessings or misfortunes to a household. An *aitvaras* that is even mildly mistreated is capable of doing a rather significant amount of damage. Even if you do treat it well, however, even a well-intentioned *aitvaras* can cause you some problems (mainly because you have no control over what it does).

Aitvarases are thieves by nature and often take nocturnal excursions in their dragon forms and steal things from neighboring houses. They will then bring these stolen wares (grain, milk, corn, livestock, jewelry, and even gold or coins) back to their household. The owners of the creature, unfortunately, often find themselves being mistakenly accused of stealing when it was the *aitvaras*. And they usually find it difficult to convince anyone of the truth. After all, you can imagine that people might find it hard to believe someone who says, "Well, you see, I have this fire-tailed rooster that hatched from an egg that one of my normal roosters laid a while back and it turns into a dragon at night and steals from everybody—and no one ever sees it." So why don't the neighbors see the dragon? Well, the legends don't really say. Perhaps it is just assumed they can become invisible by some magical means.

As already stated, someone troubled by an *aitvaras* is going to have one heck of a time getting the thing to leave because, according to the lore, the only way to rid a household of an *aitvaras* is to kill it. But this must be done when it's inside the house and in rooster form. It would seem this is the only time in which an *aitvaras* is vulnerable, and the lore explains that the creature has no magical powers of protection when it is in rooster form. So unless you just have some strange, overwhelming desire to slay a dragon (though you are more likely to be the slain one in that scenario), this "rooster-killing" method would probably be the best (and safest) way to go about getting rid of the creature.

According to one Lithuanian story, a young bride went into the barn of her mistress every morning to hand-grind her grain. Every night, she would leave behind the empty grain bucket, and every single morning, she'd return to the barn to find it (quite unexplainably) full of grain again. One night, she decided to spy on the barn to see if she could solve the mystery of the grain bucket's miraculous nature. She was shocked to see a black rooster with a fiery tail, standing beside a candle and coughing/vomiting (versions vary) up grains into the empty bucket. Certain that such a creature must be an abomination of the devil, she took up a knife that hung from the barn wall and stabbed it to death.

The young bride then ran to the nearby abode of her mistress and told her what she'd seen and done. The elderly mistress immediately went into a sobbing fit. As it turned out, the black rooster had been the household *aitvaras*. In addition, it was the source of her wealth and her only remaining source of revenue. Left without it, she now had no way to support herself in her old age. Strangely enough, the story sort of cuts off at this point. The ultimate fates of the young bride as well as her elderly mistress are never explained.

The Least You Need to Know

◆ While lycanthropy is certainly one form of therianthropy, it is not the only one.

◆ By overfeeding a cat for too long, one runs the risk of creating a human-eating *bakeneko*.

◆ *Tanuki* and *kitsune* are usually kind to humans, not counting humans who are mean or disrespectful to them.

◆ Unlike the similar Japanese *kitsune*, the Korean kumiho fox is usually portrayed as troublesome by nature.

◆ Were-lions exist in many African legends, but one cult's misrepresentation used this legend to violently extort many Tanzanians.

◆ An *aitvaras* usually turns out to be more trouble than it is worth, especially when you consider the price.

Part 4

Unexplained Phenomena

Science has a hard time explaining many things in this world. For example, why have a multitude of people, aircraft, and sea vessels gone missing in the infamous Bermuda Triangle? Science cannot definitively explain the causes behind true clairvoyance or other psychic phenomena and even refuses to acknowledge the validity of Spontaneous Combustion, despite contrary evidence. Perhaps one day you will be the one who succeeds where so many scientists and skeptics have failed. You could be the one who finally uncovers the hidden truths behind these unsolved mysteries.

Chapter 16

Psychic Phenomena

In This Chapter

- ◆ The various forms of psychic phenomena and abilities
- ◆ Recent discoveries regarding the validity of the mind-body connection
- ◆ Experiments on the phenomenon of Extrasensory Perception (ESP)
- ◆ The difference between precognition and retrocognition
- ◆ A possible explanation for déjà vu
- ◆ A look at telepathy and telekinesis

The word *psychic* literally means "of the mind." Today, saying a person is psychic often conjures up the connotation of mind readers and fortune tellers. However, this is not what the term actually means. Psychic phenomena or abilities refer to those related to or believed to be caused by the unexplained, unidentified, or unknown functions of the human mind. These psychic phenomena can often vary greatly in both form and type. Some psychic phenomena occur regularly in certain people and follow them throughout much of their lives. In other cases, psychic phenomena are isolated incidents that only occur once or twice in a person's life. What follows is a sampling of the most impressive, common, or well-known types of psychic phenomena.

Mind-Body Connection

For many years, science scoffed at the idea that the human mind was anything more than the awareness and perception of the brain. In recent decades, however, even the scientific community (especially in the medical fields) has come to realize that this may not be the case. Evidence is mounting to prove that the brain, which is a part of the body, is ruled by a more inclusive consciousness called the mind. We can no longer deny the connection between the mind and brain/body.

> **Conjuring Words**
>
> The word *psychosomatic* comes from the Greek words *psycho*, meaning "spirit" or "mind," and *somatic*, meaning "the body" or "cells." It basically refers to the mind's ability to affect physiological changes over the body. Most commonly, it is used to refer to people who develop physical illnesses due to psychological reasons.

For years, the scientific and medical communities have accepted the idea of *psychosomatic* influence, which means that a person can affect physiological changes in the body by way of their thoughts, feelings, or emotions. This makes it difficult to understand why they are so reluctant to accept that such a mind-body connection exists.

That Really Burns Her Up!

Consider the story of a woman who began experiencing episodes of what she at first thought to be "hot flashes," caused by the onset of menopause. She wasn't quite middle-aged yet, so she consulted her ob-gyn physician to make sure. He informed her she was not in menopause and referred her to another physician for testing.

After consulting several other physicians, no physical cause for her strange episodes could be found. Several times a day, she would experience episodes during which her skin would go red, becoming hot to the touch, and sweat would pour by the bucket-load. One doctor finally suggested that she seek psychiatric treatment, suspecting that her experiences might have some sort of mental cause. When the woman went to see a psychiatric therapist, the doctor asked her to talk about any stresses she was experiencing in her life.

As the woman told him about the things that were frustrating her, the psychologist noticed she would often use phrases like, "It really *burns me up* when my husband contradicts me," or "My morning commute is so stressful, and I get *burned up* at how terribly some people drive." The psychologist also noticed that she began to sweat and turn a shade of red, as if she was feeling overheated. At that point (probably wanting to avoid worsening her episode), the psychotherapist stopped the woman from speaking and replayed the recording of what she had said. He now pointed out how frequently she had used these "burn phrases," and suggested that she do her best to stop saying "burned up" when referring to sources of stress or frustration. The woman tried this, and her symptoms ceased. She was never bothered by these "burning" episodes again, which showed that her condition was psychosomatic. She was actually making her body temperature reach fever levels by her frequent claims that things were "burning her up."

Psychosomatic influence is not the only aspect of the mind-body connection. For example, recent experiments have uncovered the fact that memories exist in the form of molecules. Such "memory molecules" are believed to be passed down through generations, likely in the form of DNA, supporting a concept that was once dismissed by scientists—that the human race possesses a "collective memory." And it would also seem that this sort of collective memory is not restricted to humans.

The Planarian Experiment

In 1962, biologist and animal psychiatrist James McConnell conducted an unusual experiment on a group of Planarian flatworms. He had tried a similar experiment in 1955 but now took things a step further. He would first flash a bright light and then deliver a small electric shock to the group of flatworms. He repeated the process over time until the flatworms had developed a learned response, coiling up in anticipation of a shock every time they were flashed with the light. He then ground up the conditioned worms and fed them to an entirely new and unconditioned group of flatworms.

Once the ground-up worms had been entirely consumed and digested, McConnell flashed a light at the new, unconditioned group. What happened was astounding. They *coiled up* in anticipation of a shock, but he did not shock them. He repeated this several times, with the new group giving the conditioned response of the worms they had eaten. By consuming the conditioned worms, this new group appeared to have assimilated their memories. Weird? Yes. Gross? Most certainly. True? Absolutely.

The Human Trinity

The mind-body connection is also directly related to a third component: the spirit. No one really understands why this is true, and much of the scientific community still denies the existence of a human soul or spirit. Among members of the medical community, however, the mind-body-spirit connection continues to gain increased acceptance with every passing year.

For years, the Joint Council for Accreditation of Healthcare Services has stressed the importance of assessing a patient's "spiritual health." At minimum, health-care professionals are encouraged to be aware of the religious beliefs of their patients.

The Bermuda Triangle

Many scientists and medical professionals view spiritual health as just a type of psychosomatic influence. They view practices of prayer and spirituality as simply a coping mechanism suffering or dying patients use. In truth, when it comes to this debate on spirituality and health, it's hard to prove either side of the argument.

Extrasensory Perception

Extrasensory Perception (ESP), often referred to as "The Sixth Sense," is somewhat of an umbrella term for psychic phenomena or abilities that allow people to gain knowledge they did not experience through the five basic senses of the human body—sight, hearing, touch, taste, and smell. The term "Extrasensory Perception" was first coined in 1870 by the famous explorer and prolific writer Sir Richard Burton.

Before the use of the ESP label became common, nineteenth-century parapsychologists referred to such phenomena as either *cryptesthesia* or *relesthesia*. At that time, these referred to situations where individuals would enter trancelike states and seem to gain extrasensory knowledge.

Conjuring Words

The word *cryptesthesia* was originally used to refer to ESP and means "hidden feeling/sensation."

The word *relesthesia* was also used to refer to the phenomena of ESP and telepathy and basically means "feeling/sensing the distance."

1882: The First Formal ESP Study

The first formal study of Extrasensory Perception was conducted in 1882 by members of the newly formed British Society for Psychical Research (BSPR). The president of the BSPR published an announcement in the organization's newsletter *Journal* that members had discovered five daughters of a clergyman who had proven they had powers of ESP.

Stranger Than Fiction

Sir Richard Burton is most well known as the first white man to set eyes on the source of the Nile River. He was a bold explorer and adventurer and once successfully entered the Islamic holy city of Mecca (entry into which was then forbidden for Christians) disguised as an Arab Muslim.

A number of independent investigators, including skeptics not affiliated with the BSPR, conducted their own investigations and interviews of the five girls. They, too, were convinced by what they saw. For example, one daughter would hold a card or drawing while sitting across the room from one or more of her sisters. Soon after, the other girls would be able to say what was on the concealed card. Unfortunately for these investigators, things are not always what they seem, especially when dealing with the paranormal.

Six years after the initial investigations, the entire thing turned out to be a hoax orchestrated by the five girls. The girls had previously developed a subtle yet complicated series of body signals, which they used to silently communicate information to one another. To the unknowing or naïve observer, it appeared as though they were exhibiting ESP. However, all they were really doing was communicating through their own form of sign language.

The 1930 Rhine Experiments

In 1930, American parapsychologist J. B. Rhine conducted a series of ESP experiments at Duke University. These experiments employed a method called "card guessing," in which an administrator placed a stack of concealed cards in front of a test subject who then attempted to guess the order of the cards. Rhine used a deck of 25 total cards, containing 5 cards of five different designs. The stack of cards were always arranged randomly (shuffled) ahead of time. This meant that for each card the test subject had a one in five chance of guessing correctly. This "chance factor" was then calculated into the total results.

While many of the test subjects guessed well within the range of chance, some exceeded it. Among those test subjects who exceeded the range of chance, a certain number were able to do so consistently. These subjects were referred to as producing "extra-chance" results and were repeatedly retested. The odds of chance guessing one card right may only be five to one, but the odds of guessing outside the range of chance for the whole deck was one in a thousand. The odds of success-fully doing this multiple times are closer to one in a million. Despite these astounding odds, a number of people defied them over and over. Rhine published his findings as proof that all people are at least capable of ESP, but that only certain individuals are sensitive enough to consistently employ it. He referred to this as General Extrasensory Perception (GESP).

One interesting result of Rhine's experiment is referred to as the "unconscious factor" or "reverse ESP." When test subjects reported they had consciously tried to score high, they would almost always score far lower than average. Sometimes they would even score so low that they defied the odds of guessing right by accident. This led Rhine to the conclusion that ESP ability is not something that can be forced through the person's conscious will. He claimed that it must be an unconscious but naturally occurring psychic ability.

Stranger Than Fiction _____

Rhine's experiment has not been without critics. In fact, many prominent mathematicians tried to claim that the math Rhine used in his
work was irredeemably flawed. However, these criticisms were permanently silenced when the current President of the American Mathematical
Institute personally examined and endorsed Rhine's mathematical methodology and results.

Precognition and Clairvoyance

Precognition, also called clairvoyance, is the ability to gain knowledge
of events or facts that have not yet occurred. Basically, it means the
ability to see or sense what is going to happen in the future. While
there are many "precognition sensitive" people, it is extremely rare to
find any who have conscious control over their abilities.

Most precognition occurs in visions, images, or flashes, which must
be interpreted before any definite meaning can be ascertained. For
example, someone with precognition might initially see a flash of a ladder falling over in a hallway but not understand what the vision means.
Later in the day, she might be walking down a hallway when a mainte-
nance worker tips over his ladder. Though the person received a vision
flash, she was initially unable to figure out what it meant.

Retrocognition

Retrocognition, or "knowing the facts or events after they occur," can
best be explained as something like the opposite of precognition. At
first, the idea of someone knowing about something that has already
happened doesn't sound all that impressive. After all, couldn't you do
that simply by opening a history book? Well, not exactly.

Retrocognition is the ability to gain knowledge of facts or events that
have happened but which you could not possibly have learned through
normal sensory experiences (such as reading a book or being present at
the time they occurred). Sometimes, a person will just spontaneously
and inexplicably know about something which they should not. In other
cases, however, retrocognition occurs in the form of direct visions.

Conjuring Words

The concept of **reincarnation** exists in many spiritual traditions of the world and basically refers to the belief that the human soul returns after death in a new physical form.

The first form of spontaneous retrocognition is referred to by some as "past life recall," which is based on the concept of *reincarnation*. Those who accept this theory believe that retrocognition is actually a sudden recall of memories from experiences that took place during one's previous lives. One of the most commonly cited types of this form of retrocognition comes from cases of children who suddenly claim to be a person who has long been deceased. There have been a handful of such cases, many of which remain unexplained or have been dismissed as fraudulent. In some cases, the child will seek out family members of the person they claim to be or spontaneously begin speaking the foreign language of that person.

Retrocognition visions, the second form of this phenomenon, are the most common. In cases such as these, individuals usually see the events of the past (often in the exact spot where they actually occurred) as if they are happening right in front of them.

One example of visionary retrocognition would be someone visiting an old battlefield and actually seeing the battle as if it were taking place in the present. Confirming the validity of such claims often requires a lot of research, since one must confirm the smallest details of the vision (for example, things that might not be commonly found in history texts).

The Bermuda Triangle

Some paranormal researchers believe that many reports of paranormal activity on past battlefields are actually occurrences of retrocognition. Whereas a haunted battlefield would suggest that ghosts inhabit the area, retrocognition would not. For now, neither explanation can be conclusively proven.

Déjà Vu

Déjà vu is a French term that literally means "already seen." In Greek it's called *paramnesia*, meaning "near to memory." Basically, déjà vu is an episode where one feels as if one is experiencing the exact same event or moment for the second time. However, it must be the first occurrence since no one can experience the exact same moment or event twice (it's a statistical impossibility).

One scientific/neurological theory suggests that the feeling of déjà vu may be caused by a malfunction in how the human brain stores memories in chronological order. For example, as soon as a present moment passes, your brain almost immediately tells you that this recent moment happened in the immediate past. According to this theory, déjà vu occurs when your brain prematurely misfires this past signal, activating a sensation of the past as the moment is still occurring. This malfunction causes the individual to mistakenly feel as if a presently experienced moment has occurred in the past.

Telepathy

Telepathy is basically mind-to-mind, nonverbal, nongesture communication. The term comes from the combination of the Greek *tele*, "across a distance," and *pathe*, "event" or "feeling of a moment." Frederic Myers, a French parapsychologist and co-founder of the Society for Psychical Research (SPR), first coined the term in 1882.

Unfortunately, experimentation with telepathic abilities has produced a lot of rather inconsistent findings. In truth, telepathy is difficult to document or record since it only occurs in the minds of those who possess it. It appears that very few telepaths are able to communicate with the mind of anyone. Most can only achieve mind-to-mind communication with other telepaths. The most common form of telepathy is not back-and-forth communication but the ability to hear or sense the thoughts of others. The rarest form of telepathy is the ability to transmit one's thoughts into the minds of others. In truth, most data suggests that the large majority of telepaths have a difficult enough time trying to communicate this way with other telepaths, let alone with people who have no such psychic abilities.

Telekinesis

The word telekinesis comes from a combination of the Greek *tele*, meaning "across a distance," and *kinesis*, meaning "energy in motion" or "movement." Basically, telekinesis is the ability to move or manipulate objects using only one's mind. While skeptics abound, there has been at least one unexplainable case of telekinetic ability in modern times.

In 1970, a woman named Felicia Parise claimed to have the telekinetic ability to move small objects without touching them. She demonstrated her abilities in front of believers and skeptics alike and even agreed to demonstrate her telekinesis in front of a committee of scientists who were openly seeking to disprove her abilities. Despite their best efforts, they were unable to find a normal cause for how Parise appeared to move the objects, nor could they successfully disprove she was telekinetic. All who investigated her abilities noted that she seemed to experience an extreme amount of physical distress in order to move even the smallest objects (a pillbox, for example). After giving multiple demonstrations for skeptics who still refused to accept the validity of her abilities, Felicia finally chose to give it up, claiming that moving the objects through telekinesis was taking too heavy a toll on her physical health.

Stranger Than Fiction

For quite some time, a number of skeptic groups have come forward with offers of hefty monetary rewards for anyone who can concretely prove the existence of psychic phenomena such as telekinesis. To this day, no one has succeeded in being convincing enough to receive these rewards.

The Least You Need to Know

- Psychic phenomena are those that are related to the functions of the human mind.

- Despite the Planarian experiment, many scientists refute that a "collective memory" is feasible.

- Extrasensory Perception (ESP), "The Sixth Sense," refers to any psychic ability that allows a person to gain knowledge without use of the five senses.

◆ Some believe visionary retrocognition is responsible for many supposed ghost sightings.

◆ Some now theorize that déjà vu is not paranormal but just a malfunction of the human brain.

◆ Telepathy is the ability to sense, receive, or transmit information from one mind to another, and telekinesis is the ability to move objects with one's mind.

Chapter 17

Spirited Away

In This Chapter

◆ Unexplained disappearances all over the world

◆ The strange series of disappearances that have plagued the Bennington, Bermuda, and Dragon's Triangles

◆ The odd true story about the vanishing of the crippled and elderly Owen Parfitt

◆ Aviators who seem to have been lost to the skies, such as Amelia Earhart

◆ The mysteries surrounding the lost colonists of Roanoke

◆ The 1971 "Stonehenge Incident"

Many ancient civilizations once believed that whenever people unexplainably or suddenly disappeared, they had been snatched away by spirits, which explains the saying that a missing or abducted person has been "spirited away." However, can people truly just vanish into thin air? Or is there something else going on? After all, it would stand to reason that these people must have gone somewhere. Were they victims of foul play? Are they dead and rotting in some unreachable location that might never be found by the living? Or have these people actually been spirited away to another realm or alternate dimension? No one can answer any of these questions with certainty. Therefore, you'll have to decide what you are willing to believe.

Unexplained Disappearances

Unexplained disappearances have occurred in the human world for unknown ages. Even in the ancient past, people who disappeared without a trace were thought to have been "spirited away" by supernatural forces. Of course, in those times people were largely restricted to a few primitive forms of direct person-to-person communication. There were no telephones or computer networks or even a public postal system. When such events as tribal warfare, raids, slavery, or natural catastrophes forcibly or unexpectedly separated ancient families and social groups, it was very difficult (if not impossible) for them to reunite. Also, when ancient people left an area without giving any notice (or leaving behind any explanatory evidence), they had almost no resources by which they could send word of their new locations. Therefore, it's not surprising that such occurrences could explain away a great many of these ancient beliefs in spirit abductions. But it can't explain all of them, and the same remains true in our own, far more technologically advanced, modern world.

Today, the statistics of human disappearances are absolutely astounding. Each and every year, an average of 500,000 adults disappear—most of them never to be seen or heard from again. For children, the numbers are even grimmer as far more children go missing every year, at varying annual rates. UNICEF reports that, even today, an average of 1.2 million children are abducted each year and sold into slavery by human traffickers. Even these staggering numbers do not account for the countless mysterious child disappearances that remain unsolved. However, it is always important to consider rational explanations first before labeling an unsolved disappearance as having paranormal causes.

The Bennington Triangle

The Bennington Triangle that encompasses Glastenbury Mountain in Vermont is one of the only land-based "mystery triangles" in the world. While the area has a long and strange history of unusual occurrences and paranormal activity, it was not always specifically referred to as the Bennington Triangle. In fact, it was not known as such until 1992, when an author named Joseph Citro referred to it in this way during a radio interview. Many paranormal researchers believe this area has long been home to some kind of portal that "leaks" supernatural forces or paranormal entities into our world.

Early European settlers claimed the local Native American tribes informed them that the land was cursed. In fact, the tribes of the area altogether avoided the mountain and surrounding land and only ventured there to (very quickly) bury their dead. One group of settlers even claimed that a very large and hairy creature, similar to descriptions of a sasquatch (for more info, see Chapter 10), attacked and overturned their stagecoach as they traveled along the rural road known as Route 9.

The original settlers who founded the town of Glastenbury, Vermont, did not meet favorable ends. For a time, the town did well and was the very epitome of prosperity. By 1937, however, it had been completely abandoned due to disease, natural catastrophe, and the resulting deaths. Some theorize that the lingering spirits of these original settlers are responsible for the paranormal activity that plagues the region. Others believe that evil spirits, angered by the trespassing settlers, were responsible for both the fate of the town and the later paranormal phenomena.

On November 12, 1975, an extremely experienced hunting and fishing guide named Middie Rivers was leading a group of hunters through the woods of Glastenbury Mountain. All reports maintain that Rivers was skilled and, despite his advanced age (he was 74 years old at the time), more than capable of navigating without a map and living off the land. In other words, if anyone could've survived long enough to find his way out of the woods, it would've been Middie Rivers. However, when the guide went ahead of the hunting party to scout the terrain as they were returning to camp, he vanished and was never seen or heard from again.

During the extensive search and rescue operation that followed his disappearance, the only trace of Middie Rivers that was found was a single rifle round lying at the edge of a nearby river. Authorities speculated that Rivers had knelt there at some point to get a drink, causing the bullet to fall from his shirt pocket. Police investigators detected no evidence of Rivers' blood, an animal attack, or foul play. To this day, the Bennington Triangle disappearance of Middie Rivers remains unsolved.

Bermuda Triangle

Of all the "mystery triangles" in the world, the most well-known is the infamous Bermuda Triangle, an area of ocean encompassed by a line spanning roughly from Miami, Florida; to the Caribbean island of Bermuda; to San Juan, Puerto Rico.

This area first entered the halls of infamy on September 16, 1950, when an article by writer E. V. W. Jones about several lost planes and sea vessels was published by the Associated Press. The fervor was further fueled by a 1952 article by George X. Sand that was published in *Fate Magazine*, titled "Sea Mystery at Our Back Door."

The Loss of Flight 19

One of the first noted disappearances to occur in the Bermuda Triangle was that of Flight 19, the official military designation for a flight of a Naval Training Bomber (TBM Avengers) that departed from the Naval Air Station in Fort Lauderdale, Florida, on December 5, 1945. The pilots were supposed to complete a routine training assignment that combined plane navigation with bombing runs.

The student bomber pilots of Flight 19 began their assignment behind schedule, at 2:10 P.M., because senior aviator Lieutenant Charles Taylor, who was supposed to observe the exercise, had arrived late to the airstrip (apparently, he was denied his immediate request to be relieved). By 3 P.M., the students had successfully completed the bombing run. After that, something went sour.

A Desperate Transmission

When another flight of student pilots entered the area, the senior aviator of the second flight, Lieutenant Robert Fox, exchanged radio chatter with the senior aviator of Flight 19. Taylor told his colleague that he and his students were completely disoriented, replying, "Both of my compasses are out. … I am over land but it's broken. I am sure I'm in the [Florida] Keys, but I don't know how far down, and I don't know how to get to Fort Lauderdale."

Lt. Fox immediately radioed the Naval Air Station that the pilots of Flight 19 were lost and then instructed Lt. Taylor to put the sun at his port wing side and proceed north along the coast. The air traffic officials at the air station then ordered Taylor to activate his aircraft's transponder, which would send out a locator signal they could use to triangulate his position. For unknown reasons, it seemed the order wasn't followed. However, some believe Taylor did activate his transponder, but the interference caused by the Bermuda Triangle disrupted the signal.

At 4:45 P.M., Lt. Taylor replied to an order that he change to a search and rescue frequency and said, "I cannot switch frequencies. I must keep my planes intact." Roughly 10 minutes later, air station officials repeated their order for Lt. Taylor to activate his transponder. Taylor did not respond. A few minutes later, he was overheard ordering his students to fly east (which would have sent them further out to sea). One of his students was overheard on the radio protesting, "Head west, damn it!"

The Scary Truth

Many have speculated as to why the student pilots of Flight 19 didn't head west on their own, disregarding Lt. Taylor's orders to fly east. Some are quick to cite that doing so would have violated military protocol. Others theorize that Taylor told his students to fly east because he believed their instruments were giving opposite readings.

Soon after, inclement weather hit the area. The last radio transmission from Lt. Taylor (and the rest of Flight 19) was received at 6:04 P.M. The transmission was broken up, either because of the triangle or because they'd traveled to the outer range of the radio. Lt. Taylor was heard saying, "All planes close up tight … we'll have to ditch unless … landfall … when the first plane hits … 10 gallons … we all go down together."

After They Vanished

After this, Lt. Taylor and every pilot of Flight 19 were never seen or heard from again. The only evidence that might hint at their fate came from the captain of an ocean tanker who reported witnessing a mid-air explosion at around 7:50 P.M. For years, the fate of Flight 19 remained a mystery.

In 1986, the crash wreckage of a TBM Avenger was found off the coast of Florida, which many believed was a plane from the lost Flight 19. However, the fuselage was so terribly deteriorated that this could not be confirmed. In 1991, five more TBM Avenger wrecks were found. However, examination of the planes' serial numbers confirmed they were not from Flight 19 but were in fact unfit planes that had been dumped into the ocean.

The Dragon's Triangle

The so-called Dragon's Triangle, also known as "The Devil's Sea," is a large chunk of strange ocean area in a part of the Philippine Sea located off the eastern coast of China. It extends from there to the northern coast of Japan. To map the encompassing line of the Dragon's Triangle (which doesn't form the shape of an exact triangle), one would have to draw a line from the Miyake Island of Japan to Guam to Palau (in the Philippines). However, many strange events attributed to the Dragon's Triangle have occurred well outside of this roughly drawn border.

The name Dragon's Triangle actually originates from an ancient Chinese myth that claims a number of titanic and powerful dragons reside at the bottom of the ocean's unexplored depths. According to these myths, the dragons use their powers over natural forces to create whirlpools, tidal waves, fog, and severe storms that capsize any ships that happen to disturb their slumbers.

Over the years, the Dragon's Triangle claimed so many fishing vessels (most of which were relatively small) that in 1950 the Japanese government declared the area a danger zone for fishermen. In 1952, the Japanese government even sent an oceanic research vessel, which was dubbed *Kaio Maru Go-Ban* ("Son of Consuming Flames" Number 5), to investigate the region. The ship was soon, and rather inexplicably, lost at sea. The 22 crewmen and 9 scientists aboard were never seen nor heard from again. Could this be coincidence? Absolutely. Is it? No one can say for certain.

The Scary Truth

The oceanic area referred to as the Dragon's Triangle is home to a large amount of volcanic activity. In ancient times, an island would seem to be present one day and then disappear the next. In truth, islands are usually formed by molten volcanic rock. Once the molten rock cooled, it would act like a cork and the pressure of magma below the surface would build until it finally reached the point of explosion. This might have caused ancient fishers to believe that dragons had swallowed the islands. Then again, maybe they did.

The Lost Colony of Roanoke (1587)

In 1585, many years before pilgrims set foot in the New World at Plymouth Rock, the first English settlement was established in Roanoke in what is now the state of Virginia. After being granted a permission patent to create a New World settlement by the Queen of England, Sir Walter Raleigh initially supervised the endeavor. Unfortunately for everyone involved, they had no idea what they'd gotten themselves into.

Raleigh remained in England and left the transportation of the colonists in the hands of a nobleman named Sir Richard Grenville. When the fledgling colony's supplies began to run out near the spring of 1585, Sir Grenville was the first one to bail out and set sail. He bestowed his authority over the Roanoke colony upon a man named Ralph Lane, explaining he was going to sail to England and immediately return with supplies. (Grenville never came back to Roanoke with the promised supplies.) It would appear that the colonists Grenville had left behind weren't exactly the "brightest crayons in the box." You see, these colonists, entirely dependent on the local Native American tribes for their food, somehow managed to anger the natives by treating them condescendingly. Without the aid of the local tribes, the stranded colonists soon found themselves besieged by famine.

Sir Francis Drake, fresh from his victorious destruction of the nearby Spanish colony, landed at the Roanoke colony in 1587 and found a village of people starving to death. He loaded as many of the worst-case survivors as he could onto his ship and took them back to England (among them Ralph Lane). However, for unknown reasons he left behind 15 of his men with the remaining colonists. What happened after that remains a mystery. None of Drake's men or the colonists were ever seen again. Aside from Drake's men, the colony was made up of 90 men, 17 women, and 9 children. No one ever discovered exactly what became of them, but the colonists did leave behind certain clues.

No one in Europe even knew the Roanoke colonists had disappeared until 1590, when the delayed supply ship finally arrived (without Sir Grenville aboard, of course). The entire settlement was nothing but a ghost town, and the only clue they found had been carved into the wood of a post near the fortification's gate, which read "Croatan." Croatan was the name of a nearby island now called Hatteras Island, near Cape Hatteras, North Carolina, where the local tribes lived. Many speculate that the colonists, in order to survive, chose to be absorbed into the Native American tribes. However, this has never been conclusively proven, and to this day, the fate of the Roanoke Colony remains unknown.

Well, He Didn't Just Walk Away!

Shepton Mallet, England, is home to one of the most baffling disappearances in history. In 1763, an elderly and crippled man by the name of Owen Parfitt disappeared without a trace. Owen had an adventurous nature and had spent most of his life traveling the globe in search of fame and fortune. By 1763, however, his body had become crippled by the hard life of adventure he'd led for so many years. It was at this time in Owen's life that he went on his final journey, though no one knows how, why, or where. Today, the mystery of his vanishing remains unsolved.

By June of 1763 (though some sources say it was 1768), Owen had moved in with his sister Susannah, who cared for the nearly invalid man hand and foot. One night, she had propped him up in his chair on the porch as she and a female neighbor friend readied his bed. When the two came to retrieve Owen, he was no longer in his chair, and a town-wide search turned up nothing. Owen Parfitt was never found.

The Scary Truth

Considering Owen Parfitt's adventurous past, many have speculated he had amassed a secret fortune. At the time, similar rumors had sprung up in the area, so it is quite possible that a gang of local treasure seekers abducted him, hoping to convince the elderly man to reveal the location of his fortune.

Into Thin Air

The occurrences of lost aviators are plentiful to say the least. The idea that someone piloting an aircraft could quite literally "vanish into thin air" has captivated the imaginations of people for decades. The idea of the lost aviator is most alive in the country that was the birthplace of aviation itself—the United States of America. Perhaps this shouldn't be surprising; Americans have lost many of their icons to the hazardous skies. From rock stars to writers, the airplane has claimed many, but perhaps the most well-known lost aviator of America is Amelia Earhart.

First and foremost, Amelia Earhart was an amazing pioneer in the world of aviation. On top of that, she was one of the most incredible women of her time. Her unexplained disappearance has baffled the world for the last seven decades.

Earhart's life was changed forever on December 28, 1920, when her father took her to visit an airfield. She took an exhilarating airplane ride with legendary air racer Frank Hawks. The result was a lifelong obsession. Amelia's life, from that day forward, revolved around flying. After completing her flying lessons, she undertook a number of very impressive avionic exploits. In 1928, she gained worldwide fame by flying across the entire breadth of the Atlantic Ocean. In 1932, Earhart successfully completed a solo transatlantic flight that secured her place in the annals of history.

In 1937, Earhart undertook her most daunting challenge ever: circumnavigating the entire globe. It would turn out to be her last great adventure. Her first two attempts ended in failure. But you know what they say, "the third time is a charm." Unfortunately, this rule did not prove true in Earhart's case. Her final transmissions were picked up by officials at her last landing point. She said, "We must be on you, but we cannot see you … gas is running low … have been unable to reach you by radio … we are flying at 1,000 feet." To this day, neither the body of Amelia Earhart nor the plane she was flying has ever been recovered. This midair disappearance remains a mystery.

Inter-Dimensional Hippies?

Back in August of 1971, Stonehenge was not yet protected from the public. One August night of that year, a band of traveling hippies decided to set up their camp next to the monolithic stone structure. They lit a fire, smoked some "wacky weed," and sacked out. Around 2 A.M., however, a violent storm disturbed their campout. Accounts claim that even Stonehenge itself was struck by bolts of lightning.

According to a local farmer and investigating policeman, the pillars of Stonehenge glowed with an eerie light after being struck by lightning. At one point, the glow grew so intense that they were forced to shield their eyes. Both men later claimed they'd heard the group of hippies screaming after they had covered their eyes.

When the light subsided, the two men rushed to the campsite, fearing they would find the dead bodies of the camping hippies. Instead, they discovered something far more baffling—absolutely nothing. Not a soul could be found at the campsite. All that was left were some tent pegs and a smoldering campfire; the hippies and their tents had just vanished. Since none of the campers were initially identified, no one could verify whether they ever turned up anywhere else. To this day, their final whereabouts are unknown.

The Least You Need to Know

♦ While many disappearances can be rationally explained, a good many cannot.

♦ So-called "mystery triangles" are dangerous at best, since no one knows for sure what sparks the strange activity within them.

♦ The most notable disappearance in the Bermuda Triangle is that of Naval Training Flight 19.

♦ To this day, the fate of Amelia Earhart remains a mystery.

♦ Owen Parfitt obviously didn't just walk away, but no one knows how he got off that porch.

♦ If you ever camp near Stonehenge and a lightning storm kicks up, you might want to relocate ... *immediately.*

Chapter 18

Unexplainable (Maybe?) Mysteries

In This Chapter

◆ The strange "Taos Hum" and similar phenomena

◆ The ongoing debate regarding Spontaneous Combustion

◆ The strange phenomenon of Human Involuntary Invisibility

◆ Sarita Bista, the Glass Girl from Nepal

◆ The mysterious nature of the 13 crystal skulls

A multitude of strange phenomena exists which we can classify as paranormal yet which manage to defy further categorization. This chapter contains a sampling of our world's many confounding mysteries, all of which continue to baffle both the scientific and medical communities. Perhaps one day the fact-based world of science will manage to catch up with the fact-eluding world of paranormal phenomena. Until then, we have no choice but to wait for answers.

The Hum of Taos, New Mexico

The southwestern state of New Mexico is no stranger to the weird and unusual. It is home to the notorious installation known as Area 51, which many believe houses the remains of a crashed spacecraft and the preserved bodies of the alien life forms that were piloting it. However, the areas in and around Taos, New Mexico, have been experiencing another rather strange phenomenon for almost 20 years now. In the early 1990s, an overwhelming number of reports began to pour in from Taos residents who complained they were hearing a constant, nearly maddening humming noise. Despite the investigations of city and state officials, no direct cause for the noise could be found.

> **The Scary Truth**
>
> Some believe there is nothing paranormal whatsoever when it comes to these unexplained hums. Humming and buzzing sounds are a well-known result of such things as power lines, generators, and power transformers. Despite this proposed explanation, no such objects are present in the areas where people hear these mysterious hums.

To make matters even more unusual, not everyone is able to hear the hum. This suggests that the sound is caused by a low-frequency vibration, which only people with sharp or sensitive hearing can detect. Similar hums have been reported in the Hawaiian Islands and Europe. Volcanic activity was found to cause at least one of the hums in Hawaii, but such an explanation doesn't work for hums in other regions of the globe.

Spontaneous Combustion

Spontaneous Combustion, more specifically Spontaneous Human Combustion (SHC), has defied explanation for centuries. This phenomenon is extremely rare, with roughly 200 known cases throughout history (only a handful of which can be confirmed as true occurrences of SHC). A person who experiences SHC is reduced to ashes in seconds, as the extreme temperatures that envelop a body are estimated to range somewhere between 1,700 and 3,000 degrees Fahrenheit.

Despite what one might think about SHC, it doesn't exactly cause a person to "burst into flames." In fact, it incinerates the person where he or she stands. Such a thing would require an enormous amount of energy, leading some to ask if SHC is even possible. So, is it? Well, yes and no. It is a fact that the average human body contains enough stored energy to consume itself entirely. However, there is no known way to release all of that energy at once. Even if there were, how would all of that released energy be converted into heat? For now, all we have are theories:

- **Body fat:** Some theorize that an ignition of human body fat causes SHC. However, victims of SHC have ranged from overweight to very skinny.

- **Alcoholism:** Early recorded victims of SHC were known alcoholics, leading many to blame excessive alcohol abuse. When non-alcoholics became victims, however, this theory was somewhat debunked.

- **Static electricity discharge:** Some theorize that an internal static discharge could cause SHC. However, no static discharge powerful enough to incinerate human flesh has ever been recorded.

- **Atomic reaction:** One theory proposes that it's possible for an electrical reaction in the human body to "backfire," causing a small internal nuclear reaction (which certainly would generate enough heat to immediately reduce a body to ashes).

The Reeser Case

The first modern case of SHC was documented on July 2, 1951, in St. Petersburg, Florida. A 67-year-old woman named Mary Reeser was found in a pile of ashes. When her neighbor had come by that morning to visit, she found the doorknob was hot. Fearing a fire, she immediately went for help, and Reeser was found when authorities arrived.

It is now believed that Mary Reeser actually died from SHC sometime on the previous evening as she was lounging in her favorite easy chair (which was burned down to the cushion springs, a portion of her spine lodged within them). The large majority of her body was a scattered pile of ashes and bone fragments about 4 feet in diameter. Her skull had shrunk due to the intense heat and was only a bit smaller than a softball.

All that remained of her corpse was part of her lower leg and a foot (all completely unburned), just outside the circle of ashes.

Initial reports claimed that Reeser had been burned alive when she fell asleep holding a lit cigarette. However, the medical examiner later invalidated these reports when he concluded that such an extreme incineration would have required a heat source of roughly 3,000°F.

This is astounding because heat that intense should have completely incinerated the whole interior of Reeser's small apartment home.

It was also documented that nothing was burned, charred, or even smoke-damaged beyond the small 4-foot area where her ashes were found. Fire investigators could not find any traces that would suggest any fire accelerants, such as gasoline or paint thinner, had fueled any fire. Besides, no known (readily available) accelerant is capable of producing such extreme heat.

> **Stranger Than Fiction**
>
> The one good thing about SHC is that it seems to be painless. According to the testimony of alleged SHC survivor Peter Jones in the first episode of the 2008 documentary series *Investigation X*, he never felt any pain. Amazingly, his SHC was only partial and did not completely consume and kill him. Jones is one of the very few known survivors of SHC.

The Martin Case

Another case of SHC occurred in Philadelphia, Pennsylvania, on May 18, 1957. A 68-year-old woman named Anna Martin was found in a pile of ashes in her home. As in the Reeser case, only the area where her ashes were located was burned. Interestingly, however, a chunk of Martin's torso and both of her shoes were found unburned.

When medical examiners performed a number of tests on Martin's incinerated remains, they estimated that her body had been struck by a sudden and powerful heat source that had reached temperatures of between 1,800°F and 2,000°F. To make the case even more impressive, a stack of newspapers found right beside her were completely free of fire or heat damage.

The Bentley Case

The next case of SHC occurred on December 5, 1966, in Coudersport, Pennsylvania (the same state as the 1957 Martin case). The victim was a 92-year old male, Dr. Irving Bentley. It is believed that Bentley (whose charred remains were found by an electric company meter reader) was killed by SHC while in his bathroom.

The intense heat of Bentley's SHC ignition burned a 3-foot-wide, 2½-foot-deep hole through the floor of the small bathroom. As in the Reeser and Martin cases, only the area where Bentley's body had ignited was burned. The ceiling and wallpaper of the very tiny bathroom were completely unburned.

Human Involuntary Invisibility

Also known as Spontaneous Human Invisibility (SHI) or Human Spontaneous Involuntary Invisibility (HSII), Human Involuntary Invisibility (HII) is perhaps one of the most unusual phenomena. Oddly enough, it appears that an impressive number of people have experienced it. Basically, HII causes an individual to become completely invisible and, sometimes, inaudible as well.

The Bermuda Triangle

Some believe that many of the unsolved disappearances are the result of permanent HII (for more on unsolved disappearances, see Chapter 17). After all, the phenomenon is called "involuntary" for a reason. Imagine suddenly becoming invisible and not knowing how to reverse the condition. This theory states that such people are forced to live out their lives in a permanent invisible state.

Hypnotherapist and paranormal/alien abduction researcher Donna Higbee has conducted most of the available research on the HII phenomenon. After compiling and researching a great many inquiry letters from people claiming to have experienced HII, she published the most believable and valid of them. Of course, since no one has ever *seen* or videotaped anyone actually turning from visible to invisible during HII, concrete evidence has not yet turned up.

Sarita: The Glass Girl

First, a strange blisterlike lump formed on the side forehead of a 12-year-old Nepalese girl named Sarita Bista. On January 18, 2006, her parents scratched the lump, believing it nothing more than a large blister. What happened next astounded everyone. The skin split, and a triangular piece of glass came out. In the beginning, they thought this was rather strange but figured it was only an isolated incident. Perhaps, they reasoned, a piece of glass had somehow gotten under her skin and only now became dislodged. However, the situation soon proved to be otherwise. More glass pieces began coming out, with increasing frequency, as time went on. On average, these glass triangles were roughly 4 centimeters in length and 1 millimeter thick.

Oddly, it was reported that Sarita's skin healed very quickly once it had emitted a glass shard (sometimes in the span of roughly a day). When a glass piece was expelled, the wound bled very little (just a few drops, according to some reports). This is very uncharacteristic of head wounds, which are notorious for bleeding heavily. At first, Sarita's family, fearing she would be shunned by the community or bullied at school, did their best to keep her condition a secret. They informed her schoolteacher but asked her to keep Sarita's condition private. In the meantime, Sarita's parents spent almost every bit of what little money they had trying to find a treatment or cure for her.

Eventually, the frequency of these glass emissions made it nearly impossible to keep things secret, leaving them no choice but to go public with Sarita's condition. By early August 2006, her forehead was emitting at least one piece of glass per day. On one occasion, she emitted a total of 12 glass pieces in a single day. By September 2006, when her story first hit newspapers, Sarita had emitted a total of 130 shards of glass.

The Scary Truth

Many skeptics have been quick to point out that it is not uncommon for people who've been in car accidents to have glass shards lodge in their skin, which are sealed when the skin heals over, until they are eventually expelled. However, such skeptics also fail to mention that all of Sarita's expelled shards were triangular (unprecedented in accident cases). Also, the volume of glass Sarita has emitted is unlikely to have occurred in one accident. Lastly, there is no evidence that she had previously been in any serious accidents, vehicular or otherwise.

Doctors and specialists from all over Nepal examined Sarita. A CT-scan (cat-scan) confirmed there was something strange about the skin of Sarita's forehead. It also showed that the glass shards were not being formed from the bone of her skull.

In fact, her skull and bone structure appeared completely normal. A rigorous investigation and a series of medical exams turned up no evidence that Sarita suffered from any physical or mental ailments (aside from the fact that she had pieces of glass coming out of her head).

> **The Scary Truth**
>
> It is interesting to note that, according to medical science, it is impossible for the human body to produce glass. However, the shards being emitted by Sarita are, in fact, glass.

Some people claim that Sarita's condition is a divine miracle. Others see it as a miraculous sign of the approaching "end of times." Many in the scientific/medical communities believe that Sarita suffers from a rare, unprecedented, and unidentified skin condition that causes her cells to produce a substance similar to glass. However, they have never been successful in definitively identifying any actual cause, effective treatment, or potential cure for her condition.

Years later, the strange story of Sarita Bista remains the same; despite the best efforts of the world's leading medical professionals, no one really knows what has caused young Sarita (who is now well into her teenage years) to become the "Glass Girl of Nepal." The true cause of her condition remains a mystery.

Crystal Skulls

Crystal skulls have been a baffling, and surprisingly frequent, mystery in the archeological world. A total of 13 such skulls have been found to date, mainly throughout Mexico, Central America, and South America. Many of the skulls have been found among the ruins of the lost Mayan and Aztec civilizations, and some are believed to be as much as 5,000 years old (though a few are hypothesized by some to be far older, as much as 30,000 years old).

There exist many theories about what the crystal skulls are, where they came from, and what they were used for. In truth, however, no conclusive evidence has ever been found to answer any of these questions. Most of the claims about these skulls are heavily based upon speculation, and more than a few run the gamut of your usual conspiracy theories—that they were used in ritualistic sacrifices (which isn't completely out of the question), that they were left behind by visiting aliens, or even that they are relics from the lost civilization of Atlantis.

There are a number of amazing factors about crystal skulls, especially when you consider that they are supposed to have been produced by ancient peoples. First of all, some of them are completely absent of any tool marks. This means that whatever tools or methods were used to create them did so without leaving behind any grooves or other marks as evidence. Even among those that do have tool marks, it often requires a powerful microscope just to see them. In addition, these skulls have no fractures, cracks, or other evidence of the usual wear and erosion caused by the passage of thousands of years. Lastly, according to what is known about the physics of carving the crystal from which they are made, the skulls should not even exist. It would be nearly impossible to create one, especially one so well polished and symmetrical, without having it shatter into pieces during the process.

The Mitchell-Hedges Skull

Probably the most well-known and widely studied crystal skull is referred to as the Mitchell-Hedges skull. The attention it has received is due to the fact that it is nearly identical to a real human skull in form, size, and proportions. In fact, it was even fitted to have a jawbone. Most of the other known crystal skulls differ from the Mitchell-Hedges skull in that they usually do not have such a realistic appearance, nor do they have hinged jawbones, but are instead just carved from a single piece. Also, even on a microscopic level, the Mitchell-Hedges skull is 100 percent flawless. This means that, even with today's best technology, it is impossible to identify any of the tools or methods used to create it. On top of this, even modern sculptors using modern equipment claim that reproducing the perfection of that Mitchell-Hedges skull would be impossible to do. It is made entirely of clear crystal quartz, measures roughly 5 inches high by 5 inches wide, and weighs 11.7 pounds.

The Mitchell-Hedges crystal skull was first discovered in 1924 by the adopted 17-year-old daughter (Anna) of British-Canadian explorer Frederick Albert Mitchell-Hedges (for whom the skull is named), who then brought it to him. The two were on an expedition of the Mayan ruins in what was then the British Honduras (modern-day Belize). Mitchell-Hedges was at the site in order to look for clues about the lost city of Atlantis. Instead, his daughter stumbled upon the skull. The documentation about how the discovery happened is based entirely on hearsay (or Mitchell-Hedges' personal, uncorroborated account). But the story basically goes like this: Anna was playing and exploring in an old temple ruin, when she came upon the skull (minus its jawbone) and rushed to show it to her father. Mitchell-Hedges discovered the missing jawbone at a site roughly 8 yards away from where his daughter first found the skull … and only after three months of searching. According to Mitchell-Hedges, he did not wish to remove the skull from its home and so returned it to the local Mayan priests. However, as he was preparing to leave, Mitchell-Hedges claimed that they bestowed the skull upon him as a gift. One must admit, his story is a little hard to swallow … and it would appear for good reason.

While the origins of the skull's construction are certainly unknown, how it came to be in Mitchell-Hedges' possession is not. Evidence later surfaced that seemed to suggest he did not find the skull at the ruins, but had purchased it at an auction in 1943 at Sotheby's of London. However, perhaps even this is questionable. The British Museum, a known rival of Mitchell-Hedges, brought forward documents that they claimed were evidence that they had bid against Mitchell-Hedges in the auction for the skull. According to the Mitchell-Hedges family's website timeline, however, he'd been forced to buy back the skull when the son of a friend (with whom Mitchell-Hedges had entrusted the skull during an extended expedition) had thoughtlessly sold the skull to Sotheby's. In all honesty, both sides of the story are equally plausible.

Then again, it is odd that there are no pictures of the skull among all the photographic evidence collected during Mitchell-Hedges' Mayan expedition. It is also odd that, despite claiming to have found the skull in 1924, Mitchell-Hedges did not display, discuss, or reveal it to the public until 1943. None of this, however, explains how the skull was made regardless of whether or not Mitchell-Hedges' story is entirely accurate.

After the death of her father, Anna Mitchell-Hedges remained the sole owner of the crystal skull. She eventually ran a hotel in Canada and lived in England for many years. In her youth, Anna had made quite a reputation of her own as an adventurer, making her hotel quite the tourist attraction. In her later years, she moved to the home of friend Bill Homann in Indiana, where she died in 2007 at the age of 100. She toured widely with and gave lectures on the skull, and always insisted that her father's story was absolutely true and that it was she who found the skull at the Mayan temple ruin back in 1924. The Mitchell-Hedges skull is now in the care of Bill Homann.

In 1970, Anna Mitchell-Hedges allowed the skull to be examined and studied by Hewlett-Packard Laboratories. At their state-of-the-art crystal research facility in Santa Clara, California, the skull was subjected to numerous tests. The results of these tests were astounding.

First of all, the lab tests discovered that the skull was somehow carved against the crystal's natural axis. As any experienced crystal sculptor will confirm, this is seemingly impossible. Crystal sculptors take great care to identify a crystal's axis and always make certain never to carve against it. Doing so, even if one uses modern laser cutters, will only cause the crystal to shatter under the pressure.

In addition to the fact that the skull had been carved against its axis, the Hewlett-Packard team could not find any evidence of scratches or tool marks, not even at the microscopic level. The only way this could be done, it was believed, was by first "rough cutting" the crystal with a diamond-edged tool, and then smoothing and polishing it (likely with a solution of sand and water). Though this would be possible, it would also be insanely time-consuming. It is estimated that this polishing method, in order to produce such perfect results, would have taken at least *300 years!* And that is just counting the hours of polishing it would require (with no breaks). On top of this, the team could not find any way to date the skull because it is made of piezoelectric quartz, which has a special type of crystal structure that remains completely unchanged with the passage of time.

Stranger Than Fiction

Piezoelectric quartz is the same material used in many kinds of modern computer circuitry. Because of this, some believe the Mitchell-Hedges skull is a computer component from some lost civilization or alien race. These theories often share the notion that it is an advanced data storage device that houses some kind of absolute knowledge. One theory even claims all 13 crystal skulls were left during ancient times by an advanced race called the "Inner Earth Society," who now reside in the center of Earth. The theory claims these 13 "Master Skulls" contain the origin, knowledge, and history of these people.

So what was the conclusion of the Hewlett-Packard team's tests? Simply put, they concluded that making a crystal sculpture as complex and perfect as the Mitchell-Hedges skull would be impossible. In fact, one of the men on the team was quoted as saying, "The damned thing simply shouldn't be." And yet ... it simply *is*.

Other Crystal Skulls

The Mitchell-Hedges skull certainly isn't the only crystal skull, though it is probably the most magnificent. Here is a brief look at some of the other crystal skulls that continue to boggle scientists and capture the imaginations of many who wish to believe that the impossible can exist.

The one crystal skull that is closest in the skill and altogether "impossibility" of the Mitchell-Hedges skull is called the "Rose Quartz Crystal Skull." Found near the border between Guatemala and Honduras, it is made from rose quartz. It is similar in shape, but slightly larger than the Mitchell-Hedges skull. And, like the Mitchell-Hedges skull, it also has a hinged, removable jawbone.

Sometime during the 1890s, two European mercenaries in Mexico are said to have both bought (or stolen) crystal skulls. The two skulls are nearly identical in every way (though they are not nearly as intricate as the Mitchell-Hedges skull), and some believe that one skull was used as a model to create the other. These two skulls are referred to as the "British Crystal Skull" and the "Paris Crystal Skull." The British Crystal Skull can be seen on display at the London Museum of Mankind, and the Paris Crystal Skull can be seen at the Trocadero Museum of Paris.

There is also the "Texas Crystal Skull," more affectionately referred to as "Max." This is a single-piece skull, cut from clear crystal and weighing in at 18 pounds. The details regarding its origins are sketchy. Apparently it was first found in Guatemala under unknown circumstances. The skull later found its way into the possession of a Tibetan spirit healer named Norbu Chen. It was this man who later bestowed the skull upon JoAnn Parks of Houston, Texas. She claims that, in 1973, Chen had used the healing powers of the skull to cure her daughter, who was dying of bone cancer. In 1980, Norbu died and gave the skull to JoAnn and her husband. She claims that the skull began to communicate with her in dreams, in increasing frequency, for the next seven years. JoAnn Parks now allows viewings of the skull and travels with it to showings all over the world.

Another very odd crystal skull is referred to as the "E.T. Skull." It received this name because it looks like an alien, with a pointy, elongated cranium and an extreme overbite. This skull is in the private collection of crystal skull enthusiast Joke Van Dietan. Van Dietan makes regular lecture tours with her crystal skull collection in order to, as she claims, share their healing powers with the rest of the world.

The Least You Need to Know

- "Mystery hums" like the one in Taos, New Mexico, cannot be heard by everyone and are difficult to pick up on most recording equipment.

- The validity of Spontaneous Human Combustion remains a matter of debate, but no one has definitively proven an alternative cause.

- Human Involuntary Invisibility is a phenomenon believed to temporarily cause a person to become invisible and, in some cases, inaudible.

- The cause of Sarita Bista's strange condition, which causes triangular glass shards to emit from her forehead, remains a mystery.

- The Mitchell-Hedges crystal skull should not be possible or even exist. Yet, it is—and it does.

Appendix A

Glossary

agent   Refers to the spirit phenomenon witnessed by a percipient. This word has largely been replaced by "entity."

aitvaras   No record explains the roots of this word, and the literal definition is totally unknown, other than as a label for the rooster/dragon/shapeshifter creature in Lithuanian folklore.

alpha   Literally means "the first" or "beginning." An alpha animal is in charge of a social group, such as a lion pride or a wolf/hyena pack. Sometimes, there can be multiple alphas, but most frequently only one rules a social group.

ancestor worship   A religious practice very common in the ancient world, in which one's deceased ancestors were believed to reach the status of deities after death. Sometimes rituals of spirit necromancy would be performed to consult with the spirits of these deified ancestors for guidance or the receiving of blessings.

angelology   A term that literally means "the study of angels." However, the term has come to mean any religious or theological doctrine that involves the roles, hierarchies, or arrangements of angels.

anthropomancy   A term that comes from the Greek *anthropos* (man/ human) and *manteia* (prophecy/divination), and refers to the ritualistic disembowelment of a live human sacrifice for purposes of divination. A practitioner of this art is called an anthropomancer.

apocryphal   Literally means "probably not true." In religious terminology, it refers to writings/texts considered questionable by a main religious body. Denominations sometimes set these texts aside but do not completely forbid them. In other cases, they may be read but not cited. In extreme situations, even the mention of an apocryphal text is strictly forbidden.

Aramaic   An ancient language widely written/spoken by the Semitic tribes of the Near East around 400 to 300 B.C.E. Eventually, it was almost completely replaced by the Hebrew language. Today, it is nearly a dead language known only by about 75,000 people worldwide.

area possession   When one or more demons occupy a physical space, often a home, building, or other structure. Sometimes this includes the possession of certain objects.

bakemono   Japanese term for spirits or monsters with supernatural (and often frightening) powers. *Bakemono* can be a blessing or a curse for humans, depending on their natural dispositions, moods, or the condition under which they are encountered. Skilled (and often mischievous) deceivers, a good number of them are also known to eat humans.

binding   A spell, ritual, prayer, or other ceremony by which a spirit or demon is bound from certain actions (such as doing harm), then usually imprisoned in, permanently barred from, or attached to a place, structure, object, or animal.

bouda   Sometimes spelled *buda*, this term means "were-hyena" in many of the African continent's current languages. However, it's believed that it had a different original meaning. In Ethiopia, Christians sometimes use it to refer to Ethiopian Jews, though without the were-hyena connotation.

breakpoint   The moment during an exorcism when the demonic force is closest to expulsion. As a possessed individual begins to regain control of his will, the demon exhausts itself trying to retain its hold. Eventually, it has no choice but to release the person and vacate.

bultungin   In the dialects of the Nigerian state of Borno, this term literally means "I become a hyena." In actual use, however, the term generally refers to any person who shapeshifts into a hyena (without the same first-person implication).

chanoyu   Literally translates as "hot water." However, the word came to refer to the ritualistic practice of the special Japanese Tea Ceremony. This is one of the most honored traditions of Japanese culture, and is viewed as a pursuit of perfection. When performed for someone else, the *chanoyu* is considered one the highest gestures of respect and honor that can be displayed in Japanese culture.

cryptesthesia   Originally used to refer to extrasensory perception and means "hidden feeling/sensation."

cryptids   Basically means "hidden animals." Many think these creatures are either extinct or restricted to the realms of legends.

cryptozoology   The study and research of animals that are considered cryptids.

Dead Sea Scrolls   A collection of manuscripts found in a series of caves near the Dead Sea between 1947 and 1956. Considered apocryphal by mainstream Christianity and the subject of much debate among historians and religious scholars for decades, these scrolls shed light on many gaps in the canonical Judeo-Christian texts.

demonization   The primary stage of demonic possession in humans, characterized by the demon infiltrating and occupying the person's body. At this stage, removing the demon remains somewhat simple as long as the possessed person honestly desires the demon's removal.

disembodied   Means "released/separated from the body." In paranormal terms, it refers to spirits, such as ghosts, thought to have once occupied a physical body. In some situations, this also applies to any human-possessing demonic entities.

Dracula/Dracul   A hereditary title given to Vlad Tepes III, the word translates in multiple ways. Dracul, the title of Vlad II (his father), means "dragon" if taken from its root word *drako*. In Romanian, it means "devil/demon." Therefore, Vlad III's title name of Dracula can mean "Little Dragon" or "Son of the Dragon" but also "Son of the Devil/Demon." In either case, the title served as a powerful psychological weapon against enemies of the Tepes clan.

Espiritismo   A Spanish word that means "spiritism." However, it is sometimes interpreted to mean "Way of the Spirits." This faith magic practice from Latin America integrates elements of Catholicism, African spiritual beliefs, and various Native American religions.

exorcism   Any spiritual rite, ritual, or ceremony meant to expel demons or other malevolent spirits that occupy a physical space or human body. Specific methods for carrying out exorcisms can be found in the spiritual practices of almost every known culture group in the world.

exsanguination   An extreme and fatal loss of blood. More or less, it is just a fancy way of saying "bleeding to death."

genuflections   A practice most commonly seen in the Roman Catholic and Anglican churches that involves touching one knee (usually the right) or both knees to the ground as a sign of worship or as a gesture of respect to God.

Go-Ryo   Roughly means "honorable ghost." While vengeful, these spirits are often male members of the noble warrior classes (especially those who were betrayed or martyred in some way). According to lore, a *Go-Ryo* can only be commanded by a *yamabushi* (a mountain-dwelling warrior monk of Zen Buddhism).

haruspicy   The practice of ritualistically sacrificing an animal (often a bull or calf) through disembowelment and then examining the entrails for divination purposes. A priest who carried out such rituals was called a haruspex.

humanoid   Any nonhuman creature that somewhat resembles a human in appearance—for example, a sasquatch or werewolf.

Kabbalah   A Judaistic tradition of mystical spiritual practice. However, the specific texts associated with Kabbalah mysticism are not a part of the Jewish canon.

kama   A short, handheld sickle used by Japanese farmers to harvest grain and rice. From the side of the handle's "business end" extends a sharp curved blade. The tool was eventually developed into a weapon by Karate *Shuri-Te* founders on the island of Okinawa.

katana   A long sword with a curved blade, which was often the secondary weapon of choice (the primary weapon being a spear or halberd) for the samurai warriors of feudal Japan. Many Samurai believed their souls were fused to their *katana*.

lycanthropy   An integration of the Greek words *lykoi* (wolf) and *anthropos* (man/human). The term refers to the state of being a werewolf, a human who assumes the form or attributes of a wolf.

medium   One endowed with a natural awareness of spirit activity, and therefore does not use necromantic rituals to communicate with the spirits of the deceased.

necromancy   From the Greek *necros* (death/corpse) and *manteia* (prophecy/divination), this term refers to the art of conjuring or actively communicating with the dead (in spiritual or physical form) by way of rituals, spells, or incantations.

Nephilim   Plural for *Nephil*, an ancient race of powerful giants who were the offspring of sexual unions between fallen angels and human women; some religious scholars contest this interpretation and believe the passage refers to either angels in general or possibly some long-extinct race of giant (or at least extremely tall) humanoids.

nigromancy   An improper combination of the Latin *nigero* (black) with the Greek *manteia* (prophecy/divination), it is sometimes used interchangeably with the term *necromancy*. However, nigromancy is a much broader term that refers to all mystical or magical arts that are dark, malevolent, or demonic in nature.

nosferatu   One translation for this term is "carrier of disease," and another (far more common) is "night creature." Regardless of its literal definition, the word has come to have the connotation of "vampire."

oni   An ogrelike demonic monster in Japanese mythology.

onryo   A Japanese term meaning "angry ghost/spirit." These are most commonly female and often are the vengeful spirits of women who were murdered, abused, betrayed, or otherwise severely mistreated by their husbands. They usually torment their living husbands in retribution.

Ouija board   From the French *oui* (yes) and German *ja* (also yes). Also called a "talking board," this flat board has the letters of the alphabet written upon it, along with the options of "yes" and "no." It is used to contact spirits.

paranormal   Literally means "above/beyond normal." The term refers to events, abilities, or phenomena that cannot be explained, identified, or understood through normal/scientific means.

parapsychology   The study of unknown or unexplained mental phenomena, often called psychic phenomenon.

percipient   Someone who witnesses a spirit apparition. In recent years, some paranormal investigators have replaced this word with simpler terms, such as "subject" or "client."

perfect possession   The final stage and ultimate form of demonic possession in humans. By this stage, those possessed have surrendered to the will of the demon (or demons) within them.

personal possession   When a demon successfully infiltrates the body of a human being and gradually exercises influence or control over his or her behavior and actions. This is also the second stage of demonic possession.

physical necromancy   Also called "traditional necromancy," this practice seeks to divine special knowledge from the dead by employing some form of physical manipulation that involves the use/mutilation of a deceased spirit's actual corpse.

psalm   From the classical Greek term *psalmos*, meaning "the plucking of a harp string." In religious text, it is the anglicization of the Greek-given title for the biblical book, *Psalmoi*. The generic meaning now refers to a sacred song or poem, often in the form of spiritual praise, and more specifically to those from the Christian Bible.

psychic   A term that means "of the mind" or "related to the mind."

psychosomatic   Comes from the Greek words *psycho*, meaning "spirit" or "mind," and *somatic*, meaning "the body" or "cells." It basically refers to the mind's ability to affect physiological changes over the body. Most commonly, it refers to people who develop physical illnesses due to psychological reasons.

reanimation   Refers to the resumed movement of dead tissue/ organisms. Literally, the word means "to return to movement" or "made to move again."

recurrent spontaneous psychokinesis   A regularly reoccurring release of psychic energy, capable of moving physical objects, usually released by someone unaware he or she is doing so. This is believed by some to be a cause of poltergeist phenomenon.

reincarnation   A concept that exists in many spiritual traditions of the world and basically refers to the belief that the human soul returns after death in a new physical form.

relesthesia   Alternate term once used for the phenomena of ESP and telepathy and basically meaning "feeling/sensing the distance."

repressed psychokinetic energy   Believed to be psychic energy un-knowingly released by an individual who possesses psychic abilities but does not know it. This form of energy is believed to build up as a result of stress or trauma. The buildup eventually reaches a peak and begins to be released, resulting in poltergeist phenomena.

Santeria   From Spanish, this literally means "holiness." Sometimes it is interpreted or translated to mean "Saintly" or "Way of Saints."

sasquatch   An anglicization of the Indian word *sesquac*, which roughly translates as "wild man." In modern times, it has become interchangeable with the word Bigfoot.

séance   A group ritual, usually led by some form of spirit medium, meant to open communication with spirits. These rituals may be done in either a passive or invocative manner.

Sefiroth   Also spelled Sephiroth (singular forms are sefira/sephira), refers to two polar opposite angelic orders. One half is the Ten Holy Sefiroth, made up of Heaven's most powerful archangels. The other half is the Ten Unholy Sefiroth, a group of evil counter-entities (mostly fallen angels).

shade   A conjured soul or spirit is referred to as a shade in necromancy.

spirit box   A special box used in spirit necromancy, in which a spirit may be bound through a necromancer's incantations, acting as a vessel for the invoked spirit(s).

spirit necromancy   Also called "psychic" necromancy in modern times, this form of necromantic divination seeks to conjure forth the spirits of the dead to gain special knowledge or power.

splanchomancy   A specific form of anthropomancy in which virgins were used as ritual sacrifices for purposes of divination.

sutras   In both Hinduism and Buddhism, short summarizations of key teachings from religious texts. In Buddhism, sutras are often recited from passages believed to have been the words of the Buddha.

talisman   Any relic, amulet, or similar trinket worn on the body (usually about the neck) and believed to provide the wearer with magical protection or abilities.

Tao   Pronounced *dow*, this term literally translates as "the way/path." This is the Chinese root word for the Japanese term *do*, which has the same basic meaning (though usually without a religious connotation). The *Tao* religion is based on a search for hidden spiritual truths and walking a righteous "path" in one's life.

tatami   Thinly cushioned mats woven from bamboo and used in the floors and certain bedding materials of traditional Japanese homes.

therianthropy   From the Greek words *therion* (wild/undomesticated animal) and *anthropos* (man/human), it refers to the condition of being able to assume the forms of both a human being and one or more animals. The original form of a therianthrope can be human or animal.

transubstantiate   Literally means "to move across substance," and the simplest definition is "changing from one substance to another." In spiritual terms, especially in the Catholic and Eastern Orthodox traditions, it refers to the miraculous changing of substances. For example, Jesus transubstantiated water into wine. In regard to angels (and sometimes demons), it means the ability to shift from their true spirit forms to substantial/physical forms. This ability can be used by spirit entities, such as angels and demons, to either blend in among or physically interact with figures and elements in the human realm.

Vodun   The root term from which the Western word "Voodoo" originated. The term comes from Africa, and literally means "spirit." In the proper context, however, it originally referred to certain indigenous African religious rituals meant for communicating with or invoking the power of ancestral spirits, divine forces, or malevolent entities.

yama   Japanese term for "mountain."

YHVH   The Hebrew title for God, it is often spelled in its more anglicized forms of Yahweh and Jehovah.

yurei   A Japanese term that literally translates as "hazy/faint spirit" but is often interpreted in English as "ghost." In ancient times, they were considered good. As time went on, however, they came to be regarded with a certain amount of fear.

zombi   Root word for "zombie," it refers to a debunked practice of the Haitian *Vodun* cult. The initial belief stated that a *zombi* was one who, through the dark powers of Voodoo, had his or her soul stolen by a priest/priestess (causing a temporary death) and was later brought back to life. After being resurrected, a *zombi* was said to be bound into the service of the acting Voodoo priest/priestess.

Paranormal Societies

If you are interested in paranormal investigation or research, begin with these organizations. Also, if you are experiencing issues with paranormal phenomenon, these are the best people to go to for help. I have provided cities of location, contact info, and websites based on Internet availability.

U.S. Paranormal Societies

Following is a list of many paranormal societies throughout the United States. There are far more paranormal groups than those listed here. In all honesty, listing every single paranormal organization would probably take up an entire book itself.

Alabama

Alabama Paranormal Society
Alabama-paranormal-society.com

Central Alabama Society for Paranormal Exploration and Research (CASPER)
Casperinvestigations.com

Arizona

The Arizona Paranormal Research Society (TAzPRS)
TAZPS.com

California

Northern California Paranormal Society
Ncpsociety.com

Pasadena Paranormal Research Society
Pasadena, CA
Pasadenaghosthunters.com

Southern California Ghost Hunters Society
Southerncaliforniaghosthunters.com
Answering service: (909) 831-8377

Southern California Society for Paranormal Research
Socalprs.com

Colorado

Colorado Researchers of Paranormal Science (CORPS)
Paranormalcolorado.com

Denver Paranormal Research Society
Denver, CO
Denverparanormal.com

Rocky Mountain Paranormal Research Society
Rockymountainparanormal.com

Southern Colorado Paranormal Research Society
Hauntedcolorado.net

Connecticut

Connecticut Paranormal Research Society
Dudleytown, CT
Cprs.info

New England Society for Psychic Research
Monroe, CT
Warrens.net

Northwest Connecticut Paranormal Society
Northwestconnecticutparanormal.com

Florida

OC Paranormal Society of Florida
Oc-fl-paranormalsociety.com

Georgia

Georgia Ghost Society
www.Georgiaghostsociety.com

South Georgia Paranormal Research Society
www.theparanormalsociety.org

West Georgia Paranormal Research Society
www.gprs.com

Hawaii

Hawaiian Island Ghost Hunters
Hawaiianislandghosthunters.com

Hawaiian Island Paranormal Research Society
Hawaiianislandparanormal.com

Idaho

Idaho Paranormal Society
www.idahoparanormal.com

Paranormal Society of Idaho
Paranormalsocietyofidaho.com

Illinois

Northern Illinois Paranormal Investigation Society (NIPIS)
Nipis.org

Tazewell Illinois Paranormal Society
Tazewell, IL
Tazewellparanormal.com

Indiana

Indiana Society for Paranormal Research (ISPR)
Indianaparanormalresearch.com

The Indiana Paranormal Society
www.indianaparanormal.us

Northern Indiana Paranormal Society
Thenorthwesternindianaparanormalsociety.com

Southern Indiana Regional Paranormal Society (SIRPS)
Indianaregionalparanormalsociety.com

Louisiana

Louisiana State Paranormal Research Society
New Orleans, LA
lspr-society.com

Maine

Central Maine Researchers and Investigators of the Paranormal
Centralmaineparanormal.com

Maine Ghost Hunter's Society
www.maineghosts.org

Maryland

Greater Maryland Paranormal Society
Baltimore, MD
www.greater-maryland-paranormal-society.com

Maryland Ghost and Spirit Association (MSGA)
Marylandghosts.com

Massachusetts

Para-Boston
Boston, MA
Para-boston.org

Paranormal Research Association of Boston
Boston, MA
www.praofb.org

Spirit Encounters Research Team
Sertma.tripod.com

Michigan

Great Lakes Paranormal and Research Society (GLPARS)
Great Lakes, MI
Greatlakespars.com

Michigan Ghost Watchers
Ghostwatchers.org

Michigan Paranormal Alliance
www.m-p-a.org

Michigan Paranormal Society, PLLC
Garden City, MI
www.michiganparanormalsociety.com

Motor City Ghost Hunters
Dearborn Heights, MI
www.motorcityghosthunters.com

Northeast Michigan Paranormal Society
Prescott, MI
www.northeastmichiganparanormalsociety.org

Mississippi

The Ellisville Mississippi Paranormal Society
Ellisville, MS
Theellisvillemississippiparanormalsociety.com

Mississippi Area Paranormal Society (MAPS)
Senatobia, MS
www.freewebs.com/msareaparanormalsociety

Mississippi Society of Paranormal Investigators
Batesville, MS, and Potts Camp, MS
www.mississippi-spi.com

Nevada

Full Moon Paranormal
Reno, NV
www.fullmoonparanormal.com

Nevada Student Paranormal Investigation
Reno, NV
www.nspisite.webs.com

Western Paranormal Society
Virginia City, NV
westernparanormalsociety.com

New Mexico

Alliance Studying Paranormal Experiences (ASPE)
Angel Fire, NM
www.aspefiles.org

New Mexico Paranormal Investigators
www.spirit-newmexico.com

New York

Albany Paranormal Research Society
Albany, NY
Paranormalalbany.com

Binghamton Area Paranormal Society (BAPS)
Binghamton, NY
Binghamtonparanormal.com

Foundation for the Study of Paranormal Phenomenon
Washingtonville, NY
fspp.net

Ghostly Knights Paranormal Society
College Point, NY
Ghostlyknights.com

Long Island Paranormal Investigators
Long Island, NY
LIparanormalinvestigators.com

Western New York Paranormal Research Group
Blasdell, NY
WNYPRG.com

Oklahoma

Chickasaw Paranormal
Ada, OK
Contact: Stephanie Scott—chicakasawparanormal@yahoo.com

Muskogee Paranormal Research Society
Muskogee, OK
Contact: Terri Cobb—kmlghosthunter@yahoo.com

Sooner Paranormal of Oklahoma (SPOOk)
Terlton, OK
SoonerparanormalofOK.com

Oregon

Oregon Ghost Hunters
Eugene, OR
Oregonghosthunters.com

Oregon Paranormal Investigation Society (OPIS)
Eugene, OR
Opisonline.net

West Coast Spectre Society
Portland, OR
Westcoastspectresociety.com

Pennsylvania

NEPA Paranormal Society
Northeast Pennsylvania
Freewebs.com/nepaparanormalsociety

Paranormal Research Society
College, PA
Paranormalresearchsociety.org

Penn State Branch—Paranormal Research Society
Penn State University, PA
Paranormalresearchsociety.org

Rhode Island

The Atlantic Paranormal Society (TAPS)
Warwick, RI
www.the-atlantic-paranormal-society.com

Texas

Central Texas Paranormal Society
Waco, TX
Centraltexasparanormalsociety.com

Houston Texas Paranormal Society
Houston, TX
Texasparanormalsociety.com

North Texas Paranormal Society
University of North Texas
Denton, TX
orgs.unt.edu/ntps

South Texas Paranormal Society
Corpus Christi, TX
Southtexasparanormalsociety.com

West Texas Paranormal Investigations Society
Lubbock, TX
WTPIS.org

Utah

Northern Utah Paranormal Society
Northernutahparanormal.com

Virginia

Virginia Paranormal Society
Virginiaparanormalsociety.com

Washington

The Evergreen Paranormal Society
Puget Sound, WA
Evergreenparanormal.com

Washington State Ghost Society
Washingtonstateghostsociety.com

West Virginia

West Virginia Paranormal Society
Wvparanormalsociety.com

Wyoming

Wyoming Paranormal Society
Wyomingparanormalsociety.com

Paranormal Societies Worldwide

Association for Scientific Study of Anomalous Phenomena (ASSAP)
London, England (Founded 1981)
www.assap.org

Bermuda Society for Paranormal Research (BSPR)
pwp.ibl.bm/~jdobson/BSPRmain.htm
E-mail: jdobson@ibl.bm

Cambridge Paranormal Research Society (CPRS)
United Kingdom
cambridgeparanormal.co.uk

Children of the City (COTC) Paranormal Investigations
United Kingdom (Founded 1996)
www.cotcpi.co.uk

College of Psychic Studies
United Kingdom (Founded 1884)
www.collegeofpsychicstudies.co.uk

The Ghost Club
United Kingdom (Founded 1862)
www.ghostclub.org.uk

Ghost Hunters of Guelph
Canada (Founded by Wanda Hewer)
ghosthuntersofguelph.com
E-mail: info@ghosthuntersofguelph.com

Ghost Research International
Melbourne—Victoria, Australia
ghostresearchinternational.com

Haunted Britain
Great Britain, UK
www.hauntedbritain.net

International Paranormal Investigators
www.international-paranormal-investigators.tk

Leinster Paranormal
Carlow, Ireland
leinsterparanormal.com

Malaysian Paranormal Research
www.malaysian-paranormal-research.org

Northern Ireland Paranormal Research Association
www.nipra.co.uk

ParaScience Psychical Research and Investigation
United Kingdom
www.parascience.org.uk

Swedish Ghost Research Society
hem.passagen.se/sjoch/ghost
E-mail: sgrs@telia.com

United Kingdom Society for Paranormal Investigation
www.ukspi.co.uk

Can't Find One?

Try the Paranormal Societies Online Directory. Paranormal research and investigation groups are constantly expanding and changing. This group runs a regularly updated list of legitimate paranormal societies.

www.paranormalsocieties.com

Index

D

R

S